Climate Change, Capitalism, and Corporations

Climate change is one of the greatest threats facing humanity, a definitive manifestation of the well-worn links between progress and devastation. This book explores the complex relationship that the corporate world has with climate change and examines the central role of corporations in shaping political and social responses to the climate crisis. The principal message of the book is that despite the need for dramatic economic and political change, corporate capitalism continues to rely on the maintenance of 'business as usual'. The authors explore the different processes through which corporations engage with climate change. Key discussion points include climate change as business risk; corporate climate politics; the role of justification and compromise; and managerial identity and emotional reactions to climate change. Written for researchers and graduate students, this book moves beyond descriptive and normative approaches to provide a sociologically and critically informed theory of corporate responses to climate change.

CHRISTOPHER WRIGHT is Professor of Organisational Studies at the University of Sydney Business School. He has researched and published widely in the areas of management knowledge diffusion, organisational change, and consultancy. His current research explores organisational and societal responses to climate change, with a particular focus on how managers and business organisations interpret and respond to climate change.

DANIEL NYBERG is Professor of Management at Newcastle Business School, Australia, and Honorary Professor at the University of Sydney. His research focuses on political activities in and by organisations. He has pursued this interest in projects on how organisations respond to climate change, adaptations of sickness absence policies, and the implementation of new technologies.

Climate Change, Capitalism, and Corporations

Processes of Creative Self-Destruction

CHRISTOPHER WRIGHT AND
DANIEL NYBERG

CAMBRIDGE
UNIVERSITY PRESS

CAMBRIDGE
UNIVERSITY PRESS

University Printing House, Cambridge CB2 8BS, United Kingdom

Cambridge University Press is part of the University of Cambridge.

It furthers the University's mission by disseminating knowledge in the pursuit of education, learning, and research at the highest international levels of excellence.

www.cambridge.org
Information on this title: www.cambridge.org/9781107435131

© Christopher Wright and Daniel Nyberg 2015

First published 2015

A catalogue record for this publication is available from the British Library

Library of Congress Cataloguing in Publication data
Wright, Christopher, 1963–
Climate change, capitalism, and corporations : processes of creative self-destruction / Christopher Wright & Daniel Nyberg.
   pages   cm
Includes bibliographical references and index.
ISBN 978-1-107-07822-2 (hardback)
1. Environmental economics.   2. Corporations–Environmental aspects.
3. Industrial management–Environmental aspects.   4. Climatic changes–Economic aspects.   5. Capitalism–Environmental aspects.   6. Social responsibility of business.   I. Nyberg, Daniel, 1974–   II. Title.
HC79.E5W74 2015
363.738'74–dc23   2015014241

ISBN 978-1-107-07822-2 Hardback
ISBN 978-1-107-43513-1 Paperback

For our kids – Genevieve and Alexander,
Linnéa and Matilda

Contents

Figures

Tables

Foreword

In his 2006 landmark report on how we should respond to the climate crisis, Nicholas Stern characterised global warming as an 'externality', a damage to others due to market activity whose cost is not met by those who cause it. Indeed, Stern characterised climate change as 'the largest ever market failure'. In other words, the problem of global warming arises because the market system is not working well enough, and if we could find a way to correct the fault then the problem would be solved.

It was a geophysicist, Brad Werner, who in 2012 argued precisely the opposite case – that we are in this mess not because the market system is not working well enough but because it is working too well. Werner's startling presentation to the annual conference of the American Geophysical Union was titled 'Is the Earth F**ked?' and he posed in public the question climate scientists and others who follow their work had been asking in private. His answer was bleak, or just possibly inspirational.

Building on the fact that humans now constitute a force of nature so powerful that we have caused the Earth to enter a new geological epoch, the Anthropocene, Werner approaches the question of the sustainability of humankind through a dynamic model known as a global, coupled human-environmental system. The activities of humans are captured in a module called 'the dominant global culture', which essentially describes the globally integrated market system of resource use and waste generation driven by the relentless need to grow. He also included a representation of the political institutions that facilitate the smooth operation of the system.

The essential problem, Werner argued, is that there is a mismatch between the short timescales of markets, and the political systems tied to them, and the much longer timescales that the Earth system needs to accommodate human activity, including soaking up our carbon dioxide and other wastes. Technological progress and globalisation of finance, transport, and communications have oiled the wheels of the human components of the planetary system allowing it to speed up. But the pace of the natural system carries on as it always has. The problem is not Stern's market failure but market success.

Brad Werner's conclusion is that the Earth is indeed f**ked, unless somehow the market system can be prevented from working so well. What we urgently need is friction; sand must be thrown into the machine to slow it down. Only resistance to the dominant culture will give some hope of avoiding collapse. For Werner, prevailing political customs, including system-compatible ideas like cost–benefit analysis, global agreements, and carbon prices, are embedded in the established structure of the human component of the planetary system. Only activism that disrupts the dominant culture – including 'protests, blockades, and sabotage' – provides an avenue for a negative answer to his rude question. It is a kind of geophysical model of Naomi Klein's recent call to arms.

In their important book Christopher Wright and Daniel Nyberg give us a detailed and fascinating analysis of what global corporations do to keep the wheels of the system spinning, a phenomenon they term 'creative self-destruction'. This extends beyond how business activities contribute to the climate crisis to how the 'dominant global culture' persuades those inclined to throw sand in the wheels to express their anger in more system-compatible ways. That is, they show how critique of corporate responsibility is incorporated and converted to the continuation of 'business as usual'.

The stakes could not be higher, on both sides.

When Bill McKibben calculated that limiting global warming to 2°C above pre-industrial levels requires that 80 per cent of proven reserves of coal, oil, and natural gas be left in the ground untouched, but that doing so would destroy the balance sheets of several of the world's largest and most powerful corporations, he showed us in the starkest possible way the fundamental incompatibility of the current structure of economic power and the survival of the world as we know it.

The hard truth is that these corporations would sooner see the world destroyed than relinquish their power. As this book shows in fascinating detail, it is not that the executives who run them are evil; they simply function the way the system dictates and the system, as we find here over and over, is structured to keep the global capitalist system growing. The executives have no choice: if they cannot stomach it then they must leave and be replaced by people with fewer scruples or an enhanced ability to deceive themselves, to believe the stories their own Public Relations (PR) people make up.

This book seeks 'to outline the *processes* through which corporations are shaping humanity's response to the climate crisis'. Its analysis is revolutionary in a way because it explains to us that these shaping processes are much deeper and subtler than we realised. They include how corporations manipulate our very identities and emotional responses to the predicament we face.

The oleaginous rhetoric about sustainable business practices, green consumerism, and green growth churned out by the clever people in marketing has proven highly effective. Even some environmental organisations believe we can somehow consume our way out of the crisis and persuade themselves that the only way to change the system is by working with it (and taking corporate money in the process). Ecologists and conservation biologists have been convinced that they have to speak the language of the market to be heard and so busy themselves with 'putting a price on the environment' so that the externalities can be internalised. Governments fall over themselves to laud corporations as 'wealth creators' who must be allowed to get on with the job (political donations help oil the wheels of that machine too), even if the job in question is killing our world.

It is astonishing how gullible we all are. In the history of greenwash rarely has there been a more cynical corporation than the oil company BP, which in July 2000 rebranded itself 'Beyond Petroleum', announcing it would over time transition out of fossil fuels and into renewable energy. Today it has sold out of its small investments in wind power and solar energy and is investing heavily in the development of shale gas and oil sands in Alberta (the worst kind of fossil energy), and, we must not forget, new oil fields under the melting Arctic.

Because it is written by two business professors with decades of research into the corporate world, a knowledge deepened for this study by intensive engagement with a range of executives, this book is a very welcome corrective to the beguiling world of mistaken ideas we carry around that have us sleepwalking into disaster.

Clive Hamilton, Professor of Public Ethics,
Charles Sturt University and author of *Requiem for a Species:
Why We Resist the Truth about Climate Change*

Acknowledgements

In the course of writing this book we have incurred debts to many people who have helped us in various ways. First, we would like to thank the many managers, consultants, employees, and activists who gave up their time to talk to us about their work and what climate change means to them both professionally and personally. We started this project with great trepidation; however, it became a viable research endeavour as a result of the many people who were willing to talk to us and share their experiences and feelings about this most critical of issues. Funding for the research into business responses to climate change was provided by the Australian Research Council under its Discovery programme (DP110104066), and without this funding, this book would not have eventuated. In the course of developing our ideas and writing up our research findings we received very valuable feedback from many individuals who read and commented on early chapter drafts and responded to our presentations. In particular, we would like to thank Glenn Albrecht, John Buchanan, Dan Cass, Christian De Cock, Marc Hudson, Lesley Hughes, Michael Mann, Jeremy Moon, Mette Morsing, Lauren Rickards, David Schlosberg, Andre Spicer, and Gary Warden. A special thanks to Frances Flanagan for her invaluable research assistance and to Neil Robinson who helped us sharpen our writing, as well as Paula Parish, Claire Wood, and the team at Cambridge University Press. Lastly we would like to thank our families without whose support this book would never have eventuated, in particular, our partners Denise and Anna who provided so much support, advice, and encouragement. We have dedicated the book to our children. Climate change presents them with a terrible legacy. We hope some of the insights in this book might help them see through our current delusions and identify more meaningful ways of responding.

1 | Climate change and corporate capitalism

Climate change is the biggest challenge of our time. It threatens the well-being of hundreds of millions of people today and many billions more in the future ... No one and no country will escape the impact of climate change.

Former UN Secretary-General Kofi Annan (2014)

The future looks bleak. As an opening remark, this might seem unduly downbeat; but it is necessarily realistic. Every day we are confronted by fresh evidence that humanity is shuffling ever closer to the abyss. New data and studies are now habitually underlined by dramatic events all around the globe. Fundamental assumptions of our weather, our climate, and our ecosystem are collapsing before our eyes. As environmental activist Bill McKibben (2013a: 745) has argued: 'We don't need to imagine the future of climate change, because it is already here.'

Of course, the notion of destruction is hardly novel. Any student of economic history knows the idea has been a grim constant in attempts to characterise the relationship between capitalist dynamism and ever-spiralling consumption. Karl Marx and Friedrich Engels ([1848] 1998) warned of *enforced* destruction. Joseph Schumpeter (1942) championed a dauntless culture of *creative* destruction. Yet we now find ourselves in a new and altogether more frightening era of so-called progress: the age of creative *self*-destruction.

We are destroying *ourselves*. It is as simple as that. Economic growth and the exploitation of nature have long gone hand-in-hand, but they now constitute the most ill-fated of bedfellows. Climate change, the greatest threat of our time, is the definitive manifestation of the well-worn links between progress and devastation. And as we continue to shamble towards a tipping point from which any meaningful return will be utterly impossible, a familiar message rings out from the corporate world: 'business as usual'.

This book is about that message. It is about the corporate world's relationship with climate change; it is about the terrible paradox at the heart of that relationship; and it is about how that relationship affects us all. It is about how such a message could come to be accepted in the face of the steady annihilation of our planet; it is about how we might recognise it for what it is – the most dangerous of fallacies – and replace it with something more in keeping with our increasingly desperate plight.

Understanding corporate responses to climate change

Scientists can pinpoint with increasing certainty humanity's role in particular climate catastrophes (Lewis and Karoly, 2013). We first began researching corporate responses to climate change for this book in 2008 and in the years since have witnessed a procession of extreme weather events linked to the worsening climate crisis.

- In 2010, Pakistan experienced its worst floods in living memory. An estimated 20 million people were directly affected (Coumou and Rahmstorf, 2012).
- In the same year Russia endured its worst-ever heatwave and drought. Around 56,000 people died as a result (Trenberth, 2012).
- In 2011, the southwestern United States was plunged into the most devastating drought in its history (an ongoing crisis that is the worst drought in this region in 1,200 years (Griffin and Anchukaitis, 2014). At the same time the Mississippi suffered massive floods that matched the 'great floods' of 1927 and 1933 (Masters, 2012).
- In 2012, Arctic summer sea ice melted to an all-time low. The decline was so great that scientists now project the Arctic Ocean could be ice-free in only a few decades (NSIDC, 2012).
- In the same year New York was hit by Hurricane Sandy (Barrett, 2012). The resulting images of one of the world's great cities succumbing to nature proved especially powerful.
- 2012/13 also saw devastating bushfires across Australia during the country's hottest-ever summer. The heat was so intense that new colours had to be found to depict its severity on weather charts (Steffen, 2013).
- In November 2013, super-typhoon Haiyan hit the Philippines, the most powerful tropical cyclone to make landfall in recorded history, resulting in an estimated 10,000 fatalities (Schiermeier, 2013).

- In 2014, scientists announced the collapse of the West Antarctic ice sheet. This process is expected to result in a sea-level rise of as much as five metres and has been described by glaciologists as 'unstoppable' (Rignot, 2014; Rignot et al., 2014).

The increasing sophistication of climate science reinforces the catastrophic implications of 'business as usual' for a twenty-first-century world. Global average temperature increases of 3–5°C by the end of the century have been projected, with much of this warming locked in as early as 2020–2030 (IPCC, 2013; New, et al., 2011; The World Bank, 2012). The worst-case scenarios paint an 'unimaginable' vision of large tracts of the Earth rendered uninhabitable, the collapse of global food production, the acidification of the oceans, substantial sea-level rises, and storms and droughts of growing intensity – a literal hell on Earth (Hansen, 2009; Lovelock, 2009).

And yet how do we choose to respond? Tangible political action remains limited to rhetorical flourishes against a background of even greater fossil fuel exploitation. While governments and international organisations pledge reductions in greenhouse gas (GHG) emissions and businesses promote 'sustainability', global emissions have increased to record levels. Despite heightened political awareness of the problem of anthropogenic climate change, as outlined in Figure 1.1, total GHG emissions have continued to grow and indeed the rate of growth has accelerated in recent years (Global Carbon Project, 2014). There is plainly a substantial disconnect between how we value our socio-economic activities and how we regard what the established body of climate science is telling us (IPCC, 2013; Melillo et al., 2014).

How can we let this happen? There is no doubt that the sheer scale of the problem makes genuinely united efforts difficult, but there are other fundamental reasons for humanity's alarmingly limited reaction to the spectre of ecological disaster. Insouciance and apathy cannot be dictated by mere logistics alone. In this book we argue that the corporate world's engagement with climate change represents a profound influence on humanity's actions – and, more significantly, its inactions – in responding to the fast-unfolding crisis.

Business plays a dual role in climate politics. On the one hand, corporations are the principal agents in the production of GHG emissions in the global economy; on the other hand, they are also seen as our best hope in reducing emissions through technological innovation.

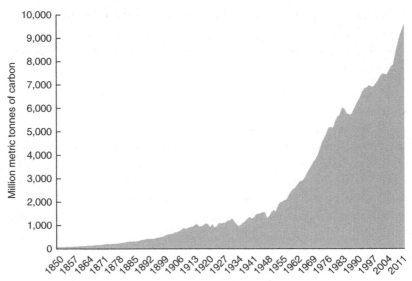

Figure 1.1 Global fossil fuel CO_2 emissions, 1850–2012.
Source: Based on data from Boden, T. A., Marland, G. and Andres, R. J. (2013) *Global, Regional, and National Fossil-Fuel CO_2 Emissions*. Oak Ridge, TN: Carbon Dioxide Information Analysis Center, Oak Ridge National Laboratory, U.S. Department of Energy, http://cdiac.ornl.gov/trends/emis/tre_glob_2010.html

Just as they are part of the disease, we dream corporations will be part of the cure. This dichotomy was neatly summed up by billionaire entrepreneur and 'green business' champion Richard Branson when he claimed that 'our only hope to stop climate change is for industry to make money from it' (Neubacher, 2012).

We contend that the particular neoliberal variant of late capitalism that now dominates the global economy places humanity at a strategic disadvantage in responding to the threat of climate change. This brand of corporate capitalism frames business and markets as the only means of dealing with the crisis, rejecting the need for state regulation and more local democratic options. In essence, the prevailing corporate view is that capitalism should be seen not as a cause of climate change but as an answer to it. A problem brought about by overconsumption, the logic goes, should be addressed through *more* consumption. By contrast, we believe the solution lies not in greater capitalism but in a strengthening of the very democracy that this strain of corporate hegemony seems determined to herd to the margins.

There are a great many books now exploring the different features of the climate crisis, but our focus is explicitly on the role of corporations as central players in the human response to climate change. Unlike popular polemics, our analysis is based on extensive research into the practices, policies, and strategies of major businesses.

Our research involved interviews with more than 70 senior managers, industry representatives, and business advisers from 25 different large corporations in Australia (see Appendix Table A.1), as well as analysis of company documentation, including strategy outlines, policy statements, and submissions to government on climate policy. Our respondents came from a diverse range of industries, including mining and resources, manufacturing, energy, consumer products, retail, banking and insurance, professional business services, transport, and aviation. The corporations involved included some of the world's biggest multinationals. The insights we were able to derive were therefore global.

From our initial sample we selected five corporations as case studies. These were subjected to a more detailed analysis of their responses to climate change. Further interviews with senior and operational managers were carried out, and an even larger body of relevant documentation was examined. The five corporations chosen were:

- A leading energy producer that was supplementing fossil fuel generation with renewable energy sources
- A large insurer that was measuring the financial risks of extreme weather events
- A major financial services company that was factoring a 'price on carbon' into its lending to corporate clients
- A global manufacturer that was reinventing itself as a 'green' company producing more efficient industrial equipment and renewable energy technologies
- A media company that had embarked on a major eco-efficiency drive to become 'carbon-neutral' (see Appendix Table A.2).

Our purpose in this book is not simply to describe what corporations are doing in response to climate change (a topic which has been documented by others, see, e.g., Hoffman, 2007; Pinkse and Kolk, 2009) but to put this empirical detail into a broader conceptual framework that contributes to our grasp of the response of humanity as a whole. In particular, in the pages that follow we aim to explain the *processes* that underpin how business corporations engage employees, customers, industry associations, the media, governments, and citizens on this issue. We believe this approach is vital to understanding the part corporations play in the politics of climate change at multiple levels in society. In particular, we seek to go beyond existing descriptive and normative approaches to develop a more sociologically and critically informed theory of corporate responses to climate change. In doing this we engage with the deeper debates that are now appearing in critical social theory about how and why humanity has been largely unable to muster a meaningful response to the crisis that is engulfing it.

Many have posited that climate change represents an especially 'wicked problem' because of its scale, its lack of immediacy, and its intangibility (Giddens, 2009; Hulme, 2009), but we suggest there are more deep-rooted reasons for our collective inaction and that these stem from the basic features of our economic system. Specifically, we argue that the threat of climate change is fundamentally connected with the expansion of global capitalism. Revoking Schumpeter's concept of 'creative destruction' as a source of economic and social dynamism, we characterise the link between economic growth, corporate innovation, and environmental destruction as a process of 'creative *self*-destruction' in which economic expansion *relies on* the continued exploitation of natural resources. We believe climate change has revealed this underlying dynamic in its starkest form: the potentially cataclysmic trade-off between economic and environmental well-being.

Before we present this argument in greater detail we set out in the remainder of this introductory chapter some necessary contextual information. This includes an outline of climate change's emergence as a political and social issue and how this has varied around the world and over time. We then provide an overview of the different roles business corporations have played in responding to climate change. Finally, we summarise the structure of the book.

Climate change: a brief overview

The science of climate change and global warming hinges on the chemical make-up of our atmosphere and its conduciveness to a habitable environment for life on Earth. The key mechanism is the way in which greenhouse gases such as carbon dioxide (CO_2), methane (CH_4), and nitrous oxide (N_2O) absorb and re-emit infrared radiation from the

Earth's surface, slowing the passage of energy back to space. The concentrations of greenhouse gases play a critical role in ensuring a balance in the Earth's energy budget, resulting in stable climatic conditions for the existence of life as we know it (Archer and Rahmstorf, 2010; Hansen et al., 2007).

Earth's climate has of course changed substantially before. Variations in the Earth's orbit around the Sun, fluctuations in solar output, volcanic activity, and other factors have all played their part. But the recent rapid rise in atmospheric concentrations of greenhouse gases resulting from human industrialisation of the past 200 years is unprecedented (Archer and Rahmstorf, 2010). Our combustion of large volumes of fossil fuels such as coal, oil, and gas for energy, manufacturing, and transport, as well as the depletion of carbon sinks such as forests and peat lands, has led to shifts of a magnitude and pace seldom witnessed before.

The growing concentration of greenhouse gases has been demonstrated through observational studies such as the famous Keeling Curve, which has charted monthly variations in the concentration of atmospheric CO_2 in parts per million (ppm) since the late 1950s, as well as comparisons with ice core samples dating back to many tens of thousands of years (Lüthi et al., 2008). In 2013, CO_2 concentrations exceeded 400ppm, a level not seen on this planet for at least 800,000 years and perhaps as much as several million years (Carrington, 2013; IPCC, 2014c) (see Figure 1.2). Moreover the link between dramatically increasing GHG concentrations and a warming climate has been demonstrated by a broad range of scientific investigation, particularly paleoclimatic research and more recent observation of temperature anomalies (IPCC, 2013; Mann et al., 1999; PAGES 2k Consortium, 2013).

While the science underlying the so-called greenhouse effect dates back nearly two centuries (Edwards, 2010; Weart, 2003), its mainstream recognition in policy and government circles did not truly occur until the 1980s. Piqued by the action of individual scientists and international organisations such as the World Meteorological Organisation (WMO) and the United Nations Environment Programme (UNEP), political acknowledgement of climate change became particularly evident in 1988, when, against the backdrop of an unseasonably warm US summer, several related events occurred on the international stage:

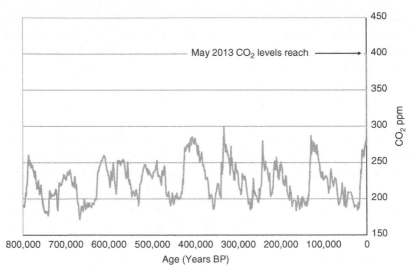

Figure 1.2 Atmospheric CO_2 concentrations in the past 800,000 years.
Source: Based on data from National Climatic Data Center/NOAA (www.ncdc.noaa
.gov/paleo/pubs/luethi2008/luethi2008.html)

- National Aeronautics and Space Administration (NASA) scientist James Hansen testified to a US congressional committee that observed temperature increase was clear evidence of global warming
- A conference of the world's leading climate scientists emphasised the need for governments to set enforceable targets for the reduction of GHG emissions
- British Conservative Prime Minister Margaret Thatcher described the dangers of global warming and the need for countries to join together in tackling the problem (Andresen and Agrawala, 2002; Weart, 2011).

In the same year this political awareness also found institutional expression with the formation of the Intergovernmental Panel on Climate Change (IPCC), an international agency of experts that assesses the latest scientific knowledge on climate change and the environmental and socio-economic impacts of the phenomenon. In producing regular reviews of climate science, the IPCC has provided a basis for ongoing international negotiations over climate change policy. Its first report, published in 1990, was soon followed by negotiations for an international agreement to limit global warming and, in 1992, a meeting of world leaders in Rio de Janeiro – the so-called First Earth Summit (Edwards, 2010; Weart, 2011).

These early political negotiations soon exposed climate change's fundamentally divisive nature. Taking meaningful action to respond to the threat would require significant reductions in the global production of GHG emissions, which in turn would demand government regulation of fossil fuel use and/or taxation. Thus a classic 'tragedy of the commons' dilemma was revealed: economic development based on fossil fuel use benefited individual countries in the short term at the cost of long-term environmental destruction. Not surprisingly, conscious of their individual economic interests, nations diverged markedly in how they approached negotiations. Early opponents of agreed emissions reductions included the world's pre-eminent economy, the United States; the oil-rich kingdoms of the Middle East; and countries, such as Canada and Australia, heavily reliant on fossil fuels as key sources of energy and export earnings.

The political implications of climate change also laid bare schisms between the so-called developed economies of the global North and the developing nations of the South. The climate crisis was an outcome of historical emissions that had facilitated the developed world's economic wealth, while many developing economies had yet to enjoy these economic gains and would be the most exposed to future climate change impacts. As Klein (2014: 181) notes, given the lack of funding from developed economies to assist in a transition away from 'dirty energy', this legacy has forced even progressive governments in countries like Bolivia and Ecuador to pursue even greater fossil fuel extraction.

These national and regional conflicts over climate change have played out over the past two decades at various UN Climate Change Conferences. The United States, in particular, influenced by domestic political considerations, has had a central role in delaying global action. Neoconservative politicians and fossil fuel interests have waged a relentless campaign against regulation, stressing 'uncertainty' and 'doubt' about climate science (Dunlap and McCright, 2011; Mooney, 2005a; Oreskes and Conway, 2010). Despite a firming of scientific findings and IPCC projections suggesting increasingly dire environmental, social, and economic impacts, global agreement on a response has remained both illusive and illusory.

Consider, for example, an alleged high watermark in global climate negotiations: the so-called Kyoto Protocol, which resulted from the 1997 UN Conference on Climate Change and committed wealthy, developed economies to undertake significant emissions cuts. Domestic political gridlock meant the United States failed to ratify the agreement – largely on the pretence that it excluded developing countries (Clark and Berners-Lee, 2013) – thereby handing other developed economies an excuse to avoid taking strong action.

Against this political conflict, public awareness and concern over climate change have also soared over the past decade or more. Several factors have played a role. We have seen extreme weather events, including the 2003 European heatwave, which resulted in tens of thousands of fatalities, and Hurricane Katrina, which decimated the US city of New Orleans in 2005 (Van Aalst, 2006). Thanks to films such as *The Day after Tomorrow* (Emmerich, 2004) and *An Inconvenient Truth* (Guggenheim, 2006), climate change has also entered the public imagination through popular culture.

Interestingly, this growth in public awareness, although in general demonstrated by opinion polls (Brulle et al., 2012; Leviston et al., 2011), has varied strikingly from country to country. Citizens in South America have registered the greatest concern, while those in the United States and China – the world's largest emitters – seem far less worried (Carrington, 2011). Indeed, there is mounting evidence that the media in the United States, the United Kingdom, Canada, and Australia has contributed to public polarisation on the issue (Boykoff, 2011; Painter, 2011).

In the wake of the fourth IPCC report, which was published in 2007 and warned of the serious harm to ecosystems and societies that would result from continued GHG emissions, hopes that the 2009 Copenhagen climate talks would lead to a meaningful international agreement were high. This optimism proved sadly misplaced. The resurfacing of national and regional tensions undermined any multilateral agreement. The so-called BRICS nations of Brazil, Russia, India, China, and South Africa emerged as key players in climate negotiations, staunchly emphasising their national economic interests, while the United States, once again hamstrung by domestic political division, failed to offer leadership (Clark and Berners-Lee, 2013).

The Copenhagen talks were also mired in the confected conspiracy of the so-called Climategate scandal, which questioned the veracity of climate science and emboldened a resurgent denial campaign (Mann, 2012). Climate change denial has now extended beyond industry-funded social movements and appears entrenched in neoconservative political parties in the United States, Australia, and Canada (Hoffman, 2012; McCright and Dunlap, 2011a). At the time of writing, for instance, neoconservative politicians in Australia have succeeded in winding back the limited regulatory and market initiatives introduced by a previous Labor government to reduce carbon emissions.

The science of anthropogenic climate change has only strengthened in the face of these myriad setbacks. Unfortunately, the science also suggests that the projections of even best-case scenarios are becoming ever more alarming.

According to the most recent IPCC report (2013), as a consequence of GHG emissions from human activities, the Earth's climate has already warmed on average by 0.85°C from pre-industrial levels. The heating of the planet and other physical impacts (e.g., ocean acidification and sea-level rise) will grow in intensity as GHG emissions continue to increase; moreover, positive feedback effects will accelerate the process, most notably through increasing methane emissions from melting tundra and the reduced albedo of shrinking Arctic ice (IPCC, 2014c; The World Bank, 2014). Both observational evidence (in the form of recorded temperatures and data on sea-level rise and declining ice mass) and climate models provide clear and direct evidence of our plight, and reviews of the cross-disciplinary science for anthropogenic climate change highlight a significant scientific 'consensus' (Cook et al., 2013).

What are the likely impacts of heightened warming of the globe? Research suggests these are both diverse and fundamental, including:

- Increasing intensity and frequency of extreme weather events such as storms, floods, droughts, and wildfires (The World Bank, 2014)
- Transformation of the terrestrial and marine ecosystems that form our life-support systems, significant levels of species extinctions, and the demise of most tropical coral reef systems (Hughes, 2011)
- Failure of crops and threats to food supplies (IPCC, 2014a)
- Increased global mobility of large volumes of people from climate-threatened regions (Bogardi and Warner, 2008)
- Heightened regional and geopolitical conflicts over scarce natural resources undermining the functioning of society (Campbell, 2009; CNA Military Advisory Board, 2014; Dyer, 2010).

Obviously, nobody can predict the future with absolute accuracy. We cannot say for sure how terrible the effects of climate change might be. But we can say with reasonable certainty how we might best try to save ourselves; and abandoning the 'business as usual' path is among the most crushingly obvious responses.

If nations around the world were to radically reduce their GHG emissions over the next 20 years there is a slim chance that average global warming could be limited to 2°C. Such an undertaking would entail genuinely dramatic change in energy production and the curtailment of all but essential fossil fuel usage (Anderson and Bows, 2011; 2012). As outlined in recent IPCC projections (see Figure 1.3), limited change in emissions or a continuation of current levels would result in estimated warming of 3 or possibly even 5°C by 2100 and even further increases thereafter (Fuss et al., 2014; IPCC, 2013). The 2° limit has been ratified politically as a level beyond which the impacts would be dangerous for human well-being, but many climate scientists have argued even this would be a prescription for disaster in light of the fact that current projections err on the 'side of least drama' (Brysse et al., 2013; Hansen and Sato, 2012).

Policy responses have to date mostly focused on attempts to cut or 'mitigate' GHG emissions, as this is the most direct way to reduce the risk of future climate change impacts (IPCC, 2014b). For instance, economic reviews in the United Kingdom (Stern, 2007) and Australia (Garnaut, 2008) have strongly advocated the 'pricing' of carbon emissions and the development of a 'market mechanism' to encourage a transition from fossil fuels to a low-carbon economy based on 'renewables' (e.g., wind, solar, tidal, biomass, and geothermal technologies) and other energy sources (e.g., nuclear). A number of regional economies and nations have launched initiatives to reduce emissions. Among the most notable have been the European Union's introduction of a 'cap and trade' carbon market in 2005; the implementation of a carbon tax in the Canadian province of British Columbia; and proposals in Australia, following the election of a Labor government in 2007, for a fixed carbon price leading to an emissions trading scheme (ETS) (Crowley, 2013; Neuhoff, 2011; Newell and Paterson, 2010; Nyberg et al., 2013).

Most recently, we have seen the introduction of carbon trading systems in a number of Chinese cities and a major climate agreement to reduce emissions negotiated between the United States and China

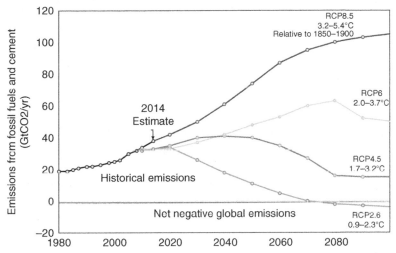

Figure 1.3 Representative Concentration Pathways (RCPs) projecting future climate change.

Source: Based on data from IPCC. (2013) *Climate Change 2013: The Physical Science Basis. Working Group I Contribution to the Fifth Assessment Report of the Intergovernmental Panel on Climate Change.* Cambridge: Cambridge University Press; Fuss, S., Canadell, J. G., Peters, G. P., Tavoni, M., Andrew, R. M., Ciais, P., Jackson, R. B., Jones, C. D., Kraxner, F., Nakicenovic, N., Le Quere, C., Raupach, M. R., Sharifi, A., Smith, P. and Yamagata, Y. (2014) 'Betting on Negative Emissions', *Nature Climate Change* 4(10): 850–3.

(Landler, 2014). Some governments have also sought to mandate targeted reductions in GHG emissions from sectors such as energy production. Other responses have included attempts to increase the 'sequestration' of carbon emissions through expanding forests, as well as expensive and untested 'carbon capture and storage' technologies.

There have even been proposals to 'geoengineer' the climate. One idea is to disperse sulphate particles in the atmosphere to dim incoming solar radiation, increase the reflectivity of clouds or 'fertilise' the oceans through encouraging algal blooms (Hamilton, 2013; Keith, 2000). Such initiatives would need to be implemented on a massive scale, and their unintended effects could be catastrophic. Indeed, plans such as these have been compared to chemotherapy for a dying planet (Wagner and Weitzman, 2012).

Irrespective of the long-term responses we choose to adopt, we must also deal with the physical manifestations of climate change that are already unavoidable. This adaptation might extend from major engineering projects – such as levees and coastal walls to protect against rising sea levels or desalination plants to tackle fresh water shortages – to social and governance responses and even individual restraint in resource use.

There is a need for psychological adjustment, too, to a changed and threatening world (Adger et al., 2009). This, again, is already unavoidable. For the reality is that mitigation and adaptation, regardless of how radical or effective they might be, cannot alter the fact that climate change is happening *now*. It is all around us. It is here. We rightly fear a climate-changed future, but we forget at our peril that we are living in a climate-changed present.

What role corporations?

While governments, politicians, and scientists figure prominently in the popular discourse of climate change, business organisations are far less apparent. Indeed, even economic analyses of climate change present a largely neoclassical view in which the firm remains hidden from view, responding to price signals dictated by the laws of supply and demand. Missing from such analysis is any concept of corporate power and agency. Yet, our contemporary economy is dominated by large multinational companies which exhibit significant influence over governments, public policy, and communities (Bakan, 2004; Barley, 2007).

The twentieth century saw the rise of 'corporate capitalism'; the twenty-first century has witnessed its further expansion under the spread of neoliberalism (Harvey, 2007). Business corporations represent around 40 per cent of the world's largest economic entities, their revenues dwarfing many national economies. Fossil-fuel-based energy giants dominate the roll-call of mega-corporations, with the revenues of the five largest – Royal Dutch Shell, ExxonMobil, BP, Sinopec, and China National Petroleum – equivalent to 3 per cent of global gross domestic product (GDP). Royal Dutch Shell's reported 2012 revenues exceeded the GDPs of 171 countries, making its 90,000 employees the 26th largest economic entity in the world – ahead of, among others, Argentina and Taiwan (Keys et al., 2013).

As the engines of the modern global economy, large business corporations underpin the production and consumption of an ever-distending cornucopia of products and services. Fossil fuels and natural resource depletion have been crucial components of economic expansion, with energy supply, industrial production, transportation, construction, and forestry/agriculture among the sectors with the most significant contributions to overall GHG emissions. The result: ever-increasing carbon emissions which in recent years have grown at around 2 per cent per annum and in 2013 reached a record high of 9.9 ± 0.5 GtC (36 billion tonnes of CO_2) – some 61 per cent above the level in 1990 (Global Carbon Project, 2014).

The globalisation of manufacturing has also led to a geographic relocation of the production of GHG emissions. China, for instance, because of its rapid economic ascent, is now the world's largest GHG emitter (see Figure 1.4). Importantly, these emissions result not only from the combustion of fossil fuels for domestic use but also from the huge industrial growth driven by demand from developed economies for cheap manufactured products (Lin and Sun, 2010). Developed economies have thus outsourced not just their manufacturing industries but also a sizeable part of their GHG emissions (Peters et al., 2011).

Although it is often assumed that GHG emissions are largely dispersed across economic sectors, recent research has shown how a relatively small number of business entities have contributed to the majority of global emissions over time. For instance, Heede's (2014) quantitative analysis found that 63 per cent of cumulative worldwide industrial GHG emissions between 1751 and 2010 could be attributed to just 90 'carbon majors' (investor-owned corporations, state-owned enterprises, and specific nation states) engaged in the production and sale of hydrocarbon fuels, cement manufacture, and associated activities. Moreover, more than half of these emissions have occurred since 1986 (Clark, 2013). Key emitters include companies such as Chevron, ExxonMobil, Saudi Aramco, BP, Gazprom, and Royal Dutch Shell, with emissions exceeding those of many small nation states (Patenaude, 2010).

The first of the roles business corporations play in relation to climate change, then, is that of a *producer* of GHG emissions. This can occur directly through business activities (e.g., energy usage, transportation, waste processing) as well as less directly through association with products and services that contribute to emissions (e.g., the sale of coal, oil, and gas for energy production or food and consumer goods that contain significant embedded emissions).

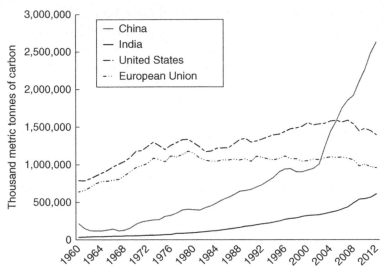

Figure 1.4 Major global CO$_2$ emitters.
Source: Based on data from Boden, T. A., Marland, G. and Andres, R. J. (2013) *Global, Regional, and National Fossil-Fuel CO$_2$ Emissions*. Oak Ridge, TN: Carbon Dioxide Information Analysis Center, Oak Ridge National Laboratory, U.S. Department of Energy, http://cdiac.ornl.gov/trends/emis/tre_glob_2010.html

The role of producer gives rise to risks. Governments might seek to reduce emissions through 'carbon pricing', 'cap and trade', or 'carbon taxes', all of which can leave high-emitting businesses facing additional costs or holding 'stranded assets' (Carbon Tracker Initiative, 2012). As the recent fossil fuel 'divestment' campaign has demonstrated, changes in public and consumer sentiment towards corporations that are major emitters can threaten these firms' 'social licence to operate' and endanger their reputation and the demand for their products and services (McKibben, 2013b).

But where there are risks there are also opportunities, and it is these that facilitate the second of the roles corporations play in relation to climate change: that of *innovator*. There is enormous scope for businesses to develop new products, services, and methods of operation that radically reduce their emissions, cut their costs, and afford them a competitive advantage as potentially 'low-carbon' or 'zero-emission' companies (Dauvergne and Lister, 2013; Hoffman, 2005). For instance, many studies of 'green' business promote the logic of process, product, and technological innovation as a way for firms to improve their market position (Esty and Winston, 2006; Orsato, 2009).

Businesses can exploit these opportunities in a number of ways. These include:

- Reducing operational costs through improved eco-efficiency (particularly as energy costs rise and GHG emissions are priced)
- Expanding eco-efficiency to broader supply chains, further reducing costs
- Identifying and developing new products and services that satisfy changing markets and social demands
- Marketing and branding themselves as 'green' companies.

For instance, corporations such as Walmart have pioneered 'green' supply chain strategies as a way to reduce costs, and new markets for environmentally friendly products and services have become an established feature in an increasing range of consumer settings (Bonini and Oppenheim, 2008; Ottman, 2011). As outlined in Table 1.1, a growing number of global corporations have introduced sustainability programmes and practices that emphasise improved environmental outcomes – although it is interesting to note that failure to achieve the targets they set is often ignored (Inez Ward, 2014).

Together with images of the green entrepreneur or 'ecopreneur' (Phillips, 2013), these programmes and practices contribute to a vision of business 'leadership' on climate change and corporations' potential role as *saviours* from the climate crisis. However, this putative quest to deliver salvation is chiefly driven by self-interest; greed, not necessity, is the mother of invention. As a South African entrepreneur at the 2011 World Climate Summit in Durban acknowledged when asked why businesses would be interested in saving the Maldives from climate catastrophe: 'Customers live there. It's a business world. It's capitalism. We need people to buy our goods ... Two, three, four hundred thousand people in the Maldives, they all buy iPads, Coca-Cola, all the products we know. If they don't exist anymore the market's gone' (Goodman, 2011).

Indeed, critics note the way in which corporate 'greening' strategies by promoting greater efficiency and cost reduction can actually result in overall increases in GHG emissions through increasing demand for their products (Owen, 2011). This paradox underpins the problem of 'decoupling' economic production from its material effects which has

Table 1.1 *Examples of corporate environmental programmes*

Company	Sustainability program	Description
Google (United States)	Google Green	Google aims to ultimately power the company with 100% renewable energy. It claims to have been carbon-neutral since 2007; using data centres that use 50% less energy than typical equivalents; and have obtained 35% of electricity from renewable sources in 2014.
Ikea (The Netherlands)	People and Planet Positive	Ikea claims to have doubled the amount of cotton bought from sustainable sources since the launch of its programme in 2012; installed over 500,000 solar panels on buildings; purchased 137 wind turbines; and increased the use of certified wood to 35%. It audits its wood supply chain and paper, food, and textile suppliers for sustainability, and has a future goal of sourcing 100% of home furnishing materials from renewable, recyclable or recycled materials by 2015. It also aims to source 50% of wood from sustainable sources by 2017 and use 100% renewable energy as a share of total consumption by 2020.
FedEx (United States)	Earth Smart	Launched 2011, the company has claimed to have saved over 7,000 metric tonnes of carbon emissions annually through the installation of solar facilities; it carbon offsets every FedEx envelope; and it has improved vehicle fuel efficiency by 30%. The company aims to reduce GHG emissions from global air operations by 20% by 2020, and plans to have 30% of jet fuel come from alternative fuels by 2030.

Table 1.1 (*cont.*)

Company	Sustainability program	Description
Sony (Japan)	Road to Zero Environmental Plan	Launched in 2010, Sony's long-term goal under its 'Road to Zero' plan is to have a zero environmental footprint in its business activities and through the life cycle of its products and services by 2050. Mid-term targets include a 30% reduction in annual energy consumption of products; 10% reduction in product mass (baseline 2008); 50% absolute reduction in waste generation; and 30% reduction in water consumption (baseline 2000).
Gazprom (Russia)	Comprehensive Environmental Program	Gazprom adopted its Environmental Policy in 1995 and Comprehensive Environmental Program in 2011. It aims to reduce gross pollutant emissions (particularly nitrogen and carbon oxides); reduce contaminated effluents in surface-water; and introduce an ISO 14001-compliant environmental management system. In 2010–2011, the company claimed gross pollutant emissions fell by 5% and 8% (2009 baseline).
Asia Pulp & Paper (Indonesia)	Sustainability Roadmap Vision 2020	Launched in 2012, Asia Pulp & Paper's 'Sustainability Roadmap Vision' is designed to achieve 'whole business' sustainability, including a reduction in carbon emissions in mills in line with national targets by 2015, and the identification and protection of high conservation value and High Carbon Stock forests. It also aims to achieve best practice peatland management and rehabilitate one million hectares of degraded forest.

Table 1.1 (*cont.*)

Company	Sustainability program	Description
Vale (Brazil)	Carbon Program	Created in 2008, the Carbon Program aims to reduce global GHGs emissions by 5% by 2020 through the use of new technologies and less carbon-intensive processes. To date, the company claims 21% of energy used by the company comes from renewable sources, 75% water is re-used in operations, and 230,000km^2 of natural areas have been protected through the Vale fund.
HSBC (United Kingdom)	Sustainable Operations Strategy	HSBC's Sustainable Operations Strategy was established in 2012, and claims to have achieved 21% reduction in waste; 30% reduction in paper consumption; and 12% reduction in overall energy consumption from 2011. It aims to increase energy consumption from renewables to 25% and reduce annual carbon emissions per employee from 3.5 to 2.5 tonnes by 2020. HSBC has partnerships with the Climate Group, Earthwatch, and WWF.
Lego (Denmark)	Planet Promise	In 2014, the company claimed an improvement of 30% in energy efficiency over a five-year period. It aims to reduce the amount of energy used to manufacture a tonne of Lego by 10% by 2016, use 100% renewable energy by 2016, and recycle all waste that is produced.
Pick n Pay (South Africa)	Social Investment Program	The company claimed a 10% reduction in carbon footprint and a reduction of 18% in packaging (2010 baseline). By 2016, it aims to send zero waste to landfill, reduce its carbon footprint by 15%, and reduce electricity consumption by 40% (2010 baseline).

Table 1.1 (*cont.*)

Company	Sustainability program	Description
Tata Motors (India)	Sustainability in Motion	Tata began publishing Sustainability Reports in 2003. In 2014, the company claims to have achieved a 9% decrease in water consumed per vehicle produced; 2.5 times increase in renewable energy consumption; and 9% of total energy consumption based on renewables. It has set up effluent treatment facilities, undertaken tree plantation programmes, and contributed to the cost of installing five pre-fabricated biogas units in its Indian operations.
Unilever (The Netherlands)	Sustainable Living Plan	Established in 2010, the plan sets the goal of halving the GHG impact of products across the lifecycle by 2020. The company claims a reduction of CO_2 emissions in manufacturing by 32% since 2008, the reduction of deforestation associated with commodity crops, and the purchase of electricity from certified renewable sources for its factory sites in North America and Europe. It acknowledges that the total GHG impact of Unilever products has increased by 5% since 2010 because of the expansions of its hair and shower product portfolio.
General Electric (United States)	Ecomagination	Established in 2005, the company claims to have reduced GHG emissions by 32% (2004 baseline) and freshwater use by 45% (2006 baseline). It has also invested $12 billion in research and development. In 2013, the company published a global white paper in support of an 'age of gas' and increased its investments in low-cost renewable technology and alternative fuel transportation.

Table 1.1 (*cont.*)

Company	Sustainability program	Description
Walmart (United States)	Sustainability Commitment	Introduced in 2005, Walmart's Sustainability Commitment set the goal for the company to create zero waste, use 100% renewable energy, source all materials sustainably. It claims that 24% of its electricity comes from renewable sources. It aims to reduce the energy intensity required to power its buildings by 20% (2010 baseline). The company's 'Acres for America' initiative involves the purchase of 1 acre of wildlife habitat in the United States for every acre of land developed.

proved elusive in both relative and absolute terms (Jackson, 2009). Nevertheless, these corporate activities feed into a broader imaginary of business 'leadership' on climate change that, as we will show, are critical for corporate legitimacy.

Corporations also play a role as major *employers*. In many service and professional settings they engage in a 'war for talent' that can be endangered if their brand is tarnished. Just as tobacco, alcohol, arms manufacture, and gambling earned a reputation as 'sin industries', so the emerging social awareness of the harm fossil fuels pose to the future well-being of society and the ecosystem may also lead to problems for these firms in attracting the 'best and brightest' employees. Many corporations now claim developing a corporate culture that promotes social and environmental sustainability can be a major factor in improved staff attraction, motivation, and retention (Renwick et al., 2013). Moreover, new functions have emerged within corporations to deal with the environment and climate change, consisting of roles such as 'environmental managers' and 'sustainability managers' (Wright et al., 2012); these point to the importance of understanding the emotional relations and activities that occur within corporations with regard to the climate crisis (Wright and Nyberg, 2012).

Finally, corporations play an active role in civil society as *corporate citizens*, particularly in the administration of citizenship rights for individuals (Matten and Crane, 2005). With the influence of the state receding under neoliberalism, there is an increasingly accepted place for businesses to supply social services (e.g., supplementing education or welfare provision), to provide economic and physical infrastructure, and to contribute to solving social and political problems (Scherer and Palazzo, 2011; Valente and Crane, 2010).

Corporate citizenship also involves engaging in political activity through marketing, lobbying, and funding. These strategies have become increasingly relevant for business interests seeking to shape government policy on climate change in areas such as 'carbon pricing', emissions regulation, and the promotion of renewable energy technologies. Fossil fuel industries have been vociferous opponents of government attempts to mitigate GHG emissions and have undertaken a range of political activities in an effort to defeat such measures (Dunlap and McCright, 2011). Ordinary citizens, among them coal miners and factory workers, are increasingly pulled into campaigns supporting corporate objectives (Nyberg et al., 2013). The political 'war of positions' has also been evident as rival firms have sought to develop renewable energy technologies and move towards more low-carbon business models (Chesbrough, 2012; Levy and Spicer, 2013).

As detailed in Table 1.2, each of these roles – *producer*, *innovator*, *saviour*, *employer*, and *corporate citizen* – is central to how businesses respond to climate change. They are the cornerstones of countless corporate sustainability programmes. From reducing GHG emissions and energy consumption to employee engagement and culture change initiatives, from corporate political activities to alliance-building with civil actors and Non-Governmental Organizations (NGOs), this is how corporations react to the greatest threat of our time. In the chapters that follow we explore these activities and the broader processes and motivations underpinning the corporate response to the climate crisis.

Book structure

This book seeks not only to document these varying corporate roles and the practices that underpin them but also – and more importantly – to outline the *processes* through which corporations are shaping humanity's response to the climate crisis.

Table 1.2 *Corporate practices in responding to climate change*

Improved energy efficiency	Practices for the measurement, recording, and reduction of energy usage and improved energy efficiency, including adoption of new technologies and processes (e.g., improved insulation, LED lighting)
Waste reduction and recycling	Minimising, separating, and reusing waste
Emissions reduction	Measurement and implementation of changed technologies and processes that reduce GHG emissions from a corporation's business activities
Green culture	Initiatives aimed at developing a corporate culture that promotes environmental sustainability and 'green' values as a way of engaging staff and customers
Green marketing and branding	Marketing and branding an organisation as environmentally aware in its products, services, and activities
Green products and services	Development of new products, services, and markets that are promoted as environmentally sustainable and 'green'
Supply chain management	Changing procurement practices and supplier relations based on an analysis of environmental impacts across the supply chain
Reporting	Gathering data on carbon emissions and other environmental activities and reporting these publicly through participation in voluntary environmental reporting schemes such as the Global Reporting Initiative (GRI) and the Carbon Disclosure Project (CDP)
Alliance-building	Building links with other businesses, industry groups, think tanks, and NGOs as a way of promoting a company's environmental and climate policies and objectives
Advocacy and lobbying	Corporate political activity aimed at shaping government policy and legislative outcomes in regard to environmental issues and climate policy

Having provided some contextual setting in this introductory chapter, in Chapter 2 we outline the conceptual framework for our analysis, which posits that climate change has revealed one of the fundamental contradictions of capitalism: the necessity to consume the natural environment to ensure continued economic growth. Building on insights from ecological sociology and the so-called treadmill of production perspective, we challenge conventional views of 'ecological modernisation' and argue that the political and economic response to climate change highlights a form of 'creative self-destruction' in which businesses are encouraged to further devour the very life-support systems of a habitable environment. We suggest that this entirely irrational path is made 'sensible' through incorporation of critique, in which criticism of corporate activities is absorbed and adapted to further justify capitalist expansion. This incorporation of critique is enacted through a range of interconnected processes. These are dealt with in the chapters that follow.

In Chapter 3 we explore how corporations have constructed climate change as a space of business risk and opportunity. We view risk as socially constructed; in other words, we suggest that corporations, by identifying, measuring, and assessing risk, are taking part in constructing the very phenomenon to which they are responding. We outline how risk has become a dominant discourse in corporations' framing and understanding of climate change and analyse the effect these risk constructions have on business and society. We argue that the construction of climate change as risk legitimises and justifies particular corporate activities and practices; moreover, we argue that the framing of societal events as risks is also a political act, since the construction of risk closes certain paths and opens others in addressing the perceived threat. We show how the practices of 'corporate environmentalism' are used to provide supposed answers to these risk framings, which present a particular future vision based on corporate self-regulation, local innovation, and market-based drivers of economic change.

Continuing our analysis of the consequences of the corporate construction of climate change, in Chapter 4 we illustrate how corporations influence the political debate and further their objectives by building coalitions with like-minded enterprises, industry groups, the media, think tanks, NGOs and by the promotion of social movements. Viewing the corporation as a political actor, we discuss corporate practices, such as lobbying, campaign funding, political marketing, and 'astroturfing', and consider how these influence debate and policy development with regard to climate change. As noted previously, this involves moving beyond a view of the 'corporate citizen' as an administrator of citizens' rights and recognising the involvement of ordinary people in a corporate 'war of positions' over climate politics and policy.

Moving beyond the level of corporate strategy and political engagement, the next three chapters explore how corporations enact climate change within the firm and what this means for employees engaged in this process.

In Chapter 5 we discuss the incompatibility of the market and the environment. We explore the process of compromise in corporate engagements with climate change and how multiple competing justifications for corporate action are internally resolved. Avoiding the simplistic black-and-white picture of corporate initiatives as either 'authentic' or 'greenwashing', we explain how the dispute between profit and the environment is conveniently and habitually settled through compromise. We argue that this involves the commensuration of competing 'orders of worth', which leads to the corruption of the environment by converting it into a market commodity.

In Chapter 6 we explore what this means for the individuals tasked with implementing corporate responses to climate change. We especially focus on the emergent occupational community of sustainability managers and advisers. These are people who may have strong personal concerns about climate change but are often faced with organisational imperatives that challenge their commitment. We explore how these individuals make sense of the paradoxes that confront them and how they develop a coherent narrative identity in situations that are fundamentally contradictory.

This analysis is further developed in Chapter 7, where we investigate how corporations have sought to define appropriate emotional responses to the climate crisis. This is an issue where cold facts have generated the most heated debate – one that we believe is associated with new 'emotionologies' (Fineman, 2010). We outline how corporate activities influence these emotionologies – in which expressions of passion, anger, fear, and hostility are common – and we explain the individual 'emotionology work' involved in dealing with the tensions and contradictions of climate change.

In Chapter 8 we synthesise our discussion of the different processes underpinning creative self-destruction by focusing on the role of political myths in creating a convincing narrative of humanity's response to climate change. In particular we focus on the myths of corporate environmentalism, corporate citizenship and corporate omnipotence as central narratives for the incorporation of critique and the maintenance of corporate legitimacy. We also identify alternative emergent narratives which to varying extents challenge the predominant focus on corporate capitalism as the solution to climate crisis.

Our analysis concludes in Chapter 9, where we return to the implications of the previous chapters and highlight six movements that can promote people's imaginations in demanding a change to our current path. These include questioning how we see our relationship to nature; disrupting the language of climate change; promoting greater democracy in climate politics; emphasising the worth of environment beyond a market commodity; developing a green identity beyond consumption; and championing the positive emotionality of climate action.

In the pages that follow we aim not only to explore how corporations have responded to climate change but also to raise questions about corporate capitalism's efficacy as the response of choice to the most significant social, political, and economic issue of our time – one that will have profound implications for the future of our societies and our very existence as a species on this planet.

Our message is that many of the corporate world's responses to climate change, despite representing a profoundly significant influence, can more accurately be described as narratives or, better still, myths. Like Plato's original Noble Lie, they function to further an agenda and maintain the status quo. It is easy enough to condemn these myths. It is easy to become angry about them and to rail against the self-serving short-termism they epitomise. But until we fully appreciate quite how brilliantly they satisfy their purpose, until we grasp how sublimely they protect the interests of their instigators and risk betraying those of everyone else, the meaningful alternatives that are so desperately required will remain disturbingly elusive. Our hope is that our overall argument will encourage and support a double-movement of much-needed regulation and more local and democratic responses.

2 | Creative self-destruction and the incorporation of critique

Anyone who believes exponential growth can go on forever in a finite world is either a madman or an economist.

(Attributed to Kenneth Boulding in
United States Government, 1973: 248)

In 2006, in a landmark report for the British government, climate change was described as 'the greatest market failure the world has ever seen' (Stern et al., 2006: viii). 'Business as usual' was not an option, said the authors. Strong, collective action was deemed imperative.

So how was this strong, collective action to be achieved? The answer, said the report, lay in creating opportunities for growth. Policies to support new technologies should be encouraged. 'Carbon pricing' and 'carbon finance' should be embraced. Every effort should be made to speed the transition to a low-carbon economy. The key message was that the cost of doing nothing would far outweigh the cost of taking action.

At first glance a manifesto such as this seems both well intentioned and, certainly nowadays, all too familiar. But at the same time it also captures the very essence of creative self-destruction: it encapsulates the bizarre notion that the only available response to a problem caused by the market's ever-expanding reach is to expand that reach further still.

This damaging conviction is the central theme of this chapter. We argue that it is the enduring promulgation of such a belief – the insidious spread and entrenchment of the idea that only *more* consumption can remedy the devastating consequences of *over* consumption – that allows inventive genius to go hand-in-hand with selective blindness, capitalism to freeride on nature and the environment itself to be rendered nothing more than a commodity. As we will see, it is a question of how corporations paper over the cracks and contradictions in our economy; and it is a question, above all, of the difference between *values* and *value*.

The age of creative self-destruction

We are living in a new geological epoch: the Anthropocene (Crutzen, 2002; Steffen et al., 2007). It is an epoch in which fossil fuel exploitation is reshaping the Earth's systems, exceeding the boundaries of what constitutes a 'safe operating space for humanity' (Rockström et al., 2009). It is an epoch that demands answers we appear determined not to provide.

We have already argued that corporate engagement in increasingly environmentally exploitative behaviour is central to the absence of effective responses to climate change. Corporate degradation of the environment is most obviously evident through the activities of the 90 or so major fossil fuel corporations and state enterprises that have managed to produce two-thirds of the world's cumulative CO_2 emissions over the past 50 years (Heede, 2014). Businesses from a range of industries continue to profit from cheap fossil-fuel-based energy, with many actively hampering the fight against the climate crisis by seeking to frame political responses in ways that suit their own objectives. Lobbying, campaign contributions, and entering into the social and public debate on climate change have all proved useful tools. Businesses have argued that the cure for the environmental ills within corporate capitalism is more corporate capitalism and that the problem, as if by magic, is therefore actually the solution.

In this chapter we further unpack this contradiction. We contend that a central reason for the lack of political and economic engagement on climate change is the uncomfortable way in which this issue reveals the underlying paradox of capitalism as an economic system that relies on the destruction of nature for its own development. We suggest that the lack of widespread societal criticism of environmental destruction demonstrates the need for a deeper explanation of the social acceptance of the climate crisis. In particular, we highlight how the narratives of corporate capitalism revolve around concealing the manifest flaws in our economic system, with the corporate politics surrounding climate change among the most extreme examples of such wilful obfuscation.

With this in mind, we subsequently turn our attention to the dynamism or 'spirit' of capitalism and the issue of how our economic system incorporates criticism and justifies further development of the market society (Boltanski and Chiapello, 2005). Environmental critique of capitalism has been recuperated through profit-seeking activities, new technologies, and novel practices – not to mention normatively appropriated through the labelling of products and services as 'green', 'sustainable', and 'environmentally-friendly' (Chiapello, 2013). Corporate environmentalism is chiefly geared towards being a little less unsustainable amid growing destruction: it is this fantasy that enables the corporate environmental movement to overlook or, better still, obstruct more radical sustainable practices (Fleming and Jones, 2013).

Building on failure

Climate change challenges the conventional wisdom of environmental economics that developed within Western liberal democracies during the later twentieth century. Based on a vision of technological progress and human betterment, environmental degradation has traditionally been seen simply as a problem of early industrialisation. According to the theory of 'ecological modernisation', increasing economic development, technological innovation, and environmental reform have over time minimised pollution and environmental harm (Hajer, 1995; Mol, 2002; Mol and Spaargaren, 2000).

   Although this comfortable assumption has been the subject of some reconsideration in the face of anthropogenic climate change, ecological modernists have continued to argue that economic progress remains the best way to respond to environmental challenges. Underpinning this view is a belief that new technologies and markets can decouple economic growth from environmental destruction at both a relative and an absolute level (Jackson, 2009). Former World Bank chief economist Sir Nicholas Stern (2007) offered a classic illustration of this mindset when he characterised climate change as a market failure, proposing the pricing of carbon emissions (defined as 'externalities') and the discipline of the market mechanism as a solution: in other words, the market should correct itself.

   Little wonder then, notwithstanding the uptake of 'sustainability', 'corporate environmentalism' and 'green growth' as both discourse and practice (Esty and Winston, 2006; Jermier et al., 2006), that humanity's degradation of the environment proceeds at an ever-accelerating pace. We can see this not only in the physical manifestations of climate change – the melting Arctic, record-breaking droughts and floods, rising sea levels and ocean acidification (IPCC, 2013; Melillo et al., 2014) – but also in the destruction of habitat and declining biodiversity. One of the defining features of the Anthropocene is the loss of vast numbers of animal and plant species – the so-called Sixth Great Extinction (Kolbert, 2014b).

A powerful and alternative explanation for humanity's destruction of a habitable environment comes from the fields of environmental sociology and political economy. Known as the 'treadmill of production' perspective, it harks back to Marx's original observation that capitalism is an economic system that depends on the unending exploitation of nature (Foster, 2000). It posits that there is a basic conflict between the political economy of global capitalism and environmental well-being; that capital investment leads to ever-growing demand for natural resources if employment and consumption are to be maintained; and that resource extraction results in the further commodification of nature through increasing profits and new investment, thus setting in train even more demand for natural resources (Schnaiberg, 1980; Schnaiberg and Gould, 1994; York, 2004).

The 'treadmill of production' also has political effects. It strengthens 'the economic and political power of shareholders (investors and managers)' who frame any resistance to ecological destruction as 'antediluvian, Luddite, old-fashioned, reactionary and doomed to failure' (Gould et al., 2004: 297). Opposition is further limited by the reliance of citizens and workers on employment and wages and by the distribution of the worst pollution and degradation to poorer, remote locations or to 'sacrifice zones' (Klein, 2014: 173), as seen in the choking smog, depleted ground water, and poisoned rivers and oceans of countries such as China (Kahn and Yardley, 2007).

In contrast to the progressive view of ecological modernisation, the 'treadmill of production' argument claims that environmental destruction is less an unfortunate by-product of industrialisation and more an essential feature of our economic system. This view provides a much more convincing explanation for the climate crisis we now face. While apparently rational from the narrow standpoint of maximising profits, the levels of environmental destruction wrought by corporate capitalism now present us with a wholly irrational future. In altering the atmosphere, biosphere, cryosphere, lithosphere and hydrosphere through our continued extraction and combustion of fossil fuels and our destruction of carbon 'sinks' such as forests, jungles, peat lands, and tundra, we are conducting a planet-wide experiment with potentially catastrophic consequences.

In trying to understand this apparently suicidal strategy, we use the term 'creative self-destruction' as a central organising concept (see also Berman, 1982: 98–104). This idea builds on the broader depiction of capitalism as an economic system based on crises and the 'enforced destruction of a mass of productive forces' (Marx and Engels, [1848] 1998: 42). Indeed, the economist Joseph Schumpeter (1942) famously characterised this process as one of 'creative destruction' in which technological innovation and entrepreneurship not only created waves of innovation but also swept away previous forms of capital accumulation and natural resources. Although 'creative destruction' has been celebrated by free market economists as central to economic efficiency and human progress, it is worth remembering Schumpeter's prescience. Crucially, he cautioned that the activity he described also involved systemic risks: 'In breaking down the pre-capitalist framework of society, capitalism thus broke not only barriers that impeded its progress but also flying buttresses that prevented its collapse ... [T]he capitalist process, in much the same way in which it destroyed the institutional framework of feudal society, also undermines its own' (Schumpeter, 1942: 139).

The corporate response to climate change mimics this process. The difference is that the definitive consequences are likely to be the destruction of the system as a whole. As we saw in the previous chapter, despite increasingly sophisticated scientific evidence of the disastrous implications of escalating GHG emissions (IPCC, 2013; Melillo et al., 2014), the global economy continues its relentless pursuit of new markets, the expansion of consumption, and new forms of capital accumulation. Rather than stopping or at least slowing our fossil fuel use, industry's innovative and creative capacities have shifted to developing new technologies and ways of exploiting 'non-traditional' fossil fuels as we exhaust more easily accessible hydrocarbon resources. For instance, the moves towards deepwater oil extraction, tar sands processing, and the 'fracking' of shale and coal seam gas (IEA, 2013) highlight both our inventive genius and our blindness to the ecological catastrophe we are fashioning.

Marx (1976) argued that crises are manifestations of the underlying contradictions of capitalism. We suggest the climate crisis is in many ways a reflection of just such a contradiction, with capital accumulation leading to the cannibalistic consumption of Earth's life-support systems. However, unlike Marx and many Marxist scholars (see, e.g., Harvey, 2014; O'Connor, 1988), we do not see this crisis as stemming from contradictions internal to the capitalist economy.

In this instance contradiction results from the endless accumulation and consumption of the basis for the capitalist system itself: nature. Nature's capacity to renew and support life on the planet constitutes the very conditions for capitalism to exist. As a result, capitalism is basically free-riding on nature, both as a source of 'inputs' to production and as a 'sink' to absorb capitalism's waste (Fraser, 2014: 63). Further, nature's CO_2 sinks are rapidly cut down and denuded for capitalist production. This is why capitalism as an economic model and social order cannot incorporate the environment. Totalising the environment, broadly speaking, would create a closed system and necessarily a collapse. Anthropogenic climate change brings forward this contradictory logic of capitalism as an economic system reliant on the destruction of nature for its further development (Schnaiberg and Gould, 1994; York, 2004); and the lack of meaningful political engagement is born of the uncomfortable way in which the issue lays bare our reliance on a capitalist imaginary of endless economic growth (Castoriadis, 1997).

Of course, industrial growth and commodity production for a market have always entailed ongoing environmental impacts such as pollution, deforestation, and over-fishing. As Harvey (2014: 3–4) observes, in the early eighteenth century, Britain faced a contradiction over the need for land for biofuel *and* for food production: the answer involved the use of fossil fuels (coal) for energy so that land could be freed up for agriculture. At a national level we still face these types of tensions over resource use, as evidenced by current debates over opening up farmland for 'fracking' or growing biofuels (Howarth et al., 2011a; Lohmann, 2006).

Yet the issue is now international in every sense of the word. The 'great acceleration' in industrial production, global markets, and escalating world population during the twentieth century have made these impacts manifest on a planetary scale. National decisions over resource exploitation now have global impacts (Steffen et al., 2007). Our awareness of the threat of climate change therefore highlights a shift from 'tension' to 'absolute contradiction', and a conflict that has always existed has now become unmanageable (Harvey, 2014: 23).

At the core of this absolute contradiction is capitalism's dependence on compound economic growth. As Harvey (2014) argues, if the economy is not continuously expanding then it is no longer a capitalist system. Over the past several decades we have witnessed this growth through consumption – both in its increasingly rapid turnover time and in the incessant identification of new products and markets. In developed and developing economies alike the rise of hyperconsumption underpins economic growth. We are encouraged to buy new clothes, phones, cars, and other 'essentials' with greater frequency and magnitude (Ritzer, 2004). We have become afflicted with 'affluenza' – 'an unsustainable addiction to economic growth' (Hamilton and Denniss, 2005: 3). Witness, too, the concomitant emergence of new commodities as assets and instruments for speculation, among them financial derivatives and carbon markets.

This being the case, we cannot uphold a 'natural' boundary or clear division between a capitalist economy and the environment. The capitalist model is *based on* the environment – at least in its broadest sense – rather than separate from it; and the boundary is partly a product of the capitalist imaginary or social order itself. It is the essential politics of capitalism to 'manage' the boundary in terms of what should be included (e.g., humans, carbon) and excluded (e.g., other species). While the boundary can be expanded to include, say, the circulation of capital through carbon markets or geoengineering, capitalism requires the destruction of the outside to support the inside. The reliance on growth through commodification further highlights the contradiction, in that turning nature into different objects for sale within self-regulating markets erodes the very support on which capitalism depends (Fraser, 2013). The physical limits of economic growth revealed by the climate crisis therefore demonstrate this contradiction at its starkest.

Managing climate crisis as opportunity

As Harvey (2014: 154) remarks, capitalism never truly solves the crises it generates: rather, 'it moves them around'. As a result, if capitalism is to survive then the climate crisis has to be managed in ways that allow – at least temporarily – for continued economic growth and consumption.

Managing and capitalising on the environment in general and climate change in particular can take myriad forms. The strategy of denying that the climate crisis really is a contradiction or even an issue of concern has been especially evident among coal, oil, and gas producers, energy companies, and significant parts of the manufacturing sector, all of which have advocated a 'fossil fuels forever' approach (Levy and Spicer, 2013: 663). As we will see in greater detail later, specific business interests and corporations have been central to funding and supporting the 'climate change denial industry' that has so effectively strangled policy responses in the United States, the United Kingdom, Australia, and Canada (Dunlap and McCright, 2011).

Beyond denial, other business groups have sought to present climate change as a space for new market opportunities. They concede capitalism needs to change but stress this should occur in a way 'so that nothing really has to change' (Swyngedouw, 2011: 264). More often than not the acknowledgement of the climate crisis merely provides a justification for expansion and further privatisation of state activities. Such a stance is analogous to what Klein (2007) has termed 'disaster capitalism'. Consider, for instance, the following recent developments:

- The expansion of mineral and fossil fuel extraction as the Arctic ice retreats
- Increasing demand for defence contractors, privatised security, and emergency workers in climate-ravaged regions
- New insurance products for increasingly extreme weather events
- Proposals for huge engineering projects to protect from future sea-level rises.

All of these illustrate how recognising the looming catastrophe validates new market-based solutions and novel means of private wealth creation (Funk, 2014).

This approach is also evident in the entrepreneurialism associated with 'geoengineering', a path championed by celebrity billionaires such as Bill Gates and Richard Branson and established players such as ExxonMobil, Shell, and BP (Hamilton, 2013). Once considered an extreme measure, geoengineering is now enjoying a swift mobilisation of money and resources (Yusoff, 2013). The example of the 'rogue' American businessman who in July 2012 dumped 100 tonnes of iron sulphate off the coast of Canada in a bid to 'fertilise' the ocean has been widely reported as the opening salvo in a frantic race to geoengineer the climate (Lukacs, 2012). Proposed initiatives include regulating solar energy through spraying sulphate particles into the upper atmosphere to mimic volcanic eruptions, 'brightening' clouds to improve the 'albedo effect', and seeking to extract pollution from the atmosphere through reforestation and industrialised carbon capture (Hamilton, 2013; Keller et al., 2014). Again, climate change can be seen as extenuating the expansion of capitalism into new areas.

Although most proponents insist these would be measures of last resort and that collective action to mitigate CO_2 emissions is preferable (Clark, 2014), the growing investment in geoengineering is used to excuse the present lack of action in reducing GHG emissions. The suggestion that it will be possible to deal with the problem later, when new technologies can save us, permits vacillation. Lack of urgency blinds us to the most obvious solution: keeping fossil fuels in the ground, transitioning to renewable, low-carbon energy sources, and slowing down material consumption.

Mounting investment in geoengineering is thus also a political statement: 'We have not the political will, imaginative largess or democratic process to respond to climate change in democratic (and just) ways' (Yusoff, 2013: 2802). This is how we have arrived at a political discourse whereby blocking out the Sun or seeding the oceans are somehow seen as sensible options in responding to climate change. This is how we have come to accept that corporate capitalism is able not only to solve the climate crisis it has created but also to actually engineer a *new* climate. Yet the alarming paradox of geoengineering is that it 'may itself be indistinguishable from the process of climate change – that is to say, equally unpredictable, incalculable and turbulent in its unfolding' (Cooper, 2010: 184).

More generally, the turn to geoengineering is symptomatic of the further marketisation and management of the ecosystem. In short, we have reached the stage at which the environment – nature itself – is commodified and priced. For instance, the UK government recently launched an 'Ecosystem Markets Task Force' to review opportunities for the business sector to 'value and protect nature's services' by incorporating the environment within the market system (DEFRA, 2012). This is a classic instance of initiatives that accord the environment a market value and portray business corporations as the central institutions through which that value can be maintained (Boyd and Banzhaf, 2007; Nordhaus and Kokkelenberg, 1999). Concepts such as 'natural capitalism' and 'corporate environmentalism' highlight a 'business case' for the environment through new products, markets, and innovation. The claim is that both the environment and corporate profitability should benefit (Esty and Winston, 2006; Hawken et al., 1999; Kurucz et al., 2008). In other words, environmental challenges are overcome by attributing a monetary value to nature – a process of commensuration that transforms 'different qualities into a common metric' (Espeland and Stevens, 1998: 314). While this approach is problematic for domains that have historically stood outside the market, the growth in neoliberalism means increasingly broad areas of civil society are now subject to such marketisation (Asdal, 2008; Crouch, 2011; Fourcade, 2011; Harvey, 2005).

The focus on carbon pricing as the dominant policy response in developed economies offers the clearest indication of the marketisation of climate change. As Newell and Paterson (2010) observe, the embrace of a 'market solution' during the late 1980s and 1990s reflected the prevailing hegemony of neoliberalism and the attendant belief that markets must be the most efficient mechanisms for achieving economic and political outcomes. Witness the economic inquiries by the UK and Australian governments during the late 2000s, both of which identified economy-wide carbon pricing as the best way to drive a technological and innovative shift away from fossil fuels and towards renewable energies (Garnaut, 2008; Stern, 2007).

Carbon pricing involves the creation of emissions trading schemes in which a total emissions limit is determined and tradeable permits are allocated. Government provides the general architecture of policy, leaving the specifics of emissions reduction to corporations (Newell and Paterson, 2010: 25–29). Emissions are accorded a price, becoming an asset as well as an instrument for speculation. This commodification of CO_2 has trigged derivative markets of futures and options (Lohmann, 2010).

Despite the failure to achieve any global agreement on cutting carbon emissions, recent studies have noted the proliferation of regional, national, and sub-national carbon pricing initiatives, including 35 countries covering around 20 per cent of global carbon emissions (Climate Commission, 2013; World Bank Group/Ecofys, 2014). Most notable has been the introduction of emission-trading schemes in California (the ninth-largest economy in the world) and major Chinese cities and provinces such as Beijing, Shanghai, and Guangdong. Although subject to resistance from existing fossil fuel interests and their political allies, carbon pricing remains the only significant policy response aimed at mitigating GHG emissions. Meanwhile, many other aspects of the natural environment, including forests, oceans, and animal species, have also been priced as market commodities – often by those who seek to defend nature – as a way to make a business case for conservation (see, e.g., Rogers et al., 2014).

The transformation of the environment into a commodity to be included in the market involves two intertwined processes: exchange and comparability. These political means for shifting the boundaries around capitalism and nature come with a frame of rules, actors, and objects.

First, for the exchange to take place, rules are needed in establishing the rationale for the market. The agenda immediately becomes profit rather than environmental well-being. The situation qualifies certain actors – the buyers and sellers – to 'trade' the commodity. Such a market set-up suggests the environment can be protected solely through the logic of the market exchange, with buyers and sellers the only actors capable of providing a 'proper' valuation. Exchange is supported by traditional market mechanisms, such as calculations of price and risk, negotiation and intermediation, governance and accountancy of assets, and speculations of futures and options. Thus the environment – and, indeed, the planet – is valued only according to a supremely narrow definition of human self-interest and it is assumed to be controlled on a presupposition of stability, predictability, and linearity – everything science suggests our changing climate is not.

The second process of commodification translates *values* into *value*. Whereas 'values' are moral, cultural, and difficult to measure (Skeggs, 2014), 'value' is economic and quantifiable. Through commensuration the former is turned into the latter: the market reduces everything to an equivalence. In the case of carbon pricing, for example, the heterogeneous and complex Earth systems involved in climate change are reduced to a single commodity. This allows the environment to be both compared to other goods and services and internally valued.

It is this sort of process that miraculously succeeds, for instance, in equalising CO_2 emissions irrespective of their source (Lohmann, 2006). To take a random case, the emissions of a car manufacturer that produces gas-guzzling four-wheel-drive vehicles are seen as equal to those of a company that builds wind farms. Whether emissions are generated in an attempt to limit future emissions is not accounted for in the market. This 'prevent[s] people from making conscious political choices or choosing priorities' (Kenis and Lievens, 2014: 11) and renders completely opposite processes comparable and interchangeable. By any standards, it is quite a feat.

Another example: the act of pumping a tonne of CO_2 into the atmosphere by a coal-fired power plant in Australia is deemed comparable to – and supposedly can be offset by – promoting forest plantations in Indonesia. As critics have argued (Lohmann, 2006), trading in carbon as a commodity does little to curtail production and consumption and in essence allows rich, developed economies to transfer the cost of emissions to poorer, developing nations that are far more vulnerable to the physical effects of extreme weather events and rising sea levels.

Ultimately, the dominance of neoliberalism as a political project places an inordinate amount of confidence in corporations to organise nature. According to neoliberalism, environmental degradation and 'eco-messes' such as oil spills, deforestation, declining biodiversity, chemical pollution, and climate change itself can be solved by the same logic that fostered them. Yet the commodification of CO_2 emissions allows capitalism to use emissions for rent but not necessarily to improve the environment or grant equal access to it.

Recognising this, we see that the current celebration of markets simply covers up the deeper crisis internal to capitalism (Connolly, 2012). In the following section we examine this further by exploring how businesses have incorporated environmental criticism of their activities as a means of further strengthening their voice and role in determining the human response to climate change.

The incorporation of environmental critique

Environmental criticism challenges assumptions that we should trust 'the capitalist system to guarantee the future of mankind': as we have outlined, 'capitalism, by its very operation, is leading directly to the destruction of our civilisation' (Chiapello, 2013: 73 and 74). Yet the fact that the muted response to climate change neatly ignores the economic causes of the crisis suggests a more sophisticated political process is at play.

As Boltanski and Chiapello (2005) have argued, the continuation of capitalism in fact depends on the recuperation and reinvention of critique. Criticism forces capitalism to adapt and change in order to maintain its social legitimacy. It is the interaction between capitalism and its critique that gives rise to the 'spirit' or ideological legitimacy of capitalism in any given period. How, then, have businesses incorporated the environmental critique surrounding climate change?

Social concern about environmental decline has a long history, particularly in response to the outcomes of industrialisation. Unfortunately, although such concern undoubtedly led to some regulatory constraint, in most countries the unfettered power of capital to exploit nature went largely unchallenged (Guha, 2000). It was perhaps only during the 1960s and 1970s, when a second wave of environmental critique highlighted the causal links between environmental degradation and industrial and economic expansion, that the deeper questioning and critique of industrial capitalism began to find something of a voice.

Symbolic of the shift was Rachel Carson's book *Silent Spring* (1962), which, in revealing the terrible environmental impact of pesticides, highlighted humanity's embeddedness and vulnerability within nature (Souder, 2012). Awareness duly gathered pace, signified through events such as the first Earth Day in 1970, the publication of the Club of Rome's *Limits to Growth* (Meadows et al., 1972), and growing social and media cognisance of industrial accidents and environmental catastrophes (e.g., the 1969 Santa Barbara oil spill, the 1976 Seveso dioxin cloud in Italy, and the 1978 Love Canal toxic waste scandal in New York State) (Hoffman, 2001). The emergence of 'Green' political parties in Europe, Australia, and elsewhere further underscored the institutionalisation of environmental critique of industrialisation and, more generally, capitalism (Dunlap and Mertig, 1992; Jermier et al., 2006).

Governments reacted by introducing regulations designed to limit environmental destruction. In the United States this included the National Environmental Policy Act (1970), the Clean Air Act (1970), and the Clean Water Act (1972) (Hoffman, 2001). Political activism and the development of governmental expertise (Bell and Warhurst, 1993; Useem, 1982), in tandem with an increased redistributive and regulatory tenor in public policy (Barley, 2010), saw many countries initiate reforms. While the initial response of many corporations and industry groups had been to dismiss or seek to silence such criticism, the acknowledgement of environmental concerns through government legislation highlighted a fundamental shift in social attitudes.

We can see these reforms as forming what Polanyi (1957) termed a 'double-movement' – society's response when the industrial process has gone too far. Destructive market forces were countered in the interests of a broader social good and conservation of 'man [*sic*] and nature … using protective legislation, restrictive associations and other instruments of intervention as its methods' (Polanyi, 1957: 132). This double-movement gained much of its political force by criticising the market and its contradictions (Blok, 2013).

However, this shift did not fundamentally challenge the legitimacy of markets in the distribution of social goods, and over the past several decades market forces and profit-seeking have come to dominate environmental thinking. This has occurred both through representations of corporate action and at the level of public policy.

Consider, for example, the emergence of 'corporate environmentalism' as a central discourse in business (Hoffman, 2001; Jermier et al., 2006). Corporate environmentalism builds on the broader concept of ecological modernisation by arguing that companies can be powerful agents in responding to environmental problems through their innovative capacity and profit motive. Unlike conventional neoclassical economic thinking, in which environmental protection is viewed as a threat to profitability (Friedman, 1970), corporate environmentalism promotes a 'win–win' vision of businesses augmenting profits by improving their environmental performance; in short, 'do well by doing good' (Falck and Heblich, 2007; see also Porter and van der Linde, 1995). As management consultancy McKinsey & Co has proclaimed: 'Any successful programme of action on climate change must support two objectives – stabilising atmospheric greenhouse gases *and* maintaining economic growth' (Beinhocker et al., 2008).

This perspective has been popularised through examples such as retail giant Walmart's 'greening' of the supply chain (Humes, 2011) and industrial conglomerate General Electric's 'ecomagination' initiative (Chesbrough, 2012). While going beyond mere marketing 'greenwash', these strategies for eco-efficiency and the development of new 'green' products and services satisfy a 'business case' and metamorphose environmental concern into business opportunity (Dauvergne and Lister, 2013). Consequently, although advocates of corporate environmentalism are seemingly sympathetic to the environment, strict regulation is seen as incompatible with 'the self-regulation of the market and thus with the market system itself' (Polanyi, 1957: 130). As critics have pointed out, these measures, through improving efficiency and cost reduction, actually encourage increasing consumption and investment and so contribute to even greater environmental damage (Foster et al., 2010; Owen, 2011).

At the same time as corporate environmentalism has promoted a vision of corporations as environmental 'saviours', businesses and their representatives have become more and more active in seeking to shape policy and regulatory outcomes (Hillman et al., 2004). Barley (2007; 2010) argues that representative democracy has been replaced by a 'corporate society' in which social and environmental relations are embedded within corporate capitalism (see also Jessop, 2001). In terms of policy agendas, corporate self-regulation and market-based approaches are emphasised as more efficient ways of responding to social and environmental problems – as illustrated by the carbon market, which is promoted as the only alternative to 'business as usual' not just by corporations and financial institutions but by governments and NGOs (Böhm et al., 2012). This behaviour has created a neoliberal hegemonic bloc (Gramsci, 1971), with the responsibility to address climate change allocated to market actors, with the state and international governing bodies serving merely to provide supportive legal and administrative structures for new markets.

The self-regulatory expansion of corporate capitalism reinforces a market society in which environmental issues are best dealt with through the commodification and exchange of new domains. There have been some notable regulatory corporate wins – 2005's infamous Halliburton 'loophole', for instance, which saw the US Congress exempt gas fracking from regulation under the Safe Drinking Water Act (Willow and Wylie, 2014) – but this is principally a hegemonic struggle over how to make sense of the situation. The problem is not the lack of environmental concern but rather the obfuscation of contradiction, which has resulted in a political incapacity to imagine alternative responses.

One of the chief strengths of neoliberalism is the rationality of the 'imagined market', with the 'assumption that "marketisation" provides the best means of satisfying a range of aspirations, collective and individual, and that markets are to be preferred to states and politics, which are at best inefficient and sclerotic and at worst threats to liberty and freedom' (du Gay and Morgan, 2013: 3). The partial acceptance of the environmental critique of human-caused climate change lends itself to a desire for further commodification and corporate self-regulation; and the ecological critique of the market society has been incorporated further by giving consumers a range of reasons to commit to the capitalist system. Both the social critique of the distribution of goods and the artistic critique of identity formation (Blok, 2013; du Gay and Morgan, 2013) have been skilfully addressed: witness the burgeoning markets for 'green', 'Fairtrade' and 'organic' products, all of which promise us the potential for 'guilt-free' consumption.

As a result, perhaps the key reason why we have yet to see an environmental double-movement around climate change in a manner reminiscent of the 1960s and 1970s is that corporate environmentalism does not attempt to impinge on the environment: rather, it strives to incorporate it within capitalism. The uptake of new standards of voluntary reporting (e.g., the Carbon Disclosure Project, the Dow Jones Sustainability Index, and the Global Reporting Initiative) (Knox-Hayes and Levy, 2011), increasing investor interest in corporate environmental performance, new sustainability-focused managerial and advisory functions – all further reinforce corporate environmentalism (Wright et al., 2012). The goal is to legitimise profit-seeking corporate behaviour in response to environmental criticism. The impression given is of opening up space for dialogue and progress. The reality is that the absolute contradiction between economy and nature is all but erased by trumpeting a possible 'win–win' relationship between corporate capitalism and climate change (Fleming and Jones, 2013).

These adapted forms of environmental critique, evident in a broader form through concepts such as 'green' or 'natural capitalism' (Hawken et al., 1999), therefore further contribute to the contradiction of creative self-destruction by ensuring that 'things remain the same, that nothing really changes, that life (or at least our lives) can go on as before' (Cook and Swyngedouw, 2012: 1973). The emphasis, as previously discussed, is on being a little less unsustainable, while the more basic issue of corporate capitalism's consumption of nature goes unchallenged and unquestioned.

Although more radical environmental and social critiques – including environmental sociology, deep ecology, and ecofeminism – do make these connections (Devall and Sessions, 1985; Foster et al.,

2010; Gaard, 1993), the hegemony of market neoliberalism within 'business as usual' and 'green capitalism' discourses guarantees that these voices are politically marginalised and frequently unheard (Kenis and Lievens, 2014). Instead corporate capitalism gains 'green' credentials through verification of its products and services by industry bodies and more 'professional' NGOs (Arts, 2002). So, for example, industry groups such as Corporate Eco Forum award annual prizes to the most 'sustainable' businesses, and environmental NGOs such as Nature Conservancy and WWF partner with major corporations, conferring legitimacy on their environmental initiatives (Dauvergne and LeBaron, 2014; Klein, 2014).

The tragedy is that in incorporating environmental critique, businesses have created a 'fantasy' of sustainability that suggests markets, innovation, and technology will solve climate change, thereby obscuring the phenomenon of creative self-destruction, and 'managing' the crisis (Fletcher, 2013). Žižek (1989: 50) refers to this as 'ideology', in that the dominant discourse effaces the impossibility of delivering on its promise.

We do not claim corporate and civil actors are unaware of these contradictions in a Marxist sense of 'false consciousness'. Rather, the 'spirit' of capitalism prevails: instead of seeing the lack of action in response to climate change as an elite conspiracy over a duped citizenry, we view such 'ideology' as a way in which corporate capitalism provides a meaningful imaginary (Castoriadis, 1997) – a 'whole way of thinking and being' (Foucault, 2008: 218).

This capitalist imaginary provides a depiction of social reality that is regarded as the truth – a hegemony of the 'truth-regime of the market' (Foucault, 2008: 144). It follows that the market solution to climate change becomes self-evident, with corporate capitalism the way the world is interpreted, lived, and understood (Harvey, 2005). As Jameson (2003: 73) has memorably argued: '[I]t is easier to imagine the end of the world than to image the end of capitalism'.

Thus, rather than suffering from 'false consciousness', people are realistic in what they can achieve (Boltanski, 2011). The hegemony of corporate capitalism does not exclude alternative narratives and imaginaries. It makes them naïve and forlorn. Corporate environmentalism and consumption offer temporary remedies for guilt and comfort in accepting the hegemony of corporate capitalism. We are aware of the self-interest of corporations and that their green products and services are not hindering escalating climate change, still we insist on both consumption and their narratives.

Conclusion

For much of its history capitalism has proved remarkably resilient in managing its internal contradictions so they do not become 'absolute' (Marx, 1976), but the climate crisis is not so easily accommodated. The processes we have unleashed through our reliance on fossil fuels and ever-spiralling production and consumption now threaten the very basis of life. We are living on a planet that is physically different from the one our ancestors inhabited (McKibben, 2010). We are stalked by the spectre of rising sea levels, ocean acidification, dramatically warming climate, and extreme weather events of unparalleled ferocity (Hansen, 2009; Lynas, 2007). It bears repeating: the future looks bleak.

Yet humanity's response has been amazingly muted, with corporations playing a pivotal role in obscuring the contradiction between endless economic growth and worsening environmental destruction. In this chapter we have characterised this as a form of creative self-destruction. Our economic system is now engaged in ever more inventive ways to consume the very life-support systems upon which we rely as a species; moreover, this irrational activity is reinvented as a perfectly normal and sensible process to which we all contribute and from which we all benefit. Perceptions of the climate crisis are challenged, market solutions provided, and consequences arranged so that the daily ritual of 'business as usual' is maintained. Climate change is invariably framed only as a topic of debate spectacularly devoid of serious suggestions that anything drastic should – or even could – be done about the problem.

In drawing attention to how businesses incorporate environmental critique, we are not simply proposing economic and social elites as the main culprits in defending the status quo. Climate change is a threat to identities and interests for most groups and classes in society. For many, even though the basic welfare of the majority of people in developed economies can equally thrive in more sustainable societies, questions of identity (of who we are in the modern economy) are inextricably intertwined with patterns of consumption and financial investment (e.g., housing, education, pensions, and retirement). We are the brands we wear, the cars we drive, the products we buy; and we are comforted to find the future portrayed as 'safe' in the hands of the market. Indicative of the emotionality and ideological hostility that surround the issue of climate change as part of the 'culture wars' (Hoffman, 2012), the uncertain alternative to 'business as usual' becomes the externalised 'enemy', the 'other', threatening the well-being of society. In the short term, being a little less unsustainable is not as threatening as being 'sustainable' (Ehrenfeld and Hoffman, 2013).

In contrast to this more radical critique, the image of 'green' or 'natural' capitalism proposed through corporate environmentalism and business sustainability promises no conflicts and no trade-offs. Under this re-varnished imaginary, it is possible to continue the current global expansion of consumption *and* address climate change. No conflict between material affluence and environmental well-being is acknowledged (Kenis and Lievens, 2014). Such an imaginary, in proposing that corporate initiatives are sufficient and that any ecological disaster can be cleaned up by the state, also fits well within the established hegemony of neoliberalism.

So this is how the creative self-destruction of our economic system is concealed. Dealing with this epic contradiction of capitalism would require material trade-offs that challenge identities and interests, which is why the alternative to 'business as usual' is much harder to imagine and much easier to construct as an opponent of social well-being – what climate change sceptics so often characterise as going back to living in caves or a return to the 'dark ages' (Neubacher, 2012). Such is the supremacy of our current capitalist imaginary that it exacts a powerful grip on our thinking and actions – a grip that is enacted whenever a 'green' product is promoted, a grip that is tightened through the establishment of sustainability functions in business and government, a grip that is defended with every 'offset' we purchase for a flight to a holiday destination.

In the end, crucially, the struggle against the hegemony of corporate capitalism is not merely environmental: it is inherently political. Whether we like it or not – or, more pertinently, whether we *realise* it or not – we are all taking part in appropriating environmental concerns into everyday behaviour; and that, maybe more than anything else, is what makes halting our slide towards the abyss such a hugely daunting prospect.

3 | Climate change and the corporate construction of risk

I am looking at this through the lens of risk – climate change is not only a risk to the environment but it is the single biggest risk that exists to the economy today ... When people say it doesn't make economic sense I want to scream out: 'Bullshit'.

Hank Paulson, former secretary of the
US Treasury (Cambone, 2014)

In the previous chapter we argued that climate change has brought to the fore corporate capitalism's continuing exploitation of the planet for gain. We called this process 'creative self-destruction' and suggested the muted response to it has been the result of not just the organised rejection of climate science but the incorporation of environmental critique through 'corporate environmentalism' and related concepts of ecological modernisation.

Corporate activities such as creating sustainability departments, submitting to voluntary reporting, and marketing products as 'green' and environmentally sound embody this trend. They seek to make climate change manageable within a corporate capitalist economy, seizing on emerging business opportunities in the face of new physical, economic, and social shifts. Unfortunately, they also obstruct desperately needed and more radical alternatives.

In this chapter we explore in more detail how corporate environmentalism is shaped and justified. In particular, we examine how business practices are moulded through the discourse of 'risk'. We investigate how, in ordering the threats and uncertainties that surround climate change, corporations construct different forms of overlapping and interrelated risks around their activities.

Consider, for instance, the development of 'green' products. This might enable a company to respond to a range of perceived market or reputational risks by seeking a first-mover advantage over competitors; or it might even be used to avoid a consumer backlash. Such an approach is manifestly rooted in being seen to be 'green'; yet it also seeks to preclude more stringent state control by emphasising the efficacy of self-regulation.

The dominant discourse of risk therefore provides a familiar language in dealing with climate change. It is the same language that businesses use in dealing with other 'threats' and 'opportunities'. Moreover, according risks a monetary value allows corporations to calculate, compare, and optimise their strategies.

We argue that corporations, in using the construct of risk, are changing the perception of climate change and turning the dangers into opportunities for capital accumulation and expansion. After all, if climate change can be portrayed as a basis for further capitalist growth then there is arguably no reason to stop it. The discursive formation of risk justifies certain actions, and it is through naming the risk, evaluating the probability, and providing responses that the future is given presence (Yusoff and Gabrys, 2011). Thus by redefining the present, corporate claims surrounding climate change lay the ground for what is to come.

Of course, we are not suggesting climate change is a solely linguistic construct. On the contrary, it is all too terribly real. Rather, we argue that how we make sense of the phenomenon sculpts our responses, which in turn materially affect the physical reality of what is happening all around us.

Take, for example, attempts to curtail GHG emissions. How we make sense of the consequences of these emissions in turn influences *future* consequences. Similarly, current physical events (e.g., occurrences of extreme weather) affect our sense-making – that is, how we understand climate change here and now. The matter and meaning of climate change are inseparable. Corporate risk constructions seek to capture future possibilities. However, in naming the risk, evaluating the probability, and providing responses, they also critically shape that future.

The framing of events as risks is also political. Corporate constructions of risk revolve around specific notions of threats and uncertainties, thereby demanding comparably specific actions – or, just as likely, *in*actions – by certain actors. This philosophy overlooks how the complexity of climate change defies such narrow framings. As a result, these performative risk categorisations 'misfire' (Austin, 1962) – nature bites back – with unequal consequences for people and societies. Often it is those not involved in calculating and categorising the event – the excluded voices and communities – that bear the brunt of these decisions. Rightly or wrongly, nature does not discriminate when it is taken for granted. Corporations may carry out the analyses, but they rarely carry the can.

'Business as usual' and unintended consequences

Advances in climate science have shown humanity must meet a defined 'carbon budget' if it is to avoid ecological disaster (Meinshausen et al., 2009). Research suggests our remaining budget to 2050, to have an 80 per cent chance of keeping average global warming under the politically agreed limit of 2°C, is around 565 $GtCO_2$. To satisfy this target it would be necessary for around two-thirds of known fossil fuel reserves to be left in the ground, which some analysts say raises the prospect of 'stranded assets' as investors revalue resource stocks that can never be realised (Carbon Tracker Initiative, 2012). This illustrates how climate change represents not only a physical threat to corporate operations – in terms of increasingly extreme weather events, droughts, floods, and hazards to global supply chains (IPCC, 2012) – but also a fundamental market, regulatory, and reputational challenge to existing business models.

Recognising this, major corporations have for some time undertaken strategic analysis of the future implications of climate change for their operations (Kolk and Pinkse, 2004; 2005). A key discourse has been the extent to which the phenomenon poses varying 'risks and opportunities' for established ways of doing business (Hoffman, 2005; Lash and Wellington, 2007). Oil multinational Shell, for instance, has for many years been engaged in scenario planning around changes in carbon emissions regulation (Shell, 2014; for other examples of climate change related scenario planning in the energy sector see Slawinski and Bansal, 2012). A number of key financial and political leaders, including former New York Mayor Michael Bloomberg and former Secretary of the US Treasury Hank Paulson, recently released *Risky Business*, a report emphasising the significant financial risks that climate change poses (Gordon, 2014).

Our own discussions with senior managers in global companies uncovered many examples of long-term strategising around the issue. For instance, a major financial services company had begun

to incorporate a de facto 'price on carbon emissions' in its investment decisions from the mid-1990s, while one of the world's largest
resource companies had been involved in scenario planning around
government policies on carbon emissions for more than 20 years.

One of the most famous instances of corporate engagement with
the risks surrounding climate change occurred in 2000 when oil
multinational, British Petroleum (BP), rebranded itself 'BP – Beyond
Petroleum' (Beder, 2002a). Conscious of growing public concern
about the company's environmental impact, John Browne, the CEO
at the time, sought to reinvent BP as not just a fossil fuel producer but
an environmentally aware energy company intent on exploring novel
and renewable technologies such as solar power. BP famously replaced
its logo with a stylised green, yellow, and white sunburst based on
Helios, the ancient Greek Sun god (BP, 2014). As the accompanying
TV advertisements intoned:

Is it possible to drive a car and still have a clean environment? To refine
a cleaner gasoline? Can solar power become mainstream? Could business
go further and be a force for good? Can a hundred thousand people in a
hundred countries come together to build a new brand of progress for the
world? We think so. And today BP, Amoco, Arco and Castrol get together to
try. Beyond Petroleum – BP. (BP, 2009)

BP's reinvention followed a 'split' among the global oil majors in the
late 1990s, when BP – and later Shell – publicly acknowledged the
problem of man-made climate change and resigned from the conservative Global Climate Coalition (GCC), a group of 50 corporations
and trade associations that claimed global warming was unproven
(Pulver, 2007). Some argued this represented a fundamental corporate reorientation regarding the risks of the climate crisis. Some highlighted BP and Shell's greater exposure to European regulation and a
socio-cultural context in which climate change was attracting mounting concern (Kolk and Levy, 2001; Levy and Kolk, 2002). Others
argued that BP was merely keen to distract attention from NGO and
media criticism of human rights abuses linked to its Colombian operations (Beder, 2002a).

Whatever the motivation, the move came to little. Despite a marketing push estimated to have cost around $600 million, as well as invest-
ment in solar power of a further several hundred million, BP soon

reverted to a 'business as usual' ethos. Following Browne's departure as CEO in 2007, the company disbanded its renewable energy divisions and refocused on oil exploration and production (Macalister, 2009). Allegations of 'greenwashing' were boosted when, in 2010, BP's Deepwater Horizon oil rig in the Gulf of Mexico exploded, killing 11 employees and causing the largest marine oil spill in the history of the petroleum industry – an unfolding tragedy that was played out for months on prime-time television (Hoffman and Devereaux Jennings, 2011).

Corporate responses to climate change are often shaped by the need to react to a broad range of risks and opportunities. As the example of BP shows, these responses themselves, in seeking to deal with perceived risks, produce further unforeseen consequences – in this case related to public perceptions of hypocrisy and 'greenwashing' and the prospect of heightened regulation.

More importantly, such 'misfires' simply do not account for the material effects of climate change. Calculated and linear risk assumptions exclude the irregular and uncertain aspects of the crisis. As mentioned earlier, the risk framing is undermined when nature eventually bites back, and the consequences are usually most sharply felt by those with limited capacity and resources – that is, local communities and the global South.

Constructing climate change as business 'risk'

The core assumption underlying risk management is that risk is 'out there': it just has to be 'found' and 'captured'. Corporations are perceived to be exposed to a variety of risks as objective facts that need to be 'managed' through rational decision making – a process employing, for example, cost–benefit analysis based on probabilities and consequences (Andersen and Schrøder, 2010; Randall, 2011). Disciplines such as finance, economics, statistics, and accounting have professionalised this approach by codifying risks into calculable entities – among them insurance costs and credit ratings – to determine the probability and consequences of events (Ailon, 2012; Lupton, 1999). The aim is to make uncertainty manageable. This is a concept that was translated into management in the 1990s after catastrophes and scandals such as the collapse of Barings Bank and the Brent Spar controversy at Shell (Power, 2004).

As confidence in the ability to manage risk has increased, risk itself has become associated with predictability and calculability. This makes for an intriguing paradox. The result is the exclusion of uncertainty and danger (Power, 2007). Risk emphasises regularities and simplification, whereas uncertainty highlights dispersion and complexity – qualitatively different meanings of the future. Despite challenges to the assumed calculability of risk, as perhaps most devastatingly evidenced by the financial crisis of 2008, risk and risk management remain powerful legitimating discourses in our society.

By contrast, a constructionist perspective on risk suggests that the meaning of what a risk is, along with how it should be addressed, depends on pre-existing knowledge and discourses (Lupton, 1999). Risk constructs are open to social definitions and contestation. This view pays greater attention to how cultural frameworks and powerful institutions influence how we understand dangers and uncertainties as risk (Lupton, 1999). It is by identifying, measuring, and assessing risks that corporations take part in constructing the very same phenomena to which they are responding.

While there are many dangers and hazards to deal with in society, only a few are constructed as risks (Lupton, 2006). As Ewald (1991: 199) has explained in an influential text: 'Nothing is a risk in itself; there is no risk in reality. On the other hand, anything can be a risk; it all depends on how one analyses the danger, considers the event.' Risks are not neutral, since responding to a risk implies a distribution of responsibilities and accountabilities serving some interests more than others (Fox, 1999). Corporate risk management programmes have both codifying effects regarding what can be known ('effects of veridiction') and prescriptive effects regarding what is to be done ('effects of jurisdiction') (Foucault, 1991: 75). The claims put forward through framing uncertainty or danger as a risk do not only aim to predict the future: more importantly, they also suggest how it should be dealt with and, crucially, by whom.

Business scholars and managers commonly distinguish between different forms of risk in ordering the threats and uncertainties around climate change. These are typically characterised as 'physical risk', 'regulatory risk', 'market risk', and 'reputational risk' (Hoffman, 2005; Lash and Wellington, 2007). The threat is broken up into a more comprehensible and 'manageable' framework by categorising these types of risk and their concomitant responses (see Table 3.1). This allows the

Table 3.1 *Risks and examples of corporate responses to climate change*

Climate change risks	Examples of corporate responses
Physical risk (e.g., risk of extreme weather events and changed climate threatening operations and infrastructure)	Climate modelling Scenario planning for physical events Safeguarding or relocation of physical infrastructure Developing emergency strategies for extreme weather events Selling off physically vulnerable activities Supply chain collaboration
Regulatory risk (e.g., risk of legislative regulation of carbon emissions via 'carbon taxes', pricing of GHG emissions in a carbon market, or mandatory restrictions)	Lobbying against carbon pollution regulation Building coalitions with opponents of action on climate change (e.g., free market think tanks, conservative political parties) Investing in low-carbon technologies and renewable energy to reduce carbon emissions intensity Incorporating carbon pricing in investment decisions Adopting a 'leadership' position advocating market forms of carbon regulation Voluntary reporting of carbon emissions to avoid mandatory requirements
Market risk (e.g., competitors gain advantage via new 'green' technologies and products)	R&D investment to identify and create 'green' products and services ahead of competitors Market scanning for competitive threats in order to mimic new technologies and products Potential to buy into 'green' technologies through takeovers and acquisitions
Reputational risk (e.g., danger that consumers view companies' activities as environmentally harmful, resulting in declining sales and reputation)	Improving environmental reputation through 'green' marketing and branding of products and services Developing alliances with environmental NGOs to pre-empt reputational shocks Stressing futility of emissions mitigation and climate change as a 'hoax' or inevitable Focusing on job creation and being a 'responsible' corporate citizen

future to be seen as challenging yet frequently interpreted in a positive light, with risks not only preventable but even representative of opportunities for corporate innovation and expansion.

Physical risk

For many businesses the most common risk framing in relation to climate change is concerned with perceived physical threats to operations. For instance, a quarter of the 250 large multinational corporations surveyed by Kolk and Pinkse (2004) cited the potential impact of weather-related catastrophes. This is especially evident in industries such as forestry, fishing, agriculture, mining, electricity production, manufacturing, and transport, which in a climate-changed world are likely to be exposed to increasingly intense floods, droughts, fires, and storms. It is not only infrastructure and facilities that are deemed in peril: productive activities and dwindling natural resources are also major considerations. Some of these threats – for instance, ocean acidification's likely effect on the marine food chain (Cooley and Doney, 2009; Sumaila et al., 2011) – are becoming clear only now. These uncertainties extend across supply chains and are seen as having significant financial implications (PREP, 2012).

Corporate awareness of these risks often results from exposure to specific instances of extreme weather. These 'surprising' events can force a reassessment of assumptions of a stable climate, revealing new operational vulnerabilities (Haigh and Griffiths, 2012). Managing these physical risks might involve efforts to better understand shifting weather patterns in order to identify the nature and extent of future threats. Mining and insurance corporations have, for instance, fostered closer relations with climate scientists in universities and have invested in internal capabilities for highlighting extreme events and long-term weather patterns (Hawker, 2007).

In one of the corporations we studied, an insurance company, a series of unprecedented storms and bushfires during the late 1990s and early 2000s markedly raised awareness of financial exposure to extreme weather events. As one of the company's executives remarked in describing the aftermath of a catastrophic bushfire event:

I think it was immediately obvious to all of us that the weather is changing and that the profile of the claims was changing over time. I think we all just sat there and said: 'We're actually sitting on a piece of data that is a great translation of these emerging trends around climate change.'

Following this realisation, the corporation established specialist groups of experts to model changing weather patterns and to carry out a much more detailed analysis of the company's exposure to regions likely to be hit by storms and fires. This resulted in a risk database that categorised varying threats to property on a postcode-by-postcode basis, facilitated amendments in policy pricing, and identified locations deemed 'uninsurable' in light of climate change.

Corporations have also developed scenario-planning methods to explore potential weather futures and to try to identify risks to their operations and ways to reduce their vulnerability. Electricity producers have introduced a range of 'climate-related operational flexibility' measures, including diversified supply, production and storage processes, alternative routing, and contingent distribution methods (Busch, 2011). Corporations with facilities at heightened risk of flooding or storm damage have begun to upgrade or relocate vulnerable infrastructure (Linnenluecke et al., 2011). We spoke to mining industry managers who outlined how they were retrofitting infrastructure in anticipation of greater storm intensity and increased flooding (see also Freed, 2012; Hodgkinson et al., 2010). Global food manufacturers are using more sophisticated models of future water supply and crop yields in planning the location of production facilities, as well as collaborating with farmers in the use of more efficient irrigation methods (Gunther, 2014; Nestlé, 2010). Risk associated with climate change has also been a powerful driver of the development of drought-resistant crops through genetic engineering by agribusinesses (Smit and Skinner, 2002).

Finally, mindful of the prospect of storms, floods, fires, and hurricanes of unknown intensity and frequency, corporations have set up an array of emergency response services (Linnenluecke and Griffiths, 2010; Mitroff and Pearson, 1993). This strategy extends beyond the obvious need for practices of this kind in geographically remote or exposed facilities such as mines and power plants. For instance, sustainability managers at a major financial services company described how they had instituted rapid-reaction teams and new procedures after storms and floods decimated communities in northern Australia and the Pacific. Significantly, the broader topic of coping with climate disasters again hints at potential opportunities for new business, as evidenced by the demand for myriad types of humanitarian and security responses (Funk, 2014).

Regulatory risk

The second category of risk commonly identified by businesses in relation to climate change is regulatory risk, which arises from perceived uncertainty over the future regulation of GHG emissions. As noted earlier, a growing number of national and regional governments have implemented or explored ways of mitigating emissions through carbon taxes and carbon trading mechanisms (Newell and Paterson, 2010). For high-emitting sectors – chief among them energy producers, resource firms, and manufacturers – new legislative requirements carry the threat of making operations increasingly costly and uneconomic. One common response has been to seek to reduce emissions through eco-efficiency programmes (Dauvergne and Lister, 2013).

For example, a major media company we studied had implemented a firm-wide drive to cut emissions, including energy audits, employee competitions to improve efficiency, the implementation of low-emission technologies, and the adoption of a goal of 'carbon-neutrality' by 2012. The professed objective of 'carbon-neutrality', to be achieved through energy efficiency and purchased carbon offsets, has also been embraced by IT giant Google and UK retailer Marks & Spencer, among others (Ernst and Young, 2012). Another important development has been the way in which financial institutions are factoring in the carbon exposure of customers to whom they lend money or provide insurance (Mills, 2009).

Some companies, in anticipating regulatory changes, have also sought to adopt a 'leadership' position by publicly championing a preferred market-based form of carbon trading (Hoffman, 2005; Kolk and Pinkse, 2005; Orsato, 2009). This has occasionally extended into explicit corporate political advocacy for action on climate change in terms of promoting emissions reductions and carbon pricing (see Chapter 4). The CEO of Duke Energy showcased this thinking when, in a classic enunciation of regulatory risk, he stressed the need to 'avoid "stroke of the pen" risk – the risk that a regulator or Congressman signing a law can change the value of our assets overnight ... If there is a high probability that there will be regulation, you try to position yourself to influence the outcome' (Hoffman and Woody, 2008: 74).

Banks and insurance companies are often leaders in these debates, so giving rise to opportunities for new financial products and services. For example, for some years one of the largest banks in Australia has been prominent in extolling the virtues of a legislated price on carbon and the movement towards a fully fledged 'carbon market' in which emissions could be traded as a commodity. As one senior manager explained: 'As a business, we already incorporate climate change or carbon risk into our lending investment.' This market approach is seen not only as a means of opening up future business opportunities but as the most effective and cost-efficient way to reduce GHG emissions.

Through schemes such as the Dow Jones Sustainability Index, the Carbon Disclosure Project, and the Global Reporting Initiative, many corporations have also engaged in voluntary reporting of social and environmental performance. This limits the need for mandatory reporting schemes (Bebbington et al., 2008; Etzion and Ferraro, 2010) and demonstrates corporate 'leadership'. As one manager in a large energy company explained, engaging with such schemes is critical in signalling to investors and customers that a firm is aware of regulatory risks and committed to more sustainable activities:

I think particularly in the investment space ... it's absolutely mainstream. So making sure that we're testing ourselves against things like the DJSI and CDP and FTSE4Good means that we're actually disclosing the kind of information that more and more analysts are going to be asking for ... I think internally it also helps, because we're able to say [to employees]: 'We're a leading organisation, and we've got international recognition that we're a leading organisation, and here's the list of our credentials.'

There has been ample evidence, however, of an alternative response to the regulatory risk of climate change: the rejection of government attempts to control carbon emissions. Especially in the United States, Canada, and Australia, fossil fuel corporations have exhibited their determination to see off the spectre of tightening restrictions by playing a pivotal role in lobbying governments in the lead-up to global negotiations on climate change. As we outline in more detail in Chapter 4, strategies here have included establishing powerful political allies, stressing the supposedly deleterious economic effects of legislative limits on GHG production, and forming industry groups to present a common front in dismissing the scientific evidence for anthropogenic global warming. As noted previously, such organised denial has had a powerful impact in shaping the US government's long-term opposition to mandatory international emission controls (Levy and Egan, 2003; McCright and Dunlap, 2010). Indeed, Canada became the first signatory to withdraw from the Kyoto Protocol, while in 2014 a new conservative Australian government dismantled the country's fledgling scheme to control carbon emissions.

Market risk

Given the genuine threat that climate change poses to the business models of fossil fuel companies, resistance to carbon regulation is perhaps to be expected. Debates over 'stranded assets', a 'carbon bubble', and the growing fossil fuel 'divestment movement' within the investor community highlight how regulatory risk links to broader market risks (Carbon Tracker Initiative, 2012; Makower, 2014).

For instance, investor groups have recently asked companies such as ExxonMobil and Shell to provide risk assessments regarding exposure to 'stranded assets'. The response of these firms has been to reject the idea of a 'carbon bubble' and argue that, because a low-carbon transition will take many decades and society will continue to rely on fossil fuels, the risk to their assets is low (Lamb and Litterman, 2014; Nichols, 2014). Possibly banking on further political reluctance to regulate emissions – and maybe also confident in their financial ability to buy back into the sector through acquisitions and mergers at a later date – the likes of Shell and Chevron have actually reduced their investments in alternative renewable energy technologies (Elgin, 2014). The issue demonstrates how the risk discourse of climate change is being adopted more broadly, both in markets and by investors, in ways that can shape corporate actions.

Market risk also extends into other areas, including the scope for new, disruptive, low-carbon technologies and enterprises. Corporations may seek to gain a competitive advantage through the early adoption of 'green' products better suited to a carbon-constrained world. The dramatic price cuts in solar photovoltaic technology, which now competes in cost terms with fossil-fuel-generated residential energy and poses a major threat to traditional models of electricity production and distribution (Feldman, D., et al., 2012; Frankel et al., 2014), offer one example.

Considerations such as these, in tandem with the threat of shifts in stakeholder perceptions of how corporations impact on the environment, can encourage established firms to invest in research and development to identify, create, and bring to market new technologies ahead of their rivals. For example, General Electric's (GE) widely documented 'ecomagination' initiative focused on the acceptance of climate science and investment in new products and services (e.g., wind turbines, fuel-efficient jet engines, electric vehicle technologies) capable of delivering significant reductions in GHG emissions (Chesbrough, 2012). Managers we spoke to positioned the company as a future leader in a 'green' economy. As a senior figure admitted: 'I'm going to be real frank here: we're not doing this to save the planet. That's not the driver. We're industrialists.'

Similarly, Toyota's launch of its hybrid Prius model in the late 1990s, while initially seen as a flawed business decision, was vindicated in an era of rising fuel costs and emerging public discourse around climate change. Market success gave the company a substantial lead in the field of 'green' cars (Porter and Kramer, 2006). The Prius and other hybrids, as well as electric counterparts such as the Nissan Leaf, have since prompted more and more manufacturers to tap into growing demand for such vehicles (Fairley, 2011). Imitation is not only the sincerest form of flattery: it is a standard retort to a new and disruptive competitive threat.

Reputational risk

The reputational risk that flows from an association with GHG pollution has also become increasingly relevant for corporations amid growing public awareness of climate change. A common response has been to use marketing and branding to promote the environmental and 'green' credentials of products (Ottman, 2011).

Take, for example, adverts for the aforementioned hybrid and electric cars. Many accentuate a link to reduced carbon emissions by employing emblematic images – say, of polar bears or melting icebergs (Garland et al., 2013). While arguably inviting further criticism for 'greenwashing'

(Pearse, 2012; Vos, 2009), marketing of this kind offers the potential to prevent reputational damage by presenting businesses as 'taking action' on climate change. The same thinking is behind airline companies' new-found enthusiasm for stressing how customers can help in limiting the environmental impact of flying by purchasing 'carbon offsets':

Join us in reducing the impact of carbon emissions on the environment. With Qantas' Fly Carbon Neutral programme you can offset your share of flight emissions for less than you'd think. Qantas is concerned about climate change and is committed to managing our operations in an environmentally sustainable manner. (www.qantas.com.au/travel/airlines/fly-carbon-neutral/global/en)

Thus the airline industry, despite being acknowledged as highly polluting, is able to fly with increased frequency, covering yet more distance, while the risk to its reputation is addressed by justifying actions that give a compelling impression of action against further climate change.

Another way of managing reputational risk is to form alliances with environmental NGOs. Many large corporations now invite NGO representatives on to their external boards and work to build close relationships with such groups (Dauvergne and LeBaron, 2014; Klein, 2014). Corporations are even engaging with the normally confrontational NGO Greenpeace in a bid to pre-empt later criticism (Arts, 2002). Pragmatism rules: these ties are viewed as instruments to achieve reputational effects or legitimacy that would otherwise be hard to obtain. For instance, a major supermarket chain we spoke to explained how this sort of strategy alerted it to the release of a documentary about unsustainable practices in fisheries, prompting it to market its fish products as 'sustainable'. The aim is to identify and guard against key reputational risks by either having an NGO 'on side' or by gaining information that permits action before a threat materialises in earnest (Beder, 2002b; Nyberg and Wright, 2012).

The performative work of risk

Translating the issue into one of physical, regulatory, market, and reputational risk has given corporations a range of powerful advantages in engaging with climate change. First and foremost, the discourse of differing forms of risk has allowed businesses to 'manage' uncertainty by breaking up a complex and amorphous concept into smaller components and shortening the timeframe of decades of scientific projection. As a sustainability adviser at a major financial services company told us: 'The long-term risk of climate change activities impacting on business is far greater than any risk from an emissions trading scheme. But that's not the sort of thing that fits into your normal three-year strategic planning project cycle.'

In addition, the risk discourse and the alleged rationality that reinforces it are already well established in the corporate lexicon. As a senior manager at a major insurer commented: 'Businesses get risk, so I think we've got to ... I don't know how ... but somehow reframe [climate change].' While the climate crisis may have become increasingly politically contested, the risk discourse has provided a more amenable way of prioritising the logic of the market. In the words of another manager at the same insurer: 'Climate change just polarises people, whereas if we internally talk about "weather risk" people tend to kind of keep listening rather than shutting off.' Thus the surrounding scientific and political intricacies can be dismissed. Perhaps the prevailing mindset is best summed up in the blunt declaration of one energy company manager: 'It's just risk management!'

Risk and risk management have also allowed a diffuse and globally complex concept to be rendered more local and relevant for business managers. The neatness and convenience of the metamorphosis are striking. 'The whole greenhouse effect is a global environmental risk,' explained one director at a major financial services company, 'which turns into a global economic risk, which turns into a business risk for our customers. So it's a risk.' This enables corporations to bypass uncertain implications and unintended consequences with enhanced confidence. Chance and dangers can be translated into probabilities and financially quantified, allowing space for managing risk and identifying business opportunities in a constructed probable future.

It should come as scant surprise, then, that a report by the Economist Intelligence Unit (2011), based on a survey of more than 700 global executives, found that two-thirds of businesses saw climate change as 'an opportunity'. The putative soundness of this process was explained by the CEO of a global manufacturing company:

Climate change has been caused by man-made activities. That's in excess of 90 per cent [of published climate research]. When was the last time you made a business decision with that degree of certainty? So I think you're foolish if you're not starting to take action around, first of all, how [to] mitigate the risk of how this is going to impact my business. Secondly, how do I create an opportunity out of this issue?

This philosophy, as mentioned earlier, is rooted in the fundamental assumption that risk is invariably 'out there' and need only be 'found' and 'captured'; and once this has been achieved, of course, the next step is to exploit it. This is how, drawing on established risk discourses, corporations now customarily transmute the uncertainty surrounding climate change into different business strategies and, ultimately, opportunities. As another senior manager conceded: 'We see [climate change] as a business risk on the one hand, but also there's a business opportunity there – perhaps if you can reposition.' When all is said and done, when all the obfuscation has been stripped away, the principal driver is revealed to be neither the destiny of the planet nor the fate of humanity: it is profitability, plain, and simple. As one energy company manager confessed: 'It's not ideological – it's purely a business case.'

Yet to deal with these risks to their own best advantage corporations also need to place a value on them. Moreover, they need then to entangle the valuation in institutions and practices and seek to ensure the most favourable conditions for their future activities. This naturalises the risk framings, allowing businesses to become hegemonic in dealing with climate change.

In the following sections we explore this process in more detail to highlight how narrow risk framings come to be taken for granted and feed into corporations' core contention that the solutions to climate change lie in the market. In particular, we show:

- How monetary valuation makes climate change implications comparable and exchangeable
- How the entanglement in market conventions provides ready-made actors and institutions to deal with the issue
- How corporate political activities fend off any challenges to this world view.

The commodification of risk

For corporations to prosper from climate change the risks associated with it have to be meaningful in a business sense. In other words, they have to be calculable and valued in monetary terms. This requires a process of commodification.

By way of example, consider the way in which carbon is treated as measurable, exchangeable, and comparable. The complex relations underlying environmental changes are thereby relegated to the act of a chemical component being assigned a value in preparation for being traded or taxed (Swyngedouw, 2010). As if by magic, the uncertainty of climate change becomes predictable. The risk is assumed to be known and is ready to be incorporated into decision making.

This process is performative, in that it is possible to calculate and compare the risk using methods of cost–benefit analysis. This allows risk distribution. In terms of regulatory risk, for instance, the calculated cost of legislation on climate change can be compared with the cost of outcomes such as job losses/gains and curtailed/new investment. This parallels the logic of 'corporate environmentalism': putting a 'price on carbon' means emissions can be factored into strategies, which duly stimulate investments in 'green' energy and technologies. In short, the valuation of risk generates economic opportunities.

'The easiest thing to do', enthused the director of carbon and energy finance at one Australian financial services company, 'is to go carbon trading. There's a way to make money!' Sure enough, firms in the financial sector tend to enjoy an especially bountiful array of opportunities from the commodification of risk in relation to climate change. One of the attractions of carbon trading in particular is that it both embeds risk within policies and processes and ensures customers are also acting on that risk. As the environmental director explained:

[Corporate customers] need price risk management tools in terms of carbon trading, but they may also need additional working capital in terms of upgrading technology or systems to reduce energy consumption. So energy efficiency or clean technology or investing in biodiversity offset projects as a way of managing their future carbon price exposure.

Moreover, woe betide those corporate customers that neglect to adhere to this school of thought. As the same manager outlined in contemplating such a stance:'We will price [the] risk higher – and then we may not do the deal, because it's no longer economic.' The lesson: once the commodification and valuation of climate change have become part of the business model, it is through risk framings that customers are themselves evaluated.

Our own interviews showed the degree to which the work of pricing risk in relation to climate change has become a central element of the insurance industry's business model. To quote one senior manager: 'We're in the business of understanding and pricing risk and weather-related events.' In this setting, risks are again easily naturalised and supported by normal business practices, enabling corporations to devise different responses and so ensure there are no surprises. Common strategies include creating carbon pricing and trading mechanisms, developing new capabilities to better estimate and price risks, upgrading technology, and cultivating internal expertise. Yet again the according of monetary value makes risk framings 'real'.

Entangling risks in institutions and practices

The commodification of climate risks is intended to reframe uncertainties to fit a market ethos and to ensure commensurability between the valuation and the system that supports it. This is how corporations strive to disentangle climate change from an environmental sphere and entangle it within an economic sphere – through, for instance, carbon markets (Callon, 2009).

Many financial services companies have frequently incorporated a 'carbon price' into planned investments. This is seen as a means of risk management that accounts for possible regulatory change. Despite the vehement and partisan political debate that has ensued over 'carbon taxes', 'cap and trade', and other proposed climate policies, particularly in countries such as Australia and the United States, a good number of these firms have regarded carbon pricing of some kind as an inevitability (Hoffman, 2011a; Nyberg et al., 2013). As one sustainability consultant responsible for advising numerous large international corporations told us: 'The reality for CEOs today is that climate change is already being factored into valuation models and portfolio management decisions.' The growing international adoption of carbon markets – including in the United States and China, the world's largest GHG-emitting economies – suggests this strategy has been prescient (Ecofys and World Bank, 2014). Irrespective of whether future government policy promotes a 'carbon tax' or a market mechanism to trade carbon emissions, investments already account for a carbon price.

Consequently, the risks surrounding climate change are now firmly entwined with corporate activities and practices. Their economic valuation is stabilised through the work of sustainability departments and managers tasked with developing an internal culture that leads to yet further risk commodification, modelling, and adherence to risk management procedures. In the words of the environment manager at a large international media corporation: 'My job is to keep their risk as low as possible – and possibly to zero – on all aspects of environment, from regulatory right through to perception and reputation.' What we see here once again is the conviction that climate change, having been tidily packaged as predictable and calculable, can be controlled.

Applying this 'logic', it follows that how risks are handled can then be evaluated both internally, through risk and performance management, and externally, through economising the risk constructs. According to the chief risk officer at a major insurance company, risk culture is even 'one of the key performance indicators for bonuses for managers'. Like the discourse of markets and profit, it is essential for managerial understanding of corporate activity in many firms and industries.

A large energy corporation that took part in our study offers a notable illustration of the entanglement of risk management in relation to climate change. As one of Australia's biggest electricity producers, the company is a significant emitter of carbon pollution and under the then government's clean energy legislation faced commercial pressure to ensure it passed on the costs of carbon pricing to consumers. As one senior manager explained: 'The largest risk is not being able to pass through to the end users the costs we're incurring upstream.' Granted, this might well have represented the largest risk; but, crucially, it was not the only one. There was also the reputational risk of mounting consumer hostility to rising electricity prices. As a senior sales manager observed: 'I think one of the biggest risks is just the organisational reputation and brand risk. What's this going to do to the brand in the broader market context?' Acknowledging this, the company established internal project teams to redesign billing processes and communicate with customers about carbon price mechanisms. The perception of 'price gouging' had to be addressed. This shows how the continuous enactment of valuations, roles, and models serves to further naturalise and stabilise the conception of climate change as involving precisely defined forms of risk.

This credo is further expanded at a macro level through efforts to establish national and international emission-trading schemes. These have created a political assemblage of actors – including specialist consultancies, banks, and risk managers – that support and facilitate the marketisation of the risks surrounding climate change. Naturally, in light of the commodification of risk, the market is portrayed as the one and only sphere that can adequately deal with commodities; other would-be solutions such as state regulation of emissions are derided as too radical or sadly naïve. Risks and remedies are habitually presented as pairs, with every framing miraculously accompanied by a perfect fit. As ever, the message, at least at its most basic, is unmistakable: the corporate answer is the only answer.

Politicisation: managing the conditions of risks

It is not enough for corporations merely to construct climate change as different forms of risk: for the risk frame to take hold, the constructions also need to be socially binding. The discursive practices of framing risks and entangling them both internally (i.e., within the organisation) and externally (i.e., in society) require a specific range of circumstances. The motivations are not necessarily political in the strictest sense – risk management, after all, is how businesses commonly deal with uncertainty – but corporate political strategies are undoubtedly involved. It is by influencing other corporations, governments, and the public that companies define the broader conditions within which risk constructions are debated.

The framing of climate change as different types of risk, along with the valuation of these risks, also involves inter-organisational collaboration. For instance, the carbon trading managers at a major financial services company told us how, in seeking to manage the carbon pricing risks they envisaged in future regulation, they arranged seminars, workshops, and conferences with senior figures from other corporations, government officials, and other key 'thought leaders' on climate change. Such activity serves to emphasise a given organisation's particular risk framing, sometimes even allowing it to spill over into the wider community of sustainability professionals – both in work and in more informal settings. As this company's environment manager remarked:

The reason I know all the guys from the other companies is also because we obviously do a lot of client engagement around carbon and so you tend to meet the treasurer or the CFO who's managing the risk and the sustainability or environment person who's reducing the risk. So in terms of all the advocacy activities we all tend to be on the same forums and so forth. So that's probably why it's a bit of a club.

Networking of this type, as we explore in greater depth in Chapter 4, also extends to the lobbying of government and rival political parties for legislative outcomes that best suit given corporate strategic positions. As one external relations manager explained: 'There's a lot of interplay between what the business does and ... how that's communicated to government and also how we position ourselves in relation to regulatory and reputational risk.'

This political work is critical in managing and reshaping climate change as both a regulatory and a market/reputational risk. Whether for or against specific government policy, corporations reframe climate change within an economic risk valuation that is often wholly divorced from the material consequences of the phenomenon. The performative risk framings are thus political, with corporations favouring particular descriptions of reality that correspond to their economic interests. Following this, there is arguably no direct benefit for financial or insurance companies to mitigate events, such as floods, fires, and hurricanes, when the possibility of pricing the risk exists. In the entanglement of climate change in the market, there are no standards or evaluations where climate change as a natural hazard is taken into account. As the environment manager at one financial services company outlined: 'If they [corporate clients] are managing it really well, no matter how "dirty" an industry they are, but if they're managing their risk really well, we will lend to them. That is our position.'

It is by hedging and spreading risks that corporations are able to manage multiple futures and distribute further uncertainties to actors who are not part of the discursive negotiations. This is a key point: the distribution of calculability is far from equal, since not all can take part in risk framing. Some, such as businesses and other market entities, have a voice and enjoy the biggest say; others, such as local communities and others with limited political impact, have no voice, yet are left to face the greatest uncertainties.

Risk channels our attention in a very narrow way, even permitting what Klein (2014: 310–12) terms 'sacrifice zones' – areas of the world where environmental degradation is allowed as a 'necessary' price

for continued economic growth. Risk allows harm to be displaced
to others, including the poor, less developed economies, and the global South. As the senior risk officer at a large insurance corporation
admitted: 'Ultimately, the insurer can always put his prices up and
cover himself ... but that just means the community's paying for the
risk at the end of the day.'

When risk constructions misfire

Corporations like to couch risk management and valuation in the
language of certainty, but recent history suggests this apparent confidence is misplaced. Nature's capacity to bite back has been demonstrated repeatedly and with mounting ferocity. The destruction of
New Orleans by Hurricane Katrina, the flooding of New York City by
Superstorm Sandy, and the procession of major floods and bushfires
in Australia are just some of the extreme weather events that have
exposed how comfortable assumptions of calculating and pricing risk
overlook the increasingly chaotic state of our climate.

The problem is that the narrow framing of climate change as corporate 'risk' or 'opportunity' disregards the innate complexities of the
phenomenon. There is no discursive closure. In analytically overex-
tending the construction of risk, these representations ultimately misfire, in that the economic valuation of climate change risk is unable
to account for extreme weather events and other unforeseeable realities. The risk frames account only for calculable and linear natural
effects, market actors, and the self-interested aspects of consumers.
As a result, excluded forces and relations continuously surprise the
performed 'reality' in a variety of ways. This invites catastrophe, and
often catastrophe does not disappoint.

There are many ways in which the performed 'reality' propa-
gated by the discourse of risk can be surprised by the nature of a
climate-changed planet. Even if we examine a construct as basic as the
measurement of carbon emissions we can see immediately that many
fundamental aspects of the environment are simply not taken into
account. Human-centric market conventions omit species and features
of the natural world that lack a market price. The critical contribution of biodiversity in the formation of soil and nutrient recycling, the
provision of natural resources, the decomposition of waste, the purification of air and water, and the moderation of the climate is unseen

and ignored (Daily, 1997). That the impacts of climate change go far beyond obvious weather events, threatening the very viability of life on Earth, encapsulates a scale of change to which risk framings pay no heed (Kolbert, 2014b).

Indeed, the calculation of carbon emissions is itself open to political interpretation, as evidenced by the issue of shale and coal seam gas fracking. Energy corporations have dramatically expanded their investments in non-conventional gas extraction through this method, promoting the resulting 'natural gas' as a 'cleaner' fossil fuel for electricity generation. 'Carbon' in terms of CO_2 emissions has become marketised and priced as risk, yet fugitive emissions from fracking, despite producing the far more powerful greenhouse gas methane (CH_4), receive far less attention and are a subject of ongoing political bargaining (Howarth et al., 2011b; Mooney, 2014).

The framing of climate change as risk also excludes the non-linear aspects of natural forces. The consequent 'misfires' are particularly evident in the insurance sector, where companies, despite their future risk projections, are regularly caught off-guard by changing weather patterns. In 2011 QBE, one of Australia's major mining insurers, suffered significant financial losses due to unprecedented floods. The company's value was halved. Even so, its chairman declared she was undecided on the subject of climate change and what it meant for risk management, insisting: 'There are always going to be changes in climate, no matter what happens or what it is caused by … Who knows? I don't have a crystal ball.' (Ryan, 2012). As a senior risk officer at one insurance company acknowledged:

Most people didn't think it hailed in Melbourne until last year. There was another one in Perth – you know, it was classic. It was known in the industry as 'un-modelled risk', which means there isn't a detailed model of the risk that you can use to price it. Hail in Perth was unknown – I mean, completely unknown.

In addition, because they are often excluded from the calculations, non-market actors sometimes intervene in ways that wrong-foot corporate risk modelling. Broader criticism of 'greenwashing' is frequently unforeseen. For example, a media corporation's internal focus on reducing emissions stood in marked contrast to the editorial line of the company's newspapers, which were widely criticised for their promotion of climate change denial. Similarly, a global manufacturer was attacked for claiming a 'green' ethos while heavily involved in coal, oil, and nuclear technologies. In these instances it is the public, not nature, that bites back.

Finally, only certain aspects or subject positions contribute to the framing of risk. Others are discarded. Market and reputational risk framings, for example, exclude aspects of consumption or consumer identification that are not based on market conventions. Such an approach again encourages misfires. So for instance, an energy company's development of coal seam gas extraction sparked a vehement public relations battle with agricultural landholders and communities. These groups denounced gas 'fracking' as environmentally harmful, a danger to their health and well-being and a threat to rural life. Here the non-market conventions of community, aesthetics, and the environment impinged on the risk calculus of claimed lower carbon emissions and increasing commodity prices. Media coverage of farmers and protestors chaining themselves to bulldozers, along with images of angry protests outside the company's city headquarters, provided vivid testament to the misfire and reputational harm that resulted.

And yet, corporations appear remarkably resilient in avoiding the impacts of these risk misfires. Claims from non-market actors or marginalised consumer voices can be countered by altering risk framings – notwithstanding, of course, that this might lead to new misfires. The act of framing climate change as risk is one that is constantly reiterated and adapted, and, as we have seen, businesses are able to spread the consequences to those who lack political and economic clout. Here there are clear parallels with the global financial crisis. That, too, was characterised by market actors 'protecting' their frames, with the assumed predictability of risk ensuring against accountability in the event of misfires. There is, though, an important distinction: in the case of climate change governments appear unwilling to take on the resulting social and financial costs.

If this stance persists it is feasible that citizens and local communities will eventually bear the consequences through higher insurance prices or, worse still, a lack of insurance altogether. As one manager acknowledged: 'It's easy to continually pass the buck, but unfortunately the risks remain. The state governments don't have any money. Local governments are trying to raise money by, in some cases, an additional levy on your rates.'

Such risk allocation is especially evident at a global level, where those most materially at risk from the climate crisis are future generations and people in poor and less developed economies. We can rest sadly assured that the individuals and entities currently enjoying the benefits of framing climate change as risk are unlikely to pay the price for the misfires that will almost inevitably ensue. In the aftermath of the catastrophic and costly climate events that lie ahead, it will become increasingly difficult to locate the corporate interests responsible, let alone hold them to account.

Conclusion

Ulrich Beck (1992) has persuasively declared that we live in a 'risk society' in which the key question is how to prevent or manage the hazardous side effects of wealth production. As we have seen in this chapter, corporate responses to climate change provide a particularly salient example of the social construction of risk, with businesses framing their responses in terms of physical, regulatory, market, and reputational risks.

These framings allow the diffuse, contested, and uncertain nature of climate change to be made more local, timely, and manageable. Moreover, they allow for strategies, practices, and local activities that seek to respond to threats and capture opportunities for further value creation. This is how the construction of climate risk becomes a performative activity, justifying new practices, roles, and relationships. A principal goal is to make climate risk calculable and, by extension, assign it a monetary value. For those involved in the process, the commodification of climate risk can broaden markets and enhance profits; for those who have no say in the matter, the impacts can bring far less auspicious consequences.

As illustrated by the growing interaction of companies and governments over carbon regulation and pricing, the corporate framing of climate risk is innately political. It is also evident at a higher level in terms of how it moulds and determines climate futures. MacKenzie (2006) has shown how theoretical models of risk management are used by finance professionals to shape the practices that the very same models are intended to predict in the first place. Defining a risk involves folding future uncertainties into the present; and the future itself can in turn be refolded on the basis of our supposed knowledge of it. As Esposito (2013: 106) argues: '[S]ince the future does not yet exist, the present expectations about the future contribute to its production.'

As a result, despite the apparent certainty that risk constructions provide corporations in particular and society more generally, observed patterns can in fact undermine the very model or construct that is supposed to predict or explain them (Butler, 2010). As we have suggested, given the lack of discursive closure in perfectly representing the represented, this produces misfires.

There are countless ways of calculating or attempting to foresee uncertainties. These combine in predicting and claiming the future. The performative account of risk suggests a continuous and pluralistic process of producing a future that surprises its predictions: what is studied or modelled will shape the calculations beyond what was predicted or assumed, and it is only under certain conditions that the models or theories bring into being what they intended to describe (Butler, 2010). Despite a consensus of climate science emphasising how increasing GHG concentrations will upset traditionally stable weather patterns, the fact that ever more extreme weather events surprise both business and governments highlights the limitations of current climate risk framing.

This brings us back to the issue of creative self-destruction. By making our climate uncertainties seemingly manageable and rendering them a basis for opportunity and profit, corporate constructions of climate risk emphasise once again a vision of human mastery over nature. Like latter-day wizardry, the calculus of risk management demonstrates the ability of markets and capital to not only control the natural world but somehow anticipate it. Our technological prowess foretells a future in which there will be no 'bad surprises' (Derrida, 2003) and we can take preventive action to escape danger.

However, the truth is that this approach closes off the possibility of the dramatic emissions reductions that scientists have shown are necessary to avoid calamitous climate change (Anderson and Bows, 2011). Tragically – some might even say scandalously – corporate risk framings remain wedded to 'business as usual' scenarios and singularly fail to acknowledge the desperate exigencies of a carbon-constrained world. Precisely the kind of devastating environmental change that is supposedly being anticipated and avoided is thus locked in to an even more terrifying degree.

4 | Corporate political activity and climate coalitions

Corporate philanthropy should not be, cannot be disinterested ... This inevitably involves efforts to shape or reshape the climate of public opinion.

(Kristol, 1977: 18)

As we saw in the previous chapter, the corporate construction of climate change as 'risk' is an inherently political activity. This is evident not just within organisations but through their interactions with other social groups and with government. In this chapter we examine more closely the role of corporations in the political struggle over the framing and definition of climate change as an economic and political issue, focusing on a number of countries – Australia, Canada, the United Kingdom, and the United States– where the battle has been most fiercely fought.

Climate change provides an especially salient example of businesses' intensifying determination to shape social and economic outcomes (Barley, 2007; 2010). Nowhere has this been more evident than in the increasingly contested sphere of climate politics. Corporations have sought to influence the agenda on climate policy and carbon regulation directly (through campaign contributions and lobbying) and indirectly (by manipulating public opinion through marketing, newspaper op-eds, 'astroturfing' and political action committees). Various features of regulation have been both favoured and opposed, but one common denominator has been conspicuous: the conviction that the answer to climate change should inevitably revolve around market expansion and economic growth.

Corporate political activities around climate change can be split into two camps. As noted in previous chapters, the first of these is rooted in the emerging discourse of 'corporate environmentalism', which sees climate change as both a business risk and an opportunity and emphasises innovation, technology, self-regulation, and marketisation as preferred responses. The second is what has been called the 'fossil fuels forever' perspective (Levy and Spicer, 2013), which seeks to downplay the threat posed by the climate crisis and rejects proposals for carbon regulation. Both positions have involved corporations in significant political activity, much of it geared towards defining government policies on GHG emissions mitigation, fossil fuel development, renewable energy, and carbon pricing and regulation. Each camp has engaged in coalition-building with like-minded enterprises, industry groups, the media, think tanks, NGOs, political parties, and individual politicians.

We argue that these practices represent a critical intervention in the broader social understanding of climate change. They not only transform what the climate crisis means and how it can be responded to: they also recalibrate our roles and identities as citizens within a world of neoliberal corporate capitalism.

Accordingly, while there may be nascent support for businesses to solve social and environmental problems (Porter and Kramer, 2011), we contend that the primary objective of corporate engagement in climate politics has been – and, indeed, remains – to maintain the hegemony of neoliberal capitalism and reinforce the conceit of the corporation as the principal agent of response. Even among corporate actors that genuinely try to address climate change, the environment is eventually compromised out of the capitalist equation. Genuine and creative solutions thus become part of our broader creative self-destruction.

Business and climate politics

A corporation's political activity revolves around influencing regulatory outcomes in ways that favour the firm's strategy and shareholder interests (Hillman et al., 2004). Of course, there is nothing new about this. The history of capitalism is littered with examples of collusion between the political and business worlds. Witness the expansion of empire and business under the British East India Company, the business co-option of government by America's late-nineteenth-century 'robber barons', and President Eisenhower's prescient warning of the merging of business and politics in the 'military–industrial complex' (Prechel, 2000; Zinn, 2003).

Yet in recent decades there have been growing calls for the world of business to intervene in civil society to a much greater degree. Perhaps unsurprisingly, many of these appeals to help to resolve various social and environmental problems have come from the business world itself.

They are reflected in the discourse of corporate social responsibility (CSR), 'corporate citizenship', and 'shared value', all of which promote the idea of business as a force for social good (Matten and Crane, 2005; Porter and Kramer, 2011).

As a result, the notion of being a 'responsible' or 'good corporate citizen' is now pervasive. Many major companies participate in corporate citizenship initiatives such as the United Nations Global Compact and the Global Reporting Initiative. The corporation is seen as playing a central role in the 'administration of citizenship rights' (Matten and Crane, 2005: 175), solving political problems where the state is lacking or has withdrawn from the provision of legal and economic infrastructure (Scherer and Palazzo, 2011; Valente and Crane, 2010). Although this is often viewed as a positive development, critical scholars have argued that the extension of corporate influence is driven by the pursuit of narrow business interests and has the potential to 'undermine representative democracy and the public good' (Banerjee, 2008b; Barley, 2007: 201).

This expansive view of corporate involvement is evident among ecological modernists and proponents of green business, who contend that technological innovation based on market mechanisms offers the most viable response to climate change (Esty and Winston, 2006; Shellenberger and Nordhaus, 2011). Moreover, there is a more immediate and instrumental motivation for businesses to engage with climate politics, in that the risks of mandatory emissions regulation are significant for corporations that rely on the production, sale, and use of fossil fuels. It is perhaps not surprising then that business has become increasingly immersed in the political debate over this issue and the potential regulatory responses.

As we saw earlier, business awareness of climate change dates back to at least the 1980s and the emergence of an international political discussion over the need to reduce GHG emissions (Weart, 2011). In 1990, against this backdrop, major US corporations from the fossil fuel, energy, and manufacturing sectors formed the Global Climate Coalition (GCC) to push back climate action – a goal they fulfilled only too well, particularly in the United States, over the course of the decade that followed.

Now, a quarter of a century later, the GCC's key strategies read like a blueprint for the art of climate denial. They included stressing the uncertainties of climate science; highlighting the economic costs of cutting emissions; promoting the views of climate 'sceptics' in government representations, media, and publications; and sponsoring ersatz environmental organisations such as the Information Council for the Environment.

Wider corporate resistance during this period included funding for major advertising campaigns, financial contributions to political parties, and appeals to broader conservative ideological values (Beder, 2011; Levy and Egan, 1998; 2003; Oreskes and Conway, 2010). By any standard, the impact of these combined efforts was profound. Vehement opposition to any form of mandatory emissions reductions hobbled US government attempts to respond to climate change throughout the 1990s; in addition, with the United States determinedly rebuffing demands for global controls, international negotiations were also negatively affected (McCright and Dunlap, 2003).

Despite this groundswell, industry rejection of climate science and carbon regulation was far from total. From the late 1990s onwards, more moderate voices emerged to stress acceptance of climate science and the need for action. As we have noted, many companies adopted a 'corporate environmentalist' perspective, highlighting the 'win–win' outcomes that could result from improved eco-efficiency and 'green' products and services. Reviewing the history of business involvement in global climate politics, Levy and Spicer (2013) argue that the years from 1998 to 2008 witnessed a 'carbon compromise' in which ecological modernisation and corporate environmentalism became more prominent business discourses.

Key examples of a more accommodating approach included oil giants BP and Shell, which during the late 1990s publicly acknowledged the danger of climate change and undertook investments in renewable energy technologies (Kolk and Levy, 2001). Other industry groups that advocated action included the Pew Center on Global Climate Change, which was established in 1998 and consisted of corporate heavyweights such as BP, Toyota, Boeing, Enron, Whirlpool, and 3M (Levy and Egan, 2003). Firms and industries around the world took on a public leadership position on climate change. European companies such as Unilever, MunichRe, and SwissRe and global bodies such as the World Business Council for Sustainable Development promoted corporate environmentalism (Holliday et al., 2002). It was a time of some hope.

But then came the global financial crisis. The economic costs of climate action were re-emphasised. Denial of climate change found renewed favour in many Western democracies. Ongoing stagnation saw the further re-entrenchment of negative views. In countries such as the United States, the United Kingdom, Australia, and Canada climate change became part of the 'culture wars' and a touchstone issue for a growing populist movement defined by its unwillingness to accept policies of emissions mitigation (Hoffman, 2012; Nyberg et al., 2013). The failure of the 2009 Copenhagen climate talks and the faux scandal of 'Climategate' stoked the politicisation process, with right-wing politicians and media propagating a narrative of climate change as a hoax and a conspiracy (Mann, 2012).

US researchers have identified a range of actors that contributed to the 'climate-change denial machine' during this period (Dunlap and McCright, 2011: 147). They included:

- Major fossil fuel corporations (e.g., ExxonMobil, Peabody Coal, Koch Industries, and the Western Fuels Association)
- Industry groups (e.g., the US Chamber of Commerce and the National Association of Manufacturers)
- Conservative industry-funded foundations (e.g., the Koch and Scaife Foundations), and think tanks (e.g., the American Enterprise Institute, the Cato Institute, the Heartland Institute, and the Heritage Foundation)
- Front groups and astroturf organisations (e.g., the Global Climate Coalition, the Cooler Heads Coalition, Americans for Prosperity, and Freedom Works).

Through interaction with Republican and Tea Party politicians, the right-wing media (most notably Fox News) and an army of sceptic bloggers, these groups have created an echo chamber of climate change denial, transforming the climate policy debate in the United States and, increasingly, in other national contexts (Brulle, 2014; Dunlap and McCright, 2011).

Arguably the most infamous corporate deniers of climate change are the Koch brothers, Charles and David. During the past decade they have directed more than $67 million to groups that share their view (Baxter, 2011). Given that their business, Koch Industries, ranks among the top 15 polluters in the United States (PERI, 2013), they have clear motivations for opposing any sort of regulation. With the restrictions on corporate electoral funding struck down by the Supreme Court in the 2010 Citizens United verdict, Koch-affiliated networks lavished more than $400 million on promoting conservative political candidates during the 2012 presidential election (Dickinson, 2014).

Corporate support for conservative think tanks has done serious damage to public understanding of climate change (Dunlap and McCright, 2011). In 2012, the Heartland Institute, which is funded by the fossil fuel industry, even ran a billboard campaign associating those who believe in climate change with mass murderers, juxtaposing a mugshot of Unabomber Ted Kaczinsky with the tag line: 'I still believe in global warming. Do you?' (Clark and Berners-Lee, 2013)

One company that highlights the critical role of corporate political engagement over climate change especially well is ExxonMobil. It grew out of the government breakup of the Rockefeller Standard Oil monopoly in 1911 under the Sherman Antitrust Act. Originally known as the Standard Oil Company of New Jersey, it merged with Humble Oil in 1972, becoming Exxon, and with Mobil in 1999, became ExxonMobil. Its diverse activities in global oil exploration, extraction, and processing have been highly profitable: annual revenues now exceed $400 billion (United States), a figure greater than the GDP of all but the top 30 national economies.

ExxonMobil has been particularly active in its opposition to any proposals for cuts in GHG emissions. It was a founding member of the GCC and, like Koch Industries, has played a leading role in funding the broader denial movement, questioning climate science, and stressing the economic costs of any attempt to reduce fossil fuel use (Brulle, 2014; Mooney, 2005b). A highly conservative company, it has also been noticeably partisan in its political activity, disproportionately funding conservative Republican politicians over rival Democrats for much of its history: during the 2010 election cycle around 90 per cent of its political funding went to Republicans. Against the context of the climate debate, ExxonMobil's strategists undertook a highly targeted lobbying campaign, grading political contributions according to four tiers:

• Senators and congressmen from oil-rich states who were strong allies (including former President George W. Bush and Vice President Dick Cheney)

- Supportive free market Republicans
- Democrats and liberal Republicans who voted against ExxonMobil's interests but could be swayed
- Democrats and environmental campaigners viewed as hostile to the company's interests – otherwise known as 'the enemy' (Coll, 2012: 75).

Tying into the 'fossil fuel forever' imaginary, ExxonMobil analysts foresee a rosy future for the company's products. Global demand for oil, gas, and coal through to the year 2040 is predicted to continue to grow. Government restrictions of fossil fuel use are deemed 'highly unlikely' (Associated Press, 2014). Engaging in the political cycle on issues such as climate change therefore constitutes part of a wider long-term corporate strategy of profit and growth. As former CEO Lee Raymond observed with spectacular insouciance: 'We see governments come and go' (Coll, 2012: 21).

Examining the practice of corporate climate politics

Australia provides a good example of the divisive politics of climate change. Australia is one of the world's largest exporters of coal and natural gas and has one of the highest levels of GHG emissions per capita among developed economies (Garnaut, 2008). It is a country in whose recent history the divisive politics of climate change are writ large. As such, it offers a prime setting in which to explore the practices and effects of corporate political engagement with government and civil society.

Early international negotiations on climate change featured Australia as an active participant, but the election of the conservative Howard government in 1996 signalled a marked shift in attitude. For the next decade the approach to carbon emissions reduction was decidedly minimalist. In line with the United States, Australia refused to ratify the Kyoto Protocol (Crowley, 2007; Griffiths et al., 2007). The government viewed regulation as a threat to economic growth and the country's competitive advantage as a fossil fuel exporter (Pearse, 2007; 2009).

A further reversal came in 2007, when the incoming Labor government, led by Kevin Rudd, committed to introducing a carbon emissions trading scheme. Failure to reach global agreement at the 2009

UN Copenhagen Climate Summit, along with conservative political opposition and growing resistance from industry, forced a deferral. Narrowly scraping back into power at the 2010 election, the minority Labor government, led by Julia Gillard and in alliance with the Greens, advocated a fixed price on carbon emissions, to be paid by the country's 500 largest GHG emitters as a precursor to a full-scale emissions trading system (Commonwealth of Australia, 2011).

This was to prove especially contentious. The conservative opposition, championing a 'people's revolt' and with backing from the media, right-wing think tanks, and industry groups, launched a highly effective public campaign against what was dubbed a 'toxic carbon tax' (ABC, 2011b; Manne, 2011). There is no doubt that the controversy played a part in Labor's defeat at the 2013 election.

Under the new conservative Liberal National Party government, led by Tony Abbott, climate politics became a central focus. One of the new government's first actions was to disband the independent Climate Commission, repeal carbon pricing, and discourage renewable energy investment. In July 2014, less than 20 years after enthusiastically supporting international negotiations on how to tackle the climate crisis, Australia had the dubious honour of being the first nation on Earth to abolish a price on carbon emissions (Bogle and Oremus, 2014; Cox, 2014a).

In the following sections we outline how these political shifts occurred and the role of corporations in shaping their context.

Corporate campaigning on climate change

One way in which corporations engage with the issue of climate change is through *campaigning* for specific legislative outcomes. Practically, this involves direct attempts to shape public policy through formal submissions to government, lobbying ministers and bureaucrats, media releases, interviews and conference presentations, as well as indirect activities such as building alliances with like-minded companies, industry associations, opposition politicians, think tanks, and NGOs. The basic argument underlying these practices is that corporations can and will act in the best interests of society.

Corporate campaigning has been evident in the policy debates on climate change in Australia, Canada, the United Kingdom, and United States. In Australia corporations submitted evidence to the government in relation to the proposed Carbon Pollution Reduction Scheme (CPRS). Setting out their formal responses to the planned legislation – including support, proposed variations, and, in many cases, opposition – they stressed the link between their competitiveness and broader national economic well-being. In essence, they drew attention to the balance between society's interests and their own. As the coal industry argued: 'Coal is vital to Australia's prosperity … It's our largest export earner – over $55 billion last year' (ACA, 2009). Corporate claims of this kind maintain that even if we accept the science of anthropogenic climate change we still need a growing economy to address the threat – an argument that conveniently ignores economic growth's central contribution to further exacerbating the crisis.

Corporations also engage in more informal practices such as lobbying of government ministers and bureaucrats for preferred policy outcomes. For instance, former US president George Bush's decision to not sign the Kyoto Protocol, allegedly resulted in part from pressure from ExxonMobil. In briefing papers the US administration thanked ExxonMobil executives for the company's 'active involvement' in helping to shape the government's climate-change policy (Vidal, 2005). In a similar manner, Pearse (2007: 227–87) documents how in Australia during the 1990s and 2000s a powerful group of corporate lobbyists known as the 'greenhouse mafia' protected the interests of the coal, oil, mining, and electricity industries by arguing against international commitments to reduce GHG emissions; and Australia duly followed the United States in rebuffing Kyoto.

These lobbying efforts often contrast with corporations' public commitments to tackling climate change. As one senior corporate sustainability adviser in Australia confided: 'In certain circles there are a lot of people who are very angry about that. There's a public persona – "Yes, climate change is important, we need to act" – but they then undermine it through public policy in Canberra.' Corporate websites and sustainability reports might publicly promote action on climate change, but behind the scenes companies that produce high levels of carbon emissions lobby intensely for more accommodating regulatory outcomes. Thus corporations address market or reputational risks through progressive public pronouncements while simultaneously limiting regulatory risks through backroom deal-chasing.

The new business opportunities that inevitably arise in the course of creative self-destruction's spread are especially ripe for this approach. A recent study of corporate lobbying in the United Kingdom (Cave and Rowell, (2014) outlines how the nuclear industry, the gas industry, and even businesses associated with tar sands production are now endeavouring to establish themselves as sources of climate-friendly energy. The trend is particularly evident in the 'selling' of hydraulic fracturing or 'fracking', with most of the championing carried out by lobbying agencies and government under the banner of energy security and carbon emissions reduction.

The Canadian tar sands offer perhaps the most ironic example of the quest to turn fossil fuel into 'clean' or 'green' energy. The average emission of greenhouse gases from the extraction of tar sands is estimated to be 4.5 times more intense than that generated by conventional crude oil extraction in the United States (Cave and Rowell, 2014: 105). Following more than a hundred events and tours of the tar sands regions in Alberta for MPs, members of the European Parliament, journalists, and friendly NGOs, the lobbying effort managed to delay EU climate legislation, which would have penalised tar sands oil (Cave and Rowell, 2014). Here corporations did not try to convince their own governments: rather, governments and politicians were used to 'sell' the concept of tar sands oil – like nuclear energy, fracking, and others before it – to a more sceptical audience at home and abroad.

Sometimes, not least when the debate over climate change intensifies, it is necessary to look beyond even these traditional paths of political influence. Corporations and industry groups often engage in more explicit public campaigning through the media, PR, and advertising activities. In Australia mining and manufacturing groups funded television and newspaper advertisements opposing the Labor government's CPRS and 'carbon tax' legislation, emphasising the threat to jobs and claiming that pricing carbon emissions would do little to solve the problem of climate change (Taylor, 2011); the coal industry in particular mounted community campaigns targeting electorates where they said jobs would be lost (ACA, 2009); and peak industry bodies and prominent mining magnates financed visits by prominent deniers of climate change, generating media attention and further eroding public support for the government's plans (ABC, 2011a).

However, public campaigning is limited not only to companies opposing carbon regulation. For instance, during the mid-2000s a number of Australia's most prominent corporations, including Westpac (banking), IAG (insurance), Visy Industries (manufacturing), BP (resources), and Origin Energy (utilities), established the Australian Business Roundtable on Climate Change. Reflecting similar activities in the United States (Kolk and Pinkse, 2007), they published reports in an attempt to build broader community support for government action to reduce GHG emissions (Hawker, 2007; Preston and Jones, 2006). The clear and urgent threat of climate change was emphasised, as was the 'leadership role' these corporations had adopted in response. One sustainability manager at a large communications company that took part in our study asserted that corporations had in fact led the fight in tackling the climate crisis: 'So far business has done more than government, I believe – in Australia definitely. I mean, anything that's happened in Australia has generally been because business has done something.' This shows the corporate world's public campaigning is by no means limited to companies that oppose carbon regulation: businesses also present themselves as 'good corporate citizens', primed to compensate for a lack of government leadership and to act in the 'national interest'.

Corporate campaigning on climate change also extends to engagement with industry associations, business coalitions, and NGOs with a view to defining the wider social debate. Many corporations have set up external boards of advice that include environmental NGO representatives who counsel senior managers on social and environmental performance and give insights into public responses to corporate activities (Dauvergne and LeBaron, 2014; Klein, 2014). Groups such as the Nature Conservancy and the Environmental Defense Fund have, for instance, forged partnerships with major companies such as BHP Billiton, Walmart, McDonald's, FedEx, AT&T, and others (Environmental Defence Fund, 2014; The Nature Conservancy, 2014). As the sustainability manager at a major retail chain explained: 'They [NGO representatives] challenge us on certain things, but they're likely to do that confidentially and help you develop your processes and policies.' Publicising such links through co-authored reports and funded initiatives bolsters a corporation's social legitimacy, which further assists in influencing government policy. As the sustainability manager at a large energy utility company outlined:

We get a lot of support for the different policy work that we've done. They [NGOs] obviously want to see the uptake of large-scale renewable energy, so [it's a case of] making sure that the messages that they're selling to government are in alignment with us. We're finding those points of common policy objectives help to strengthen the message, because if government is hearing the same thing from multiple different camps they're more likely to listen.

Corporations also use more indirect practices to sway the debate on climate change. One strategy for those opposed to carbon regulation is to provide funding and support for proxy organisations, which can manipulate public attitudes through organised media campaigns and the formation of aligned social movements ('astroturfing') (Cho et al., 2011). Just as funding from ExxonMobil and Koch Industries was vital in giving a voice to right-wing US think tanks such as the Competitive Enterprise Institute and the Heartland Institute, corporate donations have been critical to the likes of Australia's Institute of Public Affairs – which has promoted the denial of climate change by targeting political parties and marginal electorates (Cubby and Lawes, 2010). In the lead-up to a parliamentary vote on carbon regulation the Australian Trade and Industry Alliance, backed by corporate financing, took out full-page newspaper adverts that read: 'Carbon Tax Pain but no Climate Change Gain … Australia produces less than 1.5 per cent of the world's carbon emissions but will pay the world's largest carbon tax.' In 2010 and 2011, the success of such proxy campaigns was starkly demonstrated by televised mass rallies at which crowds of mostly older citizens voiced their hostility to the Australian government's 'carbon tax' and angrily denounced climate change as a conspiracy and a hoax (ABC, 2011b; Godfrey and Tranter, 2011).

In Australia the instrumental advantages flowing from corporate political action have been particularly manifest for the fossil fuel sector since the election of a conservative government in September 2013. This has resulted in not only the repeal of carbon pricing but also the dismantling of advisory groups and renewable energy initiatives; it has also seen the winding back of environmental protections – pejoratively labelled 'green tape' – in order to facilitate major fossil fuel developments, including new 'mega-mines' in Queensland's Galilee coal basin (Potter, 2014). The government's advisers have been notably drawn from corporate elites with close links to the country's major fossil fuel interests and have long promoted the denial of anthropogenic climate change (Readfearn, 2013). The revolving door between government and the coal, gas, and energy industries was perhaps at its most visible when a 2014 inquiry called for the country's Renewable Energy Target to be scrapped, thereby killing off Australia's fledgling renewables industry and delivering billions of dollars' worth of future revenues to established fossil-fuel-based providers (Taylor, 2014). The inquiry was led by business man and climate sceptic Dick Warburton, who previously chaired lobby group Manufacturing Australia in their campaigning against climate-change regulation.

Exemplifying the good corporate climate citizen

Corporations also engage with civil society by promoting themselves as responsible organisations concerned about the environment. This is a political practice we term 'exemplifying'. Legitimacy is claimed through self-regulation, marketing, and public relations. Businesses present themselves as role models that embody many of the ideal practices and innovative capabilities required to ensure the well-being of present and future generations. Sustainability reports, webpages, and other documents showcase companies' own voluntary initiatives, along with new products and technologies, as the best response to climate change. For example, as of 2014, more than 300 major corporations have signed up to Caring for Climate, a United Nations Global Compact project that seeks to mobilise businesses to demonstrate leadership on climate action by pricing carbon; signatories include oil giants such as China Petroleum, Statoil, and Repsol (http://caringfor-climate.org/workstreams/carbon-pricing/).

Voluntary reporting is a strategy common among corporations keen to exemplify their standing as good 'corporate citizens' on climate change. Through engagement with international institutions and ratings agencies such as the Global Reporting Initiative and the Carbon Disclosure Project, businesses produce extensive public reports that detail their contributions to social and environmental sustainability. As a senior manager at a mining company explained: 'That's where you can stand up [and be] accountable to your industry peers and to NGOs and say that [this company] has got world's best practice in risk management or in a climate change response.' Sustainability reporting is a form of public relations through which corporations can proclaim their environmental friendliness – highlighting, say, the attaining of 'carbon-neutral' status through energy efficiencies. As noted by one of the interviewees, a senior figure at a major resource company: 'Our sustainability reports are a vehicle that we use to engage with stakeholders, showcase our values and disclose our performance. So the look and feel of the message we deliver in our report is important – it says a lot about who we are as a company.'

Exemplifying is also evident in the marketing and branding of corporations' products as environmentally friendly and in the underlining of their broader social contribution. Witness adverts featuring hybrid or electric vehicles as responses to melting icebergs; or PR-savvy pictures of smiling children playing against a background of wind turbines. This is how corporations engage with public concern over climate change while at the same time using their public stance to further profitability and shareholder returns. The debate is framed within the business discourse of a 'win–win' for the corporate sphere and society as a whole. One senior manager characterised the practice as 'building a better world and a better business at the same time'.

This is not just public posturing: managers in these corporations are often strongly committed to the idea of carbon pricing and eco-efficiency as 'win–win' scenarios. In such cases a public admission helps to turn up the heat on internal corporate politics. As the sustainability director of a major manufacturing firm remarked: 'If we're going to talk the talk on sustainability we have to walk the walk as a company. So our factories should be showcases in terms of environmental efficiency.' The benefits include reducing GHG emissions – 'putting our own house in order', in the words of one interviewee – fostering innovation in new technologies and energy production and promoting national competitiveness. Public-facing marketing sometimes incorporates NGO branding and images of endangered species – orang-utans and polar bears have emerged as the icons of choice – to underscore 'green' credentials. As the tagline of an advert for oil giant Chevron proclaimed: 'Yes, we are an oil company, but right now we're also providing natural gas, solar, hydrogen, geothermal – *because we live on this planet, too*' (Sawyer, 2010: 68).

Exemplifying also helps companies deal with public criticism of their activities, as illustrated by the PR campaign launched by the Australian coal industry in a bid to fashion a 'green' image. Australia is one of the world's largest exporters of coal, and its economy benefits significantly from the continued expansion of mining; yet coal is a major contributor to escalating global GHG emissions – not to mention local environmental degradation – and attracts public censure (Pearse, 2010). Using media releases, adverts, and an interactive website, the industry sought a new look. It acknowledged the science of climate change and boasted of financial investment in new technologies such as carbon capture and storage (CCS – so-called clean coal) (ACA, 2010). Outlining the motivations behind the move, one senior industry insider said:

You've got this fabulous coal resource, which has given you low-cost electricity. How do you keep that resource in a carbon-constrained world? And that's where the technology comes in – carbon capture and storage. At the same time you've got an industry that's been cast as anti-climate-change-policy and anti-emissions-trading. So there's a job there to change people's attitudes.

Other companies stress how their exploitation of non-conventional fossil fuels (e.g., coal seam and shale gas) represents a more 'environmentally-friendly' source of energy because of its lower emissions profile in comparison to coal. These claims even extend to the marketing of 'natural' gas as a 'cleaner' energy source in schools and other pubic venues (West, 2014). Resource firms do not even have to convince governments, which often support these initiatives in the name of energy security. UK Energy Secretary Ed Davey recently gave fracking the green light by declaring: 'Shale gas represents a promising new potential energy resource for the UK … as we move to a low-carbon economy' (Cave and Rowell, 2014: 105). Yet again corporations succeed in generating a vision of new fossil-fuel-based energy sources as solutions to the climate crisis.

Exemplifying 'sustainable business' allows companies to present themselves as concerned corporate citizens while at the same time framing appropriate responses around self-regulation and market-based solutions. As ever, the message is that the answer to climate change lies in continued economic growth and, in this instance, more 'green' consumerism. The role of government becomes one of supporting the interests of 'green' capitalism by introducing the market mechanisms to price carbon while simultaneously fostering further economic expansion. The 'win–win' rhetoric portrays the good corporate citizen as both actor *and* benefactor. This creates an opportunistic position for corporations. The noble call for citizenly behaviour is in reality a blaring trumpet charge for extending commercial interests.

Crafting hegemony

One way of understanding corporate political engagement with climate change is via the concept of hegemony, as developed by Italian Marxist Antonio Gramsci (1971). Hegemony entails attempts to ensure that the interests and identities of dominant groups – formerly the state but more recently corporations – are identified with or overlap those of others in society. It is typically contrasted with violence as a mechanism for advancing one's cause.

Establishing hegemony requires what Gramsci called a 'war of position'. This involves reshaping the broad interests and values evident within society. Traditionally, the church, the media, schools, and universities are seen as central institutions in which hegemony is manufactured. This results in what Gramsci termed a 'historic bloc' – a group of actors who understand themselves as having a set of similar interests and are linked in particular and enduring ways. Corporations, through indirect and direct communication, create 'chains of equivalence' that connect disparate social groups within common identities and interests (Laclau and Mouffe, 2001).

A growing body of research has focused on how corporations, in response to challenges to their activities and authority, have sought to establish hegemony on a range of issues (e.g., Levy, 2008; Shamir, 2005). There are two clear hegemonic strategies at work with regard to the politics of climate change and the practices of campaigning and exemplifying.

First, corporations look to *build a common identity* with like-minded organisations and groups. The objective is to fashion a shared sense of subjectivity, so enticing people to identify with corporate projects (Laclau and Mouffe, 2001). Corporations espousing action on climate change develop relationships with 'green' (but market-friendly) NGOs, progressive think tanks, and even elements of the academic community to assemble a 'chain of equivalence' in support of a price on carbon through a market mechanism. This is bound up with businesses seeking to gain stakeholder 'buy-in' and legitimacy not just for their actions but for a larger set of ideas (Yaziji and Doh, 2009).

Similarly, those against carbon regulation enrol conservative think tanks and media commentators to proselytise doubt and scepticism about climate science and legislative change. This augments corporate influence in defining the public discourse and expands political frontiers in resisting or endorsing the implementation of climate policy. US energy companies have even sought to engage with schools as a way to question climate science and promote their products, often under the guise of energy education (Gerken, 2014). Through their connections with the media, NGOs, industry groups, and ratings agencies, businesses emphasise that the virtuous circle of 'building a better world and a better business at the same time' is enabled by creating and selling 'green' products and services. Companies also stress their links to employees, local communities, and those ideologically opposed to carbon regulation (ACA, 2010; Clarke, 2011).

The second hegemonic strategy involves persuading governments and citizens of the correctness of corporate positions on climate change. This is how businesses strive to *synchronise their interests* with broader national or societal principles. The goal here is to ensure a concrete link – at least in the short term – between the concerns of corporations and the concerns of subordinate groups (Burawoy, 1979). Here it is necessary to go beyond narrow self-interest and find more inclusive justifications for policy positions, including regional impacts (e.g., loss of jobs or new 'green' opportunities) and national economic and ecological considerations (e.g., enhancing competitiveness and ensuring a sustainable environment).

Even those firms less accepting of climate science stress how their activities contribute to social well-being through employment and economic development. Environmental costs or problems, if acknowledged at all, are presented as best solved through improved management and novel technologies (e.g., carbon capture and storage). With many companies portraying climate change as a source of business 'opportunities', as we have already seen, it is possible to link the public rationalisation of being a responsible corporate citizen to more traditional market defences of profitability and shareholder value (Nyberg and Wright, 2012; see also Chapter 5). As ever, the principles of capitalism remain agreeably unchallenged.

Reconstructing citizens within climate politics

It is by building common identities and synchronising interests that corporations mobilise particular subject positions for citizens to enact. Rather than obfuscating citizens' rights, these hegemonic strategies encourage and provide 'spaces' for citizenship activities that promote business interests. Take Unilever, the multinational consumer goods company, whose sustainability programme, Project Sunlight, is framed as follows:

In the first stage of Project Sunlight we are inviting people to take three simple actions. We want to help people SEE a brighter future; in order to do this, we are inviting people to watch a film online which aims to inspire and motivate people. We want to encourage them to ACT by doing small things which, added together, contribute to a better society and environment. Ultimately, we want people to JOIN the movement and become part of a growing community of like-minded people and organisations who all want to play their part in building a brighter future. (Unilever, 2013)

As the quote makes plain, there is often no clear frontier in which corporations and citizens choose sides in a war of positions. On the contrary, just as corporations' positions are at times contradictory, so citizens can enact multiple roles in promoting and identifying with opposing interests.

The political debate surrounding climate change has seen corporations use public campaigns that reach out to individuals and groups in support of their agendas. Such an approach is designed to provide space for citizens to engage with companies' political ideas as *active constituents*. Businesses offer competing discourses to government proposals, to which 'believers' and 'non-believers' alike can attach their interests and identities.

The Australian coal industry, for example, fought against the government's 'carbon tax' with adverts that accentuated the voices of factory workers, miners, consumers, and owners of small businesses, all of whom came to see the pricing of emissions as a threat to their jobs, their livelihoods, and the economy (ACA, 2009). In tandem, major manufacturers stressed that regulation would lead to the closure of factories and harm local communities. Appealing to conservative and nationalist identities, corporations claimed it was 'un-Australian to hide the carbon in someone else's backyard' (Clarke, 2011: 24). Crowds of older citizens duly highlighted their role as active constituents by waving anti-government placards and chanting 'No carbon tax!' during public rallies outside parliament (ABC, 2011b). The episode offered a classic instance of how corporate-funded campaigns serve to protect conservative citizens' cultural identity by reinforcing the sanctity of the industrial capitalist order (see also McCright and Dunlap, 2011a).

From a somewhat different perspective, Peabody Energy's recent Advanced Energy for Life campaign promotes the benefits of coal as an affordable energy source for the world's poor. On its website the company invites the public to become involved with this humanitarian issue. Its headline message is unequivocal: 'Join our campaign ... Learn more, be part of the solution' (www.advancedenergyforlife.com/).

Another, more common technique is to channel citizens as *responsible consumers*. This encourages them to exercise their political rights by buying into the fantasies and ideologies that companies produce through the images and information in their advertising and PR initiatives. Corporations often position themselves as sustainability authorities, providing advice on how to reduce carbon emissions through consumption choices; sometimes sustainability tools and 'carbon calculators' are made available on their websites. For instance, we identified an energy company which created a green image for itself through the careful construction of a green brand; a resource company that used reporting to push its positive environmental credentials; and a media company which used its 'carbon-neutral' status as a way of articulating its environmental credentials.

In each of these instances members of the public were positioned as consumers who could enjoy the 'citizenly spectacle' of corporations parading their environmental awareness. Several firms in our study used a 'green' image as a means of attracting a niche of new consumers, many of them willing to pay higher prices – so demonstrating that exercising one's citizenship rights can often equate to purchasing products or, to put it even more bluntly, voting with one's dollar.

Businesses also incorporate citizenship activities by linking employees' personal environmental concerns with corporate sustainability initiatives (Tams and Marshall, 2011; Wright and Nyberg, 2012). This subject position of the *ethical employee* is especially evident in firms keen to nurture a 'green culture' to better attract and retain staff. Many companies rank among the most sought-after employers because of their sustainability and responsible business programmes (Blackburne, 2013). In 2007, financial giant HSBC partnered with NGO Earthwatch to develop the world's largest employee engagement scheme focused on climate change, targeting 100,000 staff and offering environmental volunteering projects, field trips, and residential

visits to Earthwatch's research centres in the United States, the United
Kingdom, Brazil, India, and China (Beavis, 2011). As the sustainability
manager at one global manufacturer said of such programmes:

We've now got groups of employees suggesting new ideas. It's great for
employee buy-in, and it's great from an HR perspective of the employee
value position. Where these days graduates come in and interview us on
what we're doing [about sustainability and the environment], we've got a
bloody good story – better than most. You can get the best people without
paying best dollars.

Exemplifying and role-modelling 'green' values ensures not only that
staff are motivated but also that they act as corporate advocates both
within and beyond their own organisations. Ideally, they bolster the
proselytising effort, spreading the word to their families, their friends,
and their communities. As a sustainability manager in the finance
industry observed: 'I think the high levels of engagement kind of speak
for themselves. People generally as employees identify that it's something that the organisation prioritises and works on, and I think most
of them feel quite proud about that.'

Finally, citizens are also repositioned as *ecopreneurs*. This entails
connecting their environmental passions with a belief in corporate and
technological innovation (see also Phillips, 2013). Several corporations
that took part in our study highlighted how their focus on reducing
carbon emissions led to a range of suggestions from employees and
communities about how they could be more efficient in their energy
use. In one instance this involved an internal competition entitled 'How
Eco Can You Go?' and the creation of 'carbon councils' across different
business divisions to vet employees' suggestions for enhancing environmental performance. Another corporation launched a public contest to
solicit ideas and technologies for reducing carbon emissions; the prize
money was significant, and the winning concept would be commercial-
ised. This kind of 'open innovation' or 'crowdsourcing' highlights the
new position of *ecopreneur* – a citizen who combines environmental
concerns with business and entrepreneurial acumen.

Corporations and fractured hegemony

Naturally, corporations cannot afford to stand still if hegemony is to
be maintained. Major businesses regularly shift their positions as the

political debate around climate change evolves and the appetite for competing regulatory proposals intensifies and diminishes. As opinion polls fluctuate and political parties' fortunes wax and wane, companies must rely on a talent for skilful anticipation and near-constant adjustment if their mastery of the situation is to endure.

One energy company we studied, while actively campaigning for government regulation of carbon emissions and stressing its leadership in the field of renewable energy, reacted to political uncertainty over carbon pricing by augmenting its investment in coal seam gas and coal-fired power stations. Similarly, the corporations that formed the Australian Business Roundtable on Climate Change were initially highly vocal in their support for action to tackle the climate crisis but have adopted a far lower profile following the ascendancy of denial within mainstream public discourse and the election of conservative governments at state and federal levels.

Corporations often articulate antagonistic positions in endeavouring to establish political and moral leadership. They might agree with progressive parties that climate change should be taken seriously while at the same time linking their interests with conservative voices opposed to carbon regulation. What makes the upholding of contrasting views possible is companies' ability to connect their particular interests to empty universals such as the 'national interest', 'strong economy', or 'working families'.

News Corporation, Rupert Murdoch's global media giant, illustrated this capacity in remarkable style in 2011. Murdoch, the company's CEO, proudly announced in a memo to staff: 'The company has reached its first major sustainability milestone: we have become carbon-neutral across all of our global operations, and we are the first company of our kind to do so' (Grim, 2011). At the same time one of News Corporation's subsidiaries, Fox News, was among the most vehement public opponents of climate science and policies intended to address climate change. Indeed, studies of media influence have found a negative association between watching Fox News and acceptance of anthropogenic climate change (Feldman, L., et al., 2012).

The need to change one's position and, indeed, to hold different positions simultaneously can fracture the 'hegemonic bloc'. Consequently, as our own research showed, there is no singular corporate position on climate change: rather, there is an assortment of rival or contesting blocs of loosely affiliated corporate actors. Some coalitions, whether progressive or reactionary, have flourished or declined even during our period of study; and even within specific corporations there are contradictory stances. This suggests that, far from being a tightly knit set of relations, hegemony around concepts like climate change is fractured, divided by internal antagonism and characterised by ambiguity.

These different standpoints are not simply the result of strategic mis-calculations, endogenous forces, or the success of counter-movements by NGOs and other 'green' activists (Levy and Egan, 2003). The reality is that corporate citizenship requires dynamism and pragmatism in order to avoid being caught by changing political dynamics. By having industry associations, affiliated interest groups, and NGOs linked to their interests, corporations can support multiple positions without being seen as contradictory. Businesses are not trying to eliminate differences by building chains of influence (Laclau, 2005): they are safeguarding their own flexibility on issues of social and political concern. It is by upholding the tensions between equivalence and difference of interests and identities that corporations can continue to expand in the face of criticism.

Moreover, responding to criticism and engaging in debates in civil society allows corporations to defend corporate capitalism more generally as the dominant realm in which crises can be imagined and addressed. The fundamental point in corporate political engagement with climate change is not necessarily to fashion a hegemonic understanding about whether the issue is important and what action should be taken: it is to establish the corporation and the market as the central mechanisms through which climate change should be tackled. In this sense both progressive and conservative corporate practices serve to limit antagonistic imaginaries (e.g., mandatory limits on carbon emissions) that might challenge corporate solutions.

The idea of fractured hegemony around climate change can be extended to other corporate citizenship activities that habitually move in different directions. Sometimes environmental sustainability might be emphasised; at other times social agendas might be placed at the forefront. The vital and ever-present underpinning dynamic is the legitimating of the corporation as the basic organisational form through which 'market failures' should be corrected. The aim is to pre-empt any serious consideration of non-corporate mechanisms, with external regulation an especially unwelcome threat that should be defied and discredited at every turn (see also Shamir, 2005).

As the climate crisis worsens, corporate political activity is likely to increase around issues such as environmental and climate regulation, fossil fuel development, energy policy, and environmental protest and activism. Indeed, the expansion of neoliberal trade agendas on a global scale suggests a recalibration of state regulation which favours multinational capital over national and local governments. As Klein (2014: 75–86) argues the promotion of global 'free trade' fundamentally conflicts with the much-needed regulatory restrictions on fossil fuel use and GHG emissions.

The negotiations over the Trans-Atlantic Trade and Investment Partnership (TTIP) and the Trans-Pacific Partnership (TPP) offer a case in point. Multinationals have played a central role in framing future regulation, which includes provision for corporations to sue national governments over policies that reduce their profits. As critics have argued, national laws designed to reduce carbon emissions, fossil fuel use, deforestation, and other environmental protections could now be subject to legal challenge and substantial financial compensation (Rimmer and Wood, 2014).

Against a background of mounting geopolitical instability and growing fears over terrorism, there are also signs that hegemony will be supplemented by more coercive means as governments intervene directly to resolve environmental disputes. Such a scenario is particularly likely where interests deemed pivotal to national economic well-being are judged to be in peril. Many developed economies have already begun to categorise civil protest and environmental activism as potential threats to national security (Ahmed, 2014; Potter, 2011). Just as resource extraction in emerging nations has been subject to coercive state control and the use of violent force (Banerjee, 2008a), so heightened social conflicts over the expansion of fossil fuel developments portend increasingly authoritarian intercession and the unswerving complicity of governments in protecting corporations' economic interests.

Conclusion

Social concern over climate change and the potential regulation of GHG emissions have placed corporations under pressure to at least appear to be contributing to the improvement of environmental well-being rather than hastening its diminution (Hart, 2010). In this chapter we have explored how businesses have met this growing regulatory and reputational risk through closer engagement with the political arena.

As we noted at the outset, for some decades the corporate world has been involved in a 'war of positions' in responding to the prospect of regulatory constraint. This has consisted of both opposition to emissions mitigation (through a focus on the economic costs of climate action and the promotion of doubt about climate science) and a more accommodating stance (through the acceptance of climate science and the promotion of market-based mechanisms, innovation, and self-regulation).

Corporate engagement with climate politics in Australia, which has been the basis for much of the material in this chapter, closely resembles events in other fossil-fuel-rich nations, chief among them the United States, the United Kingdom, and Canada. Structural and economic reliance on fossil fuels as a source of energy and export earnings in these countries has led to a powerful synergy between business and government. As climate change has become a dominant political issue, corporations have sought to position themselves in ways that reduce regulatory threats and advance their economic interests.

The practice of *campaigning* has enabled them to directly shape the pattern of regulation and climate policy. This has been achieved through interactions with government, as well as through building alliances with like-minded companies, industry associations, opposition politicians, think tanks, and NGOs.

Exemplifying has involved a more indirect political strategy of propagating the public image of responsible social actors and playing a leading role in responding to climate change through business activities. As we have shown, this has seen the recasting of citizenship around subject positions that favour and reinforce corporate value creation. Moreover, by suggesting that they are acting in the interests of the broader public and by establishing links with civil society groups, corporations are able to portray themselves as champions of the common good rather than narrow, self-interested actors; and engaging in practices such as the public reporting of environmental data and 'green marketing' allows them to present themselves as paradigms of what that common good might be.

We have argued that these activities can be best understood as a process in which corporations are seeking to establish hegemony by building social acceptance of the merits of a neoliberal approach to the climate crisis. Here we differ somewhat from other critical commentators. We believe the expansion of corporations into civil society does not simply constrain citizens' rights (e.g., Banerjee, 2008b): we argue it also *incorporates* citizenship activities to benefit corporate political agendas.

This is achieved by building a common identity with citizens and synchronising their interests with those of corporations. This might include inviting citizens to engage in corporate political campaigns as constituents, linking the consumption of products and services with personal and group identities (e.g., 'green consumers') or encouraging individuals to apply their personal and political concerns at work (e.g., ethical employees and ecopreneurs). This leads us to posit that corporate citizenship programmes are less about protecting (Scherer and Palazzo, 2011) or obstructing citizens' rights (Barley, 2010) and more about pre-emptively reshaping understandings of citizenship in ways that further the longer-term interests of the business world.

While corporations occasionally appear to differ in their approaches to climate politics (Levy and Egan, 2003), at a general level a common 'historic bloc' has been produced around a neoliberal hegemonic closure (Torfing, 2009). There is rarely any questioning of a neoliberal project, and when groups do speak up for the environment they are inevitably demonised for wanting to 'destroy the economy'. Within this dominant perspective, there can be only one solution to the problems of capitalism: *more* capitalism.

5 | Justification, compromise, and corruption

But what all these climate numbers make painfully, usefully clear is that the planet does indeed have an enemy – one far more committed to action than governments or individuals. Given this hard math, we need to view the fossil fuel industry in a new light. It has become a rogue industry, reckless like no other force on Earth. It is Public Enemy Number One to the survival of our planetary civilisation.

(McKibben, 2012)

Mounting concern over climate change highlights the fundamental conflict between economic expansion and a finite environment (Jackson, 2009). The implications of this tension are profound. Yet an increasingly common response is to further incorporate the environment within market capitalism. As noted earlier for instance, the UK government recently initiated an 'Ecosystem Markets Task Force' to review opportunities for the business sector to 'value and protect nature's services' by incorporating the environment within the market system (DEFRA, 2012). It is illustrative of a growing and disturbing trend for the environment to be accorded a market value and for corporations to be portrayed as the central institutions through which that value should be maintained.

Concepts such as 'natural capitalism' and 'corporate environmentalism' further underline the 'business case' for the environment through new products, markets, and forms of technological innovation. The central argument is that the environment and corporate profitability can benefit concurrently (Esty and Winston, 2006; Hawken et al., 1999; Kurucz et al., 2008). Thus through a process of commensuration the resolution of environmental problems is presented as best achieved through assigning a monetary value to nature – converting 'different qualities into a common metric' (Espeland and Stevens, 1998: 314).

We have already examined how environmental 'risks' are calculated and exchanged. This, too, demands the convenient incorporation of the environment into the market. The overriding lesson is that domains that have historically stood outside the capitalist system now find themselves, along with a much broader swath of civil society, far more susceptible to marketisation in the face of neoliberalism's continued rise (Asdal, 2008; Crouch, 2011; Fourcade, 2011; Harvey, 2005).

In this chapter we explore the process through which the environment has become more and more absorbed within corporate activities. We investigate how both the environment and the market are now habitually treated as social goods; how it is inevitable that their respective interests will occasionally compete; and how the market almost invariably prevails when any kind of conciliation is required. We look at the work of sustainability managers and consultants and begin to consider the delicate balancing act that those who feel a duty both to the planet and to their employers and shareholders are nowadays repeatedly asked to perform; and we reveal the near-impossibility, even in the presence of the best intentions, of governing innocently.

We start by teasing out the dialectical relationship between corporate environmentalism and critique, studying how businesses and managers attempt to justify their actions and inactions in relation to climate change. These corporate justifications can, for example, be profit motivated (a market justification), focused on employee loyalty (a domestic justification), seeking recognition as a good corporate citizen (the justification of opinion), as well as directed towards environmental well-being (a green justification). We examine the different strategies which are involved in resolving conflicts and tensions between different reasons for engaging with climate change. We then go on to show how these justifications contribute to the legitimation of corporate engagement with climate change.

Avoiding the black-and-white picture of initiatives as either 'authentic' or 'greenwashing', we explain how the corporate actors involved in these deliberations settle the dispute between profit and the environment through a process of *compromise*. We contend that this demands the commensuration of competing 'orders of worth' (Boltanski and Thévenot, 2006) – that is, the bases for the justifications – and that the process has a powerful effect on corporate visions of the market's role in relation to competing social goods.

Most importantly, we argue that this leads to the corruption of the environment by converting it into a market commodity. Shareholder value and the bottom line rule, and even those managers who sincerely believe in the cause of sustainability ultimately find themselves playing a central role in the furtherance of creative self-destruction. It is one of the cruellest ironies of the fight to save the Earth that those who are most environmentally attuned are frequently also those who are customarily complicit in destroying the very thing they yearn to preserve.

Corporations and climate change – responding to critique

Corporate environmentalism has become a key response to public criticism of the business world's contribution to the climate crisis. As outlined in the previous chapter, different companies and industries strive to exemplify their role as 'good corporate citizens' in the face of calls for greater government regulation of GHG emissions. Corporations stress their leadership and their capacity for innovation in developing 'green' products and services that might assist in climate mitigation and adaptation. Fossil fuel, energy, and manufacturing firms defuse censure of their environmentally harmful actions by drawing attention to their investments in renewable energy and emissions-lowering technologies. The objective is always much the same: to deflect critique and, in so doing, to preserve corporate social legitimacy.

A prime example is the reinvention of US industrial conglomerate General Electric (GE) under the banner of 'ecomagination'. With 305,000 employees and global revenues in excess of $145 billion, GE is one of the world's largest industrial corporations – a huge, diversified multinational with interests in advanced technology, energy, and financial services. Founded in 1892 from Thomas Edison's business interests, it is the only surviving company from the original 12 enterprises listed on the Dow Jones Industrial Average in 1896. Ecomagination was launched in 2005 by CEO Jeff Immelt and aimed to distinguish GE as a trailblazer in the development of new technologies to respond to climate change. As the company proclaimed:

Ecomagination is GE's commitment to address challenges such as the need for cleaner, more efficient sources of energy, reduced emissions and abundant sources of clean water … We will focus our unique energy, technology, manufacturing and infrastructure capabilities to develop tomorrow's solutions such as solar energy, hybrid locomotives, fuel cells, lower-emission aircraft engines, lighter and stronger materials, efficient lighting and water purification technology. (GE, 2005)

The initiative saw GE make a number of major commitments, including:

- Doubling its investments in research into clean technologies (e.g., renewable energy and improved energy efficiency) to $1.5 billion annually
- Doubling its revenues from 'green' products and services to $20 billion by 2010
- Reducing the intensity of its own GHG emissions by 30 per cent by 2008.

Ecomagination's launch was backed by a $90-million marketing campaign. This included eight-page newspaper inserts featuring visuals of smokestacks morphing into trees, jet engines resembling spiral seashells, and videos of 'scantily clad models dusted with soot and shovelling coal in a dingy mine as a voiceover announces: "Now, thanks to emissions-reducing technologies from GE, the power of coal is getting more beautiful every day"' (Little, 2005).

Although some commentators warned of the potential for 'greenwashing', the scale of the proposed investments and emissions savings dulled criticism. GE went on to not only meet but also exceed its targets. Later innovations included partnerships with venture capital firms and funding for 'green' start-ups and entrepreneurs (Chesbrough, 2012). Significantly, ecomagination framed the climate crisis as a space in which businesses could not just make money but also contribute to social and environmental well-being.

This echoed the ecological modernisation argument. The message was that 'green' business could provide a 'win–win' outcome in which the environment could benefit through corporate profit-making. As Immelt pointed out: 'We plan to make money doing it. Increasingly for business, "green" is green' (GE, 2005). Such a triumphant doctrine undoubtedly struck a chord. Although for many years a target of environmentalists because of its efforts to avoid paying for the clean-up operation necessitated by its chemical pollution of the Hudson River, GE showed how appeals to innovation, hope, environmental well-being, and business acumen could respond to critique.

In recent years, however, there have been signs that the ecomagination dream is beginning to sour. GE's energy agnosticism – it remains a major producer of coal-fired and nuclear power stations – and expansion into more traditional carbon-polluting industries have sparked renewed criticism from NGOs, activists, and even corporate environmental promoters. For instance, 'green business' guru Andrew Winston (2014) recently questioned the company's broadening of eco-magination into improving the efficiency of tar sands processing and gas fracking, two of the most environmentally harmful sources of fossil fuel extraction. Winston noted that, while justified by GE as part of its desire to make 'dirty forms of energy cleaner', such schemes could only reinforce fossil fuel reliance, 'move the world in the wrong direction on carbon and suck up intellectual and fiscal capital that we could allocate differently'.

With the 'win–win' imaginary seemingly coming unstuck, hard choices inexorably loom. As Winston concluded: 'Will we turn to the future and put all we've got into building the clean economy? Or will we try to have it both ways?'. Ecomagination's descent into compromise parallels the broader dilemma of corporate environmentalism: the conceit that we can have ceaseless economic growth and corporate value creation while also responding to the urgent environmental challenge of climate change.

As the climate crisis exacerbates, justification is becoming increasingly central to corporate efforts to stave off criticism and maintain legitimacy. In the sections that follow we consider the different paths such justifications can take, the processes they involve, and the consequences of compromise that all too frequently ensue.

Corporate environmentalism, justification, and social goods

Businesses often face criticism from an assortment of public actors, including NGOs, the media, and social commentators. This is particularly so with regard to corporate environmental impact. This being the case, corporations depend on the congruence of their activities with surrounding norms and values to uphold their legitimacy in society (Parsons, 1960; Scott, 1991).

The legitimacy to operate is a dialogical social construction that corporations undertake to manage perceptions of their actions' appropriateness and value (Suchman, 1995). Corporations, and the managers within them, make links to a range of social goods in seeking to justify their actions and inactions in regard to climate change. This is particularly evident in response to criticism, where justification for corporate action extends beyond just a market logic (maximising profit and returns to shareholders) and brings in wider appeals to social, community, and environmental well-being.

A useful framework for understanding the process of critique and justification in areas of social dispute is the concept of 'orders of worth' outlined by Boltanski and Thévenot (2006), who drew various images of the 'common good' from the classic works of political philosophy. Their initial six orders of worth were labelled 'inspired', 'domestic', 'opinion', 'civic', 'market', and 'industrial' (Boltanski and Thévenot, 1999; 2006); 'project' and 'green' were later added to the list (Boltanski and Chiapello, 2005; Thévenot et al., 2000). Actors within organisations and in the marketplace are considered by Boltanski and Thévenot (2000: 213) to be 'moral beings, in the sense that they are capable of taking abstraction from their particularity in order to agree on external goods, which are universally listed and defined'. Using this framework, we can see managers in corporations as drawing on broader social goods to justify their actions in response to critique.

As summarised in Table 5.1, each of these justifications is based on different principles for evaluating worth in a social situation of dispute or uncertainty. Each order of worth has a different mode of evaluation and tests as to whether the justification is applicable and will lead to a common good. If a person invokes the world of the market, for example, the reality test is whether the decision leads to increased competitiveness. In the 'green' world the test is one of 'green-ness' through, say, 'protection of wilderness, stewardship of environmental resources and cultivation of various attachments to nature' (Thévenot et al., 2000: 257).

Each of these 'legitimate orders of worth' also relies on different forms of argumentative proof supporting the superior principle (Thévenot, 2007: 415). In each world particular individuals and objects have a stronger say and ability to reduce uncertainty. The proof for the market world, for instance, is monetary, and this can be applied in the local situation of goods and services, with customers and traders qualified to evaluate worth. A justification based on the civic world is evaluated in terms of collective welfare, with the test based on concepts of equality and solidarity and the qualified objects including rules, regulations, rights, and policies.

Given that these different principles of goods are incompatible with one another, with each having its own test, qualified objects, and subjects, ending a public dispute – at least beyond the use of domination

Table 5.1 *Empirically grounded orders of worth*

	Market	Industrial	Civic	Domestic	Inspired	Opinion	Green
Mode of evaluation	Price, cost	Productivity, efficiency	Collective welfare	Reputation, loyalty, tradition, locality	Inspiration, creativity, grace	Renown, fame	Environmental well-being
Test	Competitiveness	Reliability, planning	Equality, solidarity	Trustworthiness	Passion, enthusiasm	Popularity, recognition	Sustainability, renewability
Form of proof	Monetary	Statistic measurement	Demonstration of a just cause	Anecdotal, oral	Emotional involvement, myths	Public support	Ecological
Qualified objects	Market goods and services	Projects, methods, plans, investments	Rules, regulations, rights, policies	Rank, title, manner	The sublime	Media, brand, interviews	Environment
Qualified human beings	Customer, consumer, trader, seller	Engineers, professionals, experts	Collective persons and officials	Authority, boss, leader	Visionaries, creative beings	Celebrity, spokespersons, PR agents	Environmentalist
Elementary relation	Exchange	Functional	Solidarity	Trust	Passion	Recognition	Ecological

Sources: Boltanski and Thévenot, 1999; 2006; Thévenot et al., 2000.

or violence – requires either an agreement about the appropriate order of worth or a compromise between them (Boltanski and Thévenot, 1999; 2006). The former suggests one legitimate worth is established as more relevant or practical in a certain situation. The latter implies cooperation without clarification of the principles used in the criticism or dispute. The solidification of compromises depends on establishing equivalence between the different goods to make them compatible (Boltanski and Thévenot, 2006). With nature accorded a price to be evaluated in the market order of worth, the perpetuation of corporate activities in the face of criticism therefore becomes a justification process that balances the creation of equivalence and the compromise of differences between social goods (Laclau and Mouffe, 2001).

Engaging different orders of worth around the environment and climate change

The appeal to different orders of worth as sources of justification is manifest in how corporations and their managers have responded to the climate crisis. Increasing social and political awareness of climate change has been accompanied by greater business acknowledgement of the natural environment as a relevant context for corporate involvement. Again and again company websites, adverts, and sustainability reports use evocative images of forests, oceans, and landscapes as backdrops, often supplemented by testimonials from managers and employees about the importance of the environment to their professional and personal lives (Garland et al., 2013).

Engagement with environmental issues has also led many managers to reconsider their personal values and even change careers. As discussed in more detail in Chapter 6, many of the managers who took part in our research voiced not just an allegiance to their employers and shareholders but a genuine concern for the environment and society. As one senior sustainability manager at an insurance company said of her job: 'It's really about getting the organisation itself to think about … the social and environmental issues that are relevant to us as a business, because that, to me, is where this stuff is really exciting.'

The orders of worth used to justify and legitimise environmental practices are wide-ranging. They inevitably include the more obvious market and industrial worlds that predominate within for-profit corporations, but they also extend to other spheres. Many of the managers we spoke to emphasised how sustainability activities would lead to competitive advantage ('market') and more efficient production ('industrial'), yet they also described their passion for the environment ('green' or 'inspirational') and creating a better society ('civic').

Of course, reference to the *market* order of worth is especially pervasive in corporate understandings of climate change. This justification is rooted in appeals to improved competitiveness, shareholder value, and profitability. As we saw in Chapter 3, the business discourse of risk and opportunity is rich in the language of markets, customers, and competitors. As the manager of climate-change strategy at a major airline explained: 'Businesses are businesses. If they can see benefit, if they can see value to the business in doing something, they'll do it as long as it competes … We're no different.'

Sustainability managers also often rely heavily on market justifications in convincing other managers of the advantages and business opportunities of new 'greener' products and services. As one remarked in describing his role within a large construction and mining company:

The opportunity here is for us to build new businesses out of a new carbon economy, and we've done a lot of work on that. We've formed an industrial energy division to take advantage of those opportunities. We've got partnerships with a number of renewable energy technology providers. We've got an ongoing research programme looking at new opportunities. A month ago we got given a $62 million grant from the government to look at a wave-power energy station. We're in on the solar bids at the moment. We've been building wind stations. There's a number of things like that that we're looking at … We see it as being a viable part of the business.

The market logic is also pronounced in the marketing of organisations as having a 'green' brand. Products such as 'low-carbon' beer, recyclable office equipment, and hybrid and electric cars are justified as appealing to new or changing consumer tastes. As one sustainability adviser told us:

I think the carbon-neutral beer [idea] is a good one. That came from a recognition that there was a market niche that seemed to be ready for a product that had lower emissions than others. I think that's driven a lot of companies' efforts. There's a recognition that somehow there's this green consumer out there that wants to buy their new green offering.

Similarly, sponsorship arrangements and other forms of engagement with NGOs and environmental groups are frequently justified as promoting a favourable public image that translates into improved sales and profits.

Closely related are references to the *industrial* world. Here activities are justified through the metrics of efficiency and productivity and qualified through planning and projects, with the engineer as the credible subject (Boltanski and Thévenot, 1999). Key practices associated with this order of worth relate to improvements in energy efficiency and reductions in production costs, which are seen as legitimate internal justifications for sustainability practices.

Numerous managers we interviewed stressed their determination to improve efficiency, eliminate waste, and use less energy and resources. 'I've a strong passion for efficiency and how you use resources', said one, 'because I think waste is the worst thing'. For these employees the industrial order of worth offers a powerful justification for gaining senior management buy-in to sustainability programmes, many of which involve developing detailed measurement systems around energy usage within an organisation and across the broader supply chain. In the words of the energy and environment director at a global automotive manufacturer: 'We have a very rigorous management system with a whole lot of different databases and processes on how to manage internal energy use.'

And what of less conventional justifications? References to the *domestic* world certainly feature prominently, both in the context of resistance to environmental initiatives viewed as impinging on traditional sales or production cultures (e.g., a mining company emphasising the jobs and communities it supports) and instances where sustainability activities are characterised as building loyalty and trust between employees. The group sustainability adviser at a financial services business surmised the value of the latter by noting: 'I think most employees feel quite proud about that ... When you look at the activities that drive engagement in our annual engagement survey, community and sustainability is always one of the top four.'

Instances of staff engagement with environmental sustainability also link to the world of *inspiration*. The environment is regarded as a topic that engenders passion and emotion by providing a source of meaning beyond material rewards. As the sustainability manager at fast-food multinational McDonald's outlined in a video about his company's sustainability programme:

I'm known as the tree-hugger around the office ... I'm in the enviable position of a job that I love, friends that are great ... I've got freedom at work, freedom in my home life, and I'd like to continue to enjoy the pure joy of being happy, I guess. It's brilliant for me – I get to follow a personal passion. And that's what makes coming into work fun. It's not just a job. It's part of who I am. (McDonald's Australia, 2014)

Many of the managers we spoke to explained how the environment had featured in their upbringing and education, as well as in their home and family lives in terms of recreational activities, lifestyles, and consumption choices (see also Chapter 7). Some evinced a passion for the environment and strong emotional engagement with the issue of climate change. As a result, the environment is in some instances treated as a justification in itself as a separate *green* order of worth (Purser et al., 1995).

Concomitantly, in the fight to maintain legitimacy, managers and corporations also accentuate the importance of the world of *opinion*. Here organisations trade on the personality and celebrity of their environmental spokespeople and senior managers who have cultivated a public profile around climate change and promoted a positive image of companies as leaders on the issue. Celebrity CEOs such as Virgin's Richard Branson, as prominent campaigners on climate change, clearly use the world of opinion in this way (Prudham, 2009). As we have already seen, building public relationships with environmental NGOs affords another form of referred legitimacy.

Finally, climate change initiatives and sustainability practices are also routinely justified using the grammar of worth of the *civic* world, which is evaluated through the collective welfare of society and even the discourse of the 'national interest'. An environment manager at a media company argued that its practices were an expression of the need to be 'good corporate environmental citizens'; others cited the need to 'give back' to society and an obligation to protect 'future generations'.

The scope for businesses to engage in social advocacy for environmental sustainability is crucial here. As we discussed in the previous chapter, some corporations have sought to create a public profile as crusaders for climate action and the pricing of carbon emissions. As a financial services company outlined in its position statement on climate change: 'We will play a pivotal role helping our customers, employees and the broader community shift to this low-carbon economy.' Corporate positions are reinforced through appeals to moral leadership on a contested political issue.

In recent years fossil fuel companies in particular have used civic justifications to repel escalating criticism of their contribution to climate change. While environmental activists have branded the industry 'Public Enemy Number One' and instigated a highly effective social movement for divestment from fossil fuel stocks (McKibben, 2012; 2013b), major resource firms have resolutely championed the benefits of their activities in solving so-called energy poverty. As mentioned in the previous chapter, US coal giant Peabody Energy's Advanced Energy for Life campaign has acclaimed the benefits of what the company terms 'clean coal' in providing energy for the poorest citizens on Earth (Peabody Energy, 2013).

Similarly, the CEO of BHP Billiton, the world's biggest mining company, has conflated the climate crisis and the plight of the poor in advocating market-centric solutions. 'Eighty per cent of the world's energy is generated from fossil fuels,' he said, 'and Asia is dependent on coal ... We have to do something [about climate change] in a way that doesn't condemn large numbers of people in the developed world to live in poverty' (Patrick, 2014). This justification is firmly entrenched in the notion that resources such as coal remain the dominant source of cheap energy for impoverished populations and that curbing the use of fossil fuels would therefore cement global economic inequality.

The governments of countries such as Australia and Canada have dutifully mimicked this sort of appeal to a broader civic justification. Ever-growing fossil fuel exports have been defended as a noble rejoinder to worldwide poverty (Parkinson, 2014a), while the Canadian tar sands have been described as a source of 'ethical oil' (Pullman, 2012). Opening a new coal mine, the Australian prime minister recently proclaimed: 'Coal is vital for the future energy needs of the world ... Coal is good for humanity' (Chan, 2014).

We see, then, that corporate responses to environmental critique use the full range of justifications and extend far beyond the conventional business case of profitability and/or efficiency. Through reference to issues of loyalty and trust (*domestic* order of worth), inspiration and creativity (*inspired* order of worth), renown and fame (order of worth of *opinion*), environmental well-being (*green* order of worth), and collective welfare (*civic* order of worth), they bid to overcome criticism and legitimatise their activities by discursively bridging incompatible goods.

Yet the difficulty of making these competing orders of worth compatible should not be underestimated. Beyond asserting a superior order of worth, resolving such conflicts requires compromise. Conflicting justifications must at least *appear* congruent. In the section that follows we examine how corporations and managers strive to strike a balance between the market and the environment – and how it is the environment that is consistently discounted when that balance proves unattainable.

Enacting corporate environmentalism through compromise

Corporations and managers often express an interest in the environment, but they also recognise the constraints they face in challenging successful business practices that exacerbate ecological degradation. Regardless of sincerity, irrespective of a determination to do right, other factors hold sway. As the director of one sustainability consultancy conceded: 'How do you act as a consultant to make a business healthy? And again it always comes down to that optimum point. You want them to be as sustainable as they can be, but you don't want them to shut down their operation. There's no simple path through this.'

Criticism of corporate environmental activities could conceivably be resolved through the purification of reality tests. Justifications could be proffered purely on the bases of competitiveness and profit, with environmental claims removed from the picture. But it is unlikely such an approach would garner widespread acceptance, less still blunt existing disapproval. A more attractive response is compromise, which involves developing new roles, products, and services to fit the social worlds of market and environment alike.

This requires making subjects, objects, and/or concepts compatible with more than one world and capable of passing two types of test. Sustainability managers and departments, renewable energy, 'carbon-friendly' beverages, culture-change initiatives, efficiency programmes, and the branding and marketing of a company as a responsible organisation are all examples of the need to bestride two contrasting spheres. They must survive both the test of the market (i.e., are they competitive?) and the test of being 'green' (i.e., can they be seen to benefit the environment?). Sometimes it is also necessary to satisfy additional strands of justification, including the civic (i.e., do they follow regulations and address societal welfare?), opinion (i.e., do they enjoy public recognition and support?), and inspired (i.e., do they engender passion and emotions?) orders of worth (see Nyberg and Wright, 2012).

Consequently, compromise between the competing social goods of the market and the environment is essential to the everyday work of those involved in managing corporate sustainability. It is also evident at an organisational level in responses to criticism from shareholders, employees, the media, and NGOs. The problem is that compromises can never be settled or fully satisfied: they are always fragile and open to reproach, since they are not constitutive of a single order of worth (Boltanski and Thévenot, 2006). The result is an unending process of temporary resolution in which practices are continuously negotiated, enacted, refined, and re-defined. In short, each new compromise is merely a stepping-stone towards the next.

Examples of corporate compromise over the climate crisis are legion. New energy sources are presented as less environmentally harmful, yet they are *still* environmentally harmful. Solar power and 'cogeneration' tick the 'green' box in validating property developments. Manufacturers stress the redesign of production processes and supply chains for a world of spiralling energy costs and limited natural resources. Polluting industries cling to the promise of carbon capture and storage, asserting that their investment in the concept of 'clean coal' is 'the key to unlocking an environmentally-friendly future for all fossil fuels' (Kosich, 2007). The intimation that the conflict between cutting GHG emissions and maintaining mining revenues can somehow be resolved shows compromise at its most fanciful. As a senior coal industry manager insisted: 'The technology [carbon capture and storage] is about addressing this problem. I mean, what else can you do, other than restructure our economy to be a low-carbon economy right now and turn a lot of things off? That's the challenge: to deliver the environmental outcome in a way that's economically doable and sensible.'

Keeping plural worlds in play is how sustainability managers exploit new opportunities to enhance profits. Such a 'bottom line' ethos is usually characterised within the framing of a 'business case' – a term that denotes the profitable rationale for environmental initiatives. Our interviewees spoke of how their practices slashed operating costs or waste; in industrial settings managers recited the dollars per working hour saved through recycling, low-energy lighting, or the cost-cutting redesign of production operations. As one of our respondents observed: 'The business case takes many forms. It's often about brand health, brand strength. It's about efficiency – resource efficiency, energy efficiency. That's what we would describe as the "low-hanging fruit" – reduce your energy and waste.'

As many of those who participated in our study underscored through their comments, compromise can render corporate 'sustainability' decidedly selective. Sometimes the environment might win, but even then the corporation is liable to 'win bigger'. Competing interests are thus concealed. As the senior sustainability manager at a construction and mining company explained, sustainability is actually about building a 'long-lasting organisation … one that continues to perform at high levels'.

In the finance and insurance industry, as we have seen, the issue revolves around 'resilience and risk'; in food production it is about 'water usage'. One manager explained how sustainability within his company centred on changing irrigation patterns and relocating processing facilities: 'I mean, in our global Creating Share Value reports we had a case study about tomatoes … We've seen shifts in the climate impacting on the availability of tomatoes in this area, so threatening the factory.' In this firm a specialist 'Water Stress Index' was introduced to plan the siting of factories and gauge existing facilities. The compromise of sustainability was thereby connected to specific organisational and material arrangements and evaluated according to new reality tests.

Analogously, in the finance industry a de facto 'price for carbon' has been developed to assess business lending risk. This highlights the linkage between the market world of profitability and an assessment of environmental impact. Another commonplace test involves the voluntary reporting of a company's sustainability, often in combination with more traditional financial reporting. Such practices are driven by external criticism of the corporate contribution to climate change, as well as nascent shareholder interest in non-financial measures of performance (Bebbington et al., 2008).

Sustainability reporting is also central to such compromise. These reports might include detailed analysis of carbon emissions, broken down by source of business activity and compared to reduction targets over time. Water usage, recycling, and even biodiversity serve as tests of a corporation's environmental – and, in tandem, financial – sustainability. Asked to outline the thinking behind such reporting, a manager at one resource company explained:

A financial report won't tell you whether they've got assets that are spilling oil into the environment. It won't tell you whether they're looking after their employees with fair and equitable wages or whether they've got a good gender balance within their organisation ... whereas the sustainability balanced scorecard will describe to you all of that management performance.

Criticism, purification, and renewed compromise

Even at best, compromises are impermanent resolutions of competing social worlds. As such, they are subject to continued adaptation and revision in the face of further criticism. Imagine that a corporation's formative act of compromise receives criticism from both within and beyond the order of worth in play. The criticism from the market world might be that the proposed practices do not lend themselves to competitiveness. The criticism from a non-market world might be that the proposed practices fail the tests of, say, equality (civic), popularity (opinion), or sustainability (green). The corporation has two options: it can give primacy to one order of worth over another, or it can find a new compromise.

'Greenwashing' is one example of the *external* criticism that can compel companies to confront this choice. Here, corporate practices are dismissed as largely symbolic and inadequate in dealing with the underlying tension between business growth and environmental degradation. For instance, a senior manager in a major accounting firm criticised the practice of airline companies inviting customers to 'offset' their carbon emissions by paying a ticket-price surcharge:

I would never go flying carbon-neutral, because what they do is they collect that money, they go out and they buy it off an organisation who then goes and plants a tree in whoop-whoop ... Well, who's giving me the guarantee for spending my money that in 25 years' time that tree is going to be there? So I just don't believe it. It's rubbish.

A corporation might respond to 'greenwashing' by removing a product or activity or by reaching a new compromise in the expectation that it will be viewed in a more positive light. Witness what happened when environmentalists accused biofuels of causing deforestation and food shortages: 'second-generation' biofuels were unveiled, with their use of non-food-based crops exploited as the 'hook' in promoting them as both more environmentally sound and offering economic competitiveness for industries looking for cost-efficient sources of fuel (CSIRO, 2011). A food company manager who took part in our study related how his firm's use of 'sustainable' palm oil evolved in response to an influential NGO-led social media campaign addressing environmental and civic concerns:

[B]ecause all of us want the same outcome. I mean, we don't want to be destroying orang-utans, and we think that de-forestation is terrible. Palm oil, though, is an important ingredient in many products around the world. Its production supports many communities in poor rural areas. So, yes, we have committed going forward to using certificates, and globally by 2015 there should be enough sustainable palm oil available to meet our needs and those of others in the industry.

This shows how corporations move the tests of the order of worth into the future to avoid criticism. What is conveniently overlooked is that by then new contingencies are highly likely to have made the tests problematic or even no longer applicable.

Internal criticism, meanwhile, is built on the detection of flaws in the claim that activities, products, or services are maximising profits. From this perspective, as our interviewees again attested, compatible practices are seen as insufficiently attuned to business goals. Responding to this criticism often involves adaptations that distil the justification process to a single test: competitiveness. As a sustainability manager at a large insurer confessed in describing how opponents of her role flatly rejected the proposition of corporate environmentalism: 'This is all about the shareholder return, and the directors' fiduciary duties and the executives' duties to the directors and to the shareholders are quite clear ... Mucking around in sustainability things for society is not the work of companies.'

We found considerable evidence of environmental compromises being undermined by the increasing demands of the market test.

A major supermarket company set an 'ambitious' carbon emissions reduction target of 40 per cent by 2015, only to later concede the expansion of its business had made such an objective 'difficult to deliver' – in spite of investment in energy-saving refrigerators and sustainable new outlets. The test of financial performance is more often than not judged of greater decisiveness than the test of environmental performance in determining how a compromise should be weighted.

In some cases previous tests are recalibrated, further exposing the crushing futility of emissions-reducing programmes as a viable organisational response. As the sustainability manager at one electricity retailer confided: 'Our goal is to get more customers, which means we're selling more energy. So that kind of emissions reduction target isn't actually the most effective way that we can contribute to dealing with climate change.'

In a situation like this the previously sought compromise of values is laid bare. Any given settlement or solution is revealed to be purely ephemeral and at the constant mercy of market interests. Refinement by refinement, profit is granted ever more precedence; adjustment by adjustment, the environment is further marginalised.

Business sustainability as compromise and noble corruption

The rhetoric of corporate environmentalism as a 'win–win' mechanism conveys the idea that the market and the environment are compatible. As we have discussed, this view is at best optimistic and at worst mendacious. Our study repeatedly showed that managers within corporations are acutely aware that the promotion of the environment can occur only when accompanied by the promotion of the market – and preferably with the latter comfortably to the fore. With no space for a diminution of profit or a reduction in company growth, compromise seeks to hide the incommensurability of different social goods.

It is to uphold the illusion of 'real' compromise that corporations have adopted concepts such as 'sustainability' and subsequent *reality tests* within which their practices can be evaluated. The compromise of 'sustainability' is consolidated through large-scale investments, committees populated by senior managers, and expensive analyses conducted by accounting firms (Lohmann, 2009); it is also supported by material arrangements in the form of environmental or sustainability managers – as opposed to environmentalists – whose deeds are evaluated and tested according to corporate metrics rather than measures of ecological well-being or biodiversity. With the burden of proof shifted from the preservation of the ecosystem to the perpetuation of the market as the answer to all crises, capitalism 'incorporates some of the values in whose name it was criticised' (Boltanski and Chiapello, 2005: 28).

Given their innate frailty, compromises are frequently the subject of further criticism, purification, and ongoing 'justification work' by organisational actors (Jagd, 2011). Those who hold sustainability roles within corporations are given the authority to question environmental practices or to support sustainability as the new, established order of worth. It is in the 'friction' between values and through querying and disrupting assumptions and methods that environmental managers and consultants prove their worth (Stark, 2009). A principal task is to connect ideas of sustainability with the market and so take part in developing novel practices, products, and services that make money for companies. Such justification work is an illustration of entrepreneurship and how corporations change through reassessing how they think and what they do (Stark, 2009).

Importantly, the managers we interviewed were cognizant of the scepticism surrounding compromise and had pondered the attendant politics long and hard. They were cognizant, too, that the 'magic' of compromise in the hegemonic alchemy of transforming the environment into a business opportunity is habitually presented as an act of pragmatism. Many voiced a concern and passion for the environment. It is an unhappy irony, then, that these individuals, the vast majority of whom are by definition the most environmentally attuned employees within their organisations, so often find themselves at the vanguard of creative self-destruction.

This being so, they accept – albeit sometimes grudgingly – that their roles are mired in the politics of 'dirty hands' and the impossibility of governing innocently (Walzer, 1973). We can see this as a sort of Machiavellian 'noble corruption' (Coady, 2008: 91): 'When the act accuses, the result excuses' (Machiavelli cited in Walzer, 1973: 175). There is a recognition that the short-term compromise of the environmental good is often necessary in striving to prevent environmental harm. Some of our interviewees went further, offering an Orwellian description of their activities based on the ends pursued (Lukes, 1991) – the implication being that they must continue to pollute the environment to save it. One senior coal industry executive argued that mining and selling more coal would provide an economic foundation for the long-term switch to a low-carbon economy. This could be an indication of the success of the capitalist market in incorporating critique and transforming itself in relentless waves of creative – and, indeed, environmental – destruction (Harvey, 1982).

Beyond stabilising the market through the resolution of disagreements (Biggart and Beamish, 2003), the compromise of alternative orders of worth also assists further domination of the market by validating the market mechanism and depoliticising political activities. Wide-scale corporate compromises are not independent applications of orders of worth: rather, they change the understanding of these orders. The business sector is now considered a 'natural' guardian of the environment through 'ecological modernisation' (Mol and Sonnenfeld, 2000) and partnerships with NGOs and governmental authorities.

Moreover, if an environmental NGO's activities are for sale to corporate sponsors, then the NGO runs the risk of undermining its own independence and undercutting the altruism of public donations for its activities (Dauvergne and LeBaron, 2014; van Huijstee et al., 2011). This shows how achieving compromise through creating compatible products or services for the market and another social good can threaten to 'crowd out' alternative experiences of that same good. A comparable event occurred in the United States when the commercialisation of blood donation impacted on the long-standing notion of giving blood as a civic duty (Lukes, 2005: 296): giving blood instead of selling it could suddenly be seen as somewhat naïve (Jagd, 2007). The success of corporate domination is to shape the meaning of other goods in its own image (Walzer, 1983).

The process of compromise also builds on the appearance of consensus between the market and the environment, thereby sidelining and excluding more antagonistic perspectives. This has been demonstrated through the failure of movements such as 'deep ecology', whose concentration on the worth of nature in and of itself is seen as lacking concern for social or economic life (Jamison, 2001). Whereas rival actors are perceived as unduly idealistic in their refusal to countenance other kinds of valuation, corporations are able to project a semblance of conciliation and are hailed as 'compromising devices' par excellence (Thévenot, 2001: 410). The expansion of the market is based on an endless capacity to reconcile competing orders of worth through the commercialisation of goods and, just as significantly, a supreme knack of dodging political battles via the laying down of one's own terms.

Conclusion

Growing public concern over the catastrophic effects of climate change has gone hand-in-hand with an increase in awareness and criticism of corporations treating the environment as an 'externality' (Stern et al., 2006). The climate crisis has thus created a critical moment and a reflexive understanding that something has to change (Boltanski and Thévenot, 1999).

Such a realisation undoubtedly challenges established economic activity, yet critique has also prompted justifications that seek to defend the legitimacy of how corporations react. As we have seen, this rejoinder has not relied exclusively on straightforward market and efficiency justifications: it has also involved engagement with issues of social, community, and environmental well-being. Competing justifications are brought together through compromise, as is manifest in the discourse of business sustainability and myriad corporate environmental practices.

Unfortunately, although a virtuous circle of advantage for companies, society, and even nature itself is presented, the truth is that compromise is only temporary. As such, it is subject to further critique, adaptation, and refinement. Consequently, while multiple justifications may well be drawn on, there remains a distinct hierarchy of worth within the modern corporation, with the market order the lodestar that is most slavishly followed.

Ironically, with environmental goals thus subsumed within the core demands of profitability and shareholder value, it is those managers who are the most environmentally aware who almost invariably find themselves at the forefront of the compromise process. This is 'noble corruption' in action. As nature itself is reconstructed into a commodity and a tool for profit, environmental and sustainability managers have to get their hands dirty – and they know it.

They acknowledge, too, that compromise is short-lived and under permanent threat of further refinement. The next step is likely to be little more than a new and 'better' compromise, if not an outright shifting of the goalposts. While there will be 'win–win' situations, not least when new 'green' products or initiatives cut costs or enhance revenues, these can be tolerated only when the benefits to the market can be guaranteed. The environment is allowed to win from time to time, but the market must be the bigger winner if the corporation is to act.

Ultimately, then, corporate responses to environmental concerns represent a process of accommodation and political struggle in which companies set out to maintain their autonomy through incorporating the environment on their terms alone (Banerjee, 2008b). The resultant corruption is increasingly plain in efforts to expand the market logic into the realm of nature itself – as seen, for example, in the pricing of carbon emissions and other kinds of 'natural capital' and 'ecosystem services' (Farber et al., 2002; Hawken et al., 1999).

As the chairman of the United Kingdom's Natural Capital Committee recently declared: 'The environment is part of the economy and needs to be properly integrated into it so that growth opportunities will not be missed' (Natural Capital Committee, 2014: 4) . Ignoring the obvious fact that an economy exists within a society, which is itself dependent on the natural environment, this remarkable inversion of the hierarchy perfectly sums up the ever-accelerating commodification of nature. It also perfectly encapsulates the alarming dominance of neoliberal thinking in which the market absorbs all areas of social and natural interaction, unfailingly prizing voracity over veracity as it surges ever onwards.

6 | Climate change, managerial identity, and narrating the self

I get out of bed because I save people and I save the planet. That's what I do. That's what I tell my kids, and that's what they tell their friends: 'My daddy saves the planet.' It's all I want to do.

(Interview, corporate sustainability manager, March 2010)

It is not only our economy that faces an unparalleled challenge from climate change. How we understand our relationships, our identities, and even ourselves as people is also at stake. For instance, in Chapter 4 we explored how businesses attempt to maintain their hegemony over climate politics by synchronising their interests with broader societal principles and building a common identity with like-minded groups and individuals. This involves incorporating citizenship roles and leads to the recalibration of subject positions, such that citizens, in enacting corporate interests, can become active constituents in campaigns, responsible consumers of 'green' products and services, ethical employees, and even ecopreneurs.

However, this vision of identity assumes acceptance of roles defined within dominant discourses and diminishes the scope for individual agency and resistance. With this in mind, in this chapter we delve deeper into the identity construction that occurs within corporate responses to climate change, focusing particularly on the activities of those tasked with implementing environmental sustainability initiatives. To what degree are the people at the heart of the business world's engagement with the climate crisis (sustainability specialists) bound by the constraints that the very same engagement routinely seeks to impose?

As an increasingly familiar feature of corporate activity, engaging with climate change has the potential to defy the dominant and privileged discourses of shareholder value and economic expansion. This situates sustainability specialists in a contradictory space in which their positions within organisations are rooted in incongruity and paradox. Navigating the consequent tensions involves assembling a coherent sense of self amid conflicting demands and social situations – a process of 'identity work' (Alvesson and Willmott, 2002).

Such a process is both regulated through prevailing organisational and occupational discourses (e.g., maximising shareholder value) and threatened by competing discourses (e.g., environmental catastrophe and well-being). Managers and employees, in dealing with the existential implications of climate change, therefore need to create a sense of coherence between their actions and their values. The friction between the market and the environment and individuals' understandings of their work and personal roles can involve substantial narrative reinvention.

As a result, managers adopt an array of different 'personas' in the day-to-day work of corporate environmentalism. We do not see these as rigid: rather, we see them as identity resources that are enacted in seeking to bridge contradictions between personal stories and competing organisational discourses. In the discussion that follows we try to make sense of the discord between actions and values and to investigate the need to nurture a more seamless and potentially affirming story of the self. We outline a range of genres managers use in building 'narrative identities' for themselves, their careers, and their understanding of a pressing and utterly fundamental question in the age of creative self-destruction: 'Who am I?'

Climate change, identity, and personal reinvention

Research into managerial attitudes to the natural environment has tended to paint a somewhat conflicting picture. This in itself underlines the inherent complexity of the situation and the contradictions and paradoxes that regularly confront those in sustainability roles. Let us look very briefly at two examples.

Steve Fineman's (1996; 1997) analysis of corporate 'greening' in UK car manufacturing and food retailing during the 1990s found little evidence of managers with a genuine personal concern about the environment. Fineman argued that much of their work instead derived from 'enlightened self-interest' and centred on endeavouring to align their own behaviour with approved 'greening' initiatives. He concluded: 'Few "green" managers exhibit moral conscience (and its concomitant emotions) when considering environmental protection … In practice, enacted "ethical" moralities are essentially pragmatic, well attuned to the organisation's profit interests and expediently adjusted to different subcultural interests' (Fineman, 1996: 492).

By contrast, Andy Hoffman (2010) identified an emerging group of employees with greater environmental awareness. These individuals, he contended, were increasingly to the fore in championing pro-environmental change within organisations. They did not subjugate their identities in favour of corporate discourses: rather, they acted as change agents, drawing on their educational backgrounds and religious and environmental values in striving to bring about more sustainable entities. In Hoffman's words:

> In the pursuit of a spiritual element to their work, environmentalists in the workplace are challenging these dominant beliefs, attempting to reconcile them with their own personal value systems. They see their attempts to bring environmental sustainability into the core values of the organisation as a spiritual cause and purpose both for maintaining their personal identity and for positively impacting society. (Hoffman, 2010: 157–58)

The reality is that employees in contemporary organisations exhibit a diversity of opinions in relation to the environment and the extent to which it is important to their personal and work identities. Studies have found a variety of managerial responses – from high levels of climate scepticism to a marked determination to regulate GHG emissions – in a number of settings, including Canada's tar sands industry (Lê, 2013; Lefsrud and Meyer, 2012).

In recent years there has been a noticeable uptake of environmental discourse within business media. Virgin CEO Richard Branson has been a very public advocate of corporate sustainability (Prudham, 2009), as illustrated by his formation of 'The B Team', a group of CEOs and other public spokespeople who aim 'to catalyse a better way of doing business for the well-being of people and the planet' (http://bteam.org/about/). Harvard strategy professor and business guru Michael Porter has become a prominent proponent of the environment in his work on 'green' capitalism and, more recently, 'creating shared value' (Porter and Kramer, 2011; Porter and van der Linde, 1995). Even News Corporation CEO Rupert Murdoch, a long-time climate sceptic, announced in 2007 that 'the planet deserves the benefit of the doubt' and that his company would pursue carbon-neutral status (Hannam, 2007). Accordingly, while the politics of climate change has become ever more partisan and vitriolic, there is now legitimate space for managerial engagement with the environment.

There is also space for engagement at a more personal level – one that lies beyond corporate-sanctioned schemes – as shown, for example, by the website of Gary Warden, a professional geologist who spent 18 years at BHP Billiton, the world's largest mining company, rising to the position of global manager of its $1 billion business improvement programme. The story of Warden's own epiphany on climate change (Warden, 2009) is in some ways exceptional, but its power in conveying the climate crisis as a source of organisational and career transformation is undeniable.

Pivotally, Warden describes how he chanced upon a *Time* special report on global warming while waiting in a doctor's surgery in 2006. The article was prefaced by a cover image of a polar bear standing on a thin strip of melting ice, seemingly all but stranded by the metamorphosis enveloping it. The headline was explicit in the urgency of its message: 'Be worried. Be very worried.' Warden recalls how he felt compelled to reappraise the issue of climate change at the most basic level:

This was the first time that I had seen the most recent data, and I was quite frankly scared by what I read. The science was compelling – CO_2 levels in the atmosphere at 380ppm, higher than at any time in the last 650,000 years. Nineteen of the twenty hottest years on record occurring since 1980, positive feedback loops from the melting of polar ice and much more – not only was climate change happening, but it was happening at an alarming rate, and we needed to act urgently to avoid catastrophic consequences … I walked away from the doctor's surgery a changed man.

Warden was inspired to question both his lifestyle and his career. He and his wife looked for more carbon-efficient options at home, replacing their gas-guzzling 4WD with a hybrid model. They engaged others in their family and community on the subject of climate change. Warden decided to leave his employer and dedicate himself to a more sustainable life. His belief in the need for a political response saw him join environmental groups. He became involved in the Climate Project, training with Al Gore to advocate action. In 2007, he ran for the Australian Senate in the Federal Election, representing the Climate Change Coalition.

Although unusual in the completeness of its trajectory, Warden's journey from scepticism to newfound purpose highlights how managers struggle to link their own identity with their organisational duties. As we show in more detail in the following sections, considerable identity work is needed to facilitate the necessary shift in attitudes and the required clarification of values.

The identity work of corporate environmentalism

Our discussions with sustainability managers and consultants uncovered a number of identities used in the daily work of corporate environmentalism. Three in particular dominated: the 'rational manager', the 'change agent', and the 'committed activist'. Crucially, these identities pertained not so much to fixed positions but rather to roles or characters (Watson, 2009; Wetherell and Potter, 1989) adopted in specific circumstances and for certain audiences (see Table 6.1).

The rational manager

Economic crisis, corporate restructuring, heightened performance expectations, job insecurity, and the breakdown of traditional career hierarchies have all posed challenges to managerial identity in recent years (Hassard et al., 2011; Martin and Wajcman, 2004). These generic pressures are especially pronounced for new jobs that lack established institutional presence and professional identification. Corporate sustainability roles could be said to represent a novel and particularly vulnerable managerial occupation in this regard, given that they have developed only during the past decade or so amid mounting disquiet over regulatory, market, and reputational risks.

In addition, sustainability managers and advisers act within an uncertain and liminal space inside a corporation. They often find themselves separated from operational business activities and so serve more as internal consultants to different units. In essence, they aim to promote change within an organisation through influence rather than through authority (Sturdy et al., 2015; Wright et al., 2012).

Perhaps not surprisingly then, an identity many stress is that they share the same concerns as their more operationally focused counterparts, not least around discourses of efficiency, profitability, and

Table 6.1 *Identities of sustainability specialists and common themes*

Identity	Indicative themes	Attitudes, relations, and activities
Rational manager	Efficiency	Improved efficiency and reduced costs as a rationale for environmental sustainability
	Professional	Being seen as 'professional' and objective
	Business case	Presenting and justifying environmental initiatives as a 'business case'
	Reputational risk	Promoting environmental sustainability as a way of preventing risks to corporate reputation and community goodwill
	New opportunities	Engaging with climate change provides new opportunities for value creation
	Being practical	Effective change agency is about being practical and pragmatic
	'Green'	Not being perceived as 'green'; 'green' as a negative identity
Green change agent	Environmental consciousness	Personally concerned about the environment and issues such as climate change
	Passion	Passionate about climate change and environmental sustainability
	Change agency	Identifying as a change agent advocating environmental sustainability
	Embedding change	Embedding environmental sustainability within organisations and having a lasting impact
	Satisfaction	Expressing satisfaction about work in environmental sustainability
	Resistance	Encountering resistance to environmental change agendas

Table 6.1 (*cont.*)

Identity	Indicative themes	Attitudes, relations, and activities
Committed activist	Values	Engagement with climate change related to personal values
	Journey	Seeing engagement with environmental sustainability as a 'journey' or a 'mission'
	Community engagement	Membership of community groups and engaging in environmental activity
	Volunteer work	Undertaking volunteer environmental work
	Sustainability community	Being part of a broader community of like-minded individuals concerned about sustainability and climate change
	Burnout	Becoming demoralised and burnt out within organisations that fail to support change initiatives

shareholder value. Presenting themselves as 'rational managers' underscores their standing as loyal corporate functionaries who act in the company's best interests. The emphasis is firmly on the primacy of business strategy and its contribution to shaping responses to environmental issues. As the sustainability manager at a large retail chain admitted: 'I'm not a crusader, greeny, tree-hugger – none of those things. When you do engineering they beat that out of you.' One young sustainability consultant, boasting of entering the profession to learn more about efficiency, told us: 'I wouldn't say I'm the greenest person. I think I'm quite business-focused.'

Managers relating to this identity view climate change and environmental sustainability in a circumspect manner. They know these issues are important, but they are also conscious that they have to be balanced against economic growth, profitability, and other competing demands. For instance, many of the consultants we interviewed, in advising their clients, asserted the discourse of 'professionalism' and the objective analysis of how the pursuit of sustainability might affect a business.

The 'business case' is undoubtedly a common refrain among rational managers, whose identity is customarily articulated using the language of mainstream management and the market order of worth. This frequently amounts to a conviction that addressing climate change has to be justified first and foremost from a business rationale of improved shareholder value. As the group sustainability manager at a major resources and construction company observed in aligning his role with the firm's strong commercial outlook: 'I think what they want to see is results. If we put up a case for pursuing a particular renewable energy initiative the management team aren't going to support it if it's a bucket load of money and there's no return. They're looking for return out of everything – which is great.'

A senior consultant advising corporations on climate policies reiterated this standpoint. Expounding the evolution of his firm's philosophy, he claimed that to have 'impact' it was vital to concentrate on clients' core strategies and then build sustainability initiatives that supported these objectives. 'What we were doing was more the strategic consulting,' he explained, 'so we leveraged more off the strategic management frameworks and introduced the sustainability concepts into that.'

Adopting the persona of the rational manager therefore means framing environmental sustainability and engagement with climate change in ways that appeal to market and efficiency logics (see also Chapter 5). For many this is a preferred and self-affirming work identity (see also Fineman, 1997), but for others emphasising the 'business case' is more a political and situational device to bridge the gap between their own desire for pro-environmental action and the prevalence of antipathetic local discourses.

Indeed, some of the sustainability professionals we interviewed remarked how engaging with climate change in corporate settings often involved presenting these issues and related initiatives in accordance with conventional business language and concepts (see also Andersson and Bateman, 2000). Several confessed that their efforts to alter corporate behaviour could easily be thwarted by emotional appeals or perceptions of being overzealous. Even being labelled 'green' might prove fatal to organisational legitimacy, as one senior sustainability adviser cautioned: ' "Oh, they're just the tree-huggers, they're not commercial, they don't understand …" So definitely there's an association. If you're "green" then you have an ideological bent – "You're part of the movement, you're not objective, you're not commercial, therefore we can put you in that box. We can't trust you."'

Yet even relying on a 'business case' for environmental sustainability is not without its contradictions. The rational manager who promotes sustainability as 'simply good business' might also sometimes acknowledge deeper and more personal feelings about climate change and the future of the planet. For instance, the head of environment at a well-known airline recognised his strictly corporate contribution revolved around improving fuel efficiency – the top cost driver of the company's business model – but insisted: 'I want to be able to leave a legacy ... so that maybe not my kids but my kids' kids can still see the sun, can still see birds flying.'

These insights demonstrate that even frequent adopters of the rational manager persona see the climate crisis as a possibly apocalyptic scenario that has a bearing on the cosy certainties of business discourse. For some this validates their work in building a more 'sustainable' corporation in the belief that the market and innovation will deliver solutions; for others it is the very identity of the rational manager that offers a retreat from such uncomfortable thoughts.

The green change agent

Public polls, the growth of environmental social movements, and the increasing presence of Green political parties have all reflected intensifying awareness and anxiety over climate change during the past several decades. A significant corollary has been the emergence of broader social discourses alongside the enduring corporate fixation on markets and competitiveness.

These contesting discourses, including the wider notion of a climate crisis and the potentially catastrophic effects of a 'business as usual' approach to GHG emissions (Levy and Spicer, 2013), can impose hugely contradictory demands on managers and employees working in corporate environmental sustainability. They do not merely serve to justify the need to manage reputational and regulatory risks: they might also provide a persuasive connection to personal fears about the escalating devastation of our ecosystems. The identity of the 'green change agent' is often central to juggling these conflicting exigencies.

Many of our interviewees demonstrated this identity. Their ingrained respect and enthusiasm for the environment underpinned their resolve to dispute corporate assumptions and stimulate organisational transformation. They spoke of furthering the cause of sustainability both inside and outside work, using professional and social networks alike; they also spoke of the environment's significance in their home and family lives. As a sustainability consultant at a leading accountancy firm explained: 'I have a huge passion around climate change, around the change side of how you move this change through organisations.'

Local discourses of 'corporate sustainability' provide an especially strong context for the enactment of this identity, as in the case of the climate-change manager at a sizeable media organisation who implemented an initiative to reduce employees' carbon footprints both at work and at home. The programme featured a dedicated website showcasing employees' stories, as well as a competition with an environmentally friendly hybrid car as a prize. Its success kick-started a pervasive 'green' office culture, from which the manager derived significant satisfaction. Other managers described how their work resulted in employees becoming keen advocates of energy efficiency, recycling campaigns, less company air travel, and other 'green' schemes. As the sustainability manager at a large bank explained: 'That's really what you're trying to do in this whole field – get people to go: "Oh, okay, there's another agenda, there's something else bigger than just me and my job."'

As 'change agents', these managers use their personal commitment to environmental sustainability to give fresh insights into organisational problems and product/process innovations. They offer different perspectives on topics such as how to achieve novel efficiencies and how to tap into new consumer trends. A commercial property company's sustainability manager told us that designing a marketing strategy around changes in environmental building certification not only gave his firm a competitive edge but also, he felt, contributed to society's longer-term well-being. An environmental manager at a multinational food company recalled how the locating of facilities was reassessed after he liaised with senior management about climate-induced adjustments in production.

Managers are able to present a positive image of themselves through stories such as these. They can regard themselves both as loyal employees and as agents of change, helping to achieve core business objectives while at the same time fostering corporate environmental responsibility. To quote one sustainability manager: 'This sounds really idealistic, but I was really looking for something where I could contribute and achieve something that was more than just making money for somebody.'

This is, though, an identity that does not fit all circumstances. Managers lacking the official sanction that might come from executive patronage can struggle to maintain it; so, too, can those employed in companies whose devotion to sustainability is unclear. Moreover, developing an identity that accentuates difference, distinctiveness, and 'otherness' carries the burden of choosing to stand outside existing organisational norms (Bartel and Dutton, 2001). Many of our interviewees admitted they attracted gibes about their opinions and their status as a 'green advocate'. A sustainability manager at an accountancy company revealed how her colleagues labelled her one of the 'hippies on the third floor', thereby not only denigrating her views but also hinting at her limited eminence within the firm's hierarchy: in short, she was regarded as a tolerated eccentric.

The committed activist

The tensions between environmental convictions and corporate commitment are arguably at their greatest in companies that are hostile or sceptical towards claims of a climate crisis. In these circumstances striking a balance is sometimes seen as coming at too high a cost and goes to the very heart of an individual's values and sense of self. It is in such situations that the identity of the 'committed activist' is most likely to surface.

Managers who adopt this identity are ready to stand firm in the face of organisational resistance. For them the personal becomes the political. Some of our interviewees told how they essentially put themselves on the line in countering corporate decisions and practices. Expressing his willingness to step outside business convention and oppose proposals entailing environmental harm, one sustainability manager at a food company said: 'I guess we have to be the voice of the environment, which can't speak ... So sometimes decisions are made and those considerations aren't there, and we've got to be the ones who stand up and say: "No!"'

More explicitly, the identity of the committed activist is evident when individuals' environmental values prompt them to leave their organisations or to refuse work from companies whose activities they deem incompatible with their principles. One sustainability consultant told how the takeover of his firm by an energy multinational left him with no choice but to resign: 'Seventy per cent of their revenue comes from hydrocarbons,' he said, 'and I just can't do it.' Explaining his decision to abandon his corporate career to lead a more 'sustainable life' as a political and community activist, one manager said: 'I never had anybody who really came back to me and said: "You're crazy." A lot of them really admired me for taking a stand on this.'

While some of the managers who articulated this identity moved to companies in which their values were more welcome, several set up their own advisory businesses or embarked on community and political activism, including volunteer work. Some of those we interviewed had participated in volunteer activities such as the Climate Project and made presentations to companies, community groups, and schools; others talked about undertaking further education in environmental issues and developing networks with like-minded sustainability professionals. Many spoke of a multi-faceted 'journey' encompassing moving in and out of corporate and consultancy roles and the intermingling of work, education, and community activities. As the group sustainability adviser at a major bank confessed: 'Most companies are a long way from being sustainable in the true sense, and so therefore anything you get through is a win on that path. I think everyone is conscious that it's a long journey and there are kind of ebbs and flows in that.'

Shifting between identities: crafting a coherent sense of self

Managers use different identities at different times and in different contexts when they engage with climate change. This is so both at work and in their social and family lives. As our research confirmed, such identity work allows them to negotiate between self-understanding and dominant local discourses.

We have already seen how some of our interviewees adopted the identity of the rational manager. They might voice strong environmental values at home or among like-minded colleagues, but they would moderate their views in the presence of scepticism over climate change. Confronted by the discourses of 'professionalism' and 'productivity', they found the identity of the rational manager not only more appropriate but also liable to prove politically effective in convincing others of the merits of pro-environmental action.

Such was the case with the media company sustainability manager who regularly sought to engage in high-level discussions on waste reduction, recycling, and reduced costs. Here the identity of the rational manager reaped rewards twice over: plant managers believed in the moral worthiness of the proposed initiatives, and senior figures within the company also began promoting them.

Similarly, a sustainability manager tasked with embedding awareness of climate change in a training programme for insurance sales staff initially met with cynicism and even hostility from many members of the target audience. The key to success was the framing of the offering: although involving basic education on the increased frequency of extreme weather events, the programme was billed as a means of improving interaction with customers and so selling more policies. In due course, not least given the additional revenue it helped to generate, the scheme was hailed as 'fantastic'. In this instance the identity of the rational manager supplied the necessary 'work-around' in the cause of environmental sustainability. As another sustainability consultant remarked: 'If you can get business to change – and it's still delivering value for the community, it's not a greenwash, it's still delivering measurable value in some way – then I don't care why they do it.'

At the other end of the spectrum is the identity of the committed activist, which many of the managers we spoke to also found useful – although some noted the importance of having sufficient senior management backing before 'speaking out'. As the climate-change manager at a multinational resource company observed: 'I'm pretty passionate, but I've learned how far I can push – and sometimes it can be a little bit counterproductive.' This identity is one that tends to be displayed only in specific contexts or where an issue is of such magnitude that risking one's career is seen as worthwhile. Some organisations might abide 'hippies on the third floor'; others might not. Comparing the respective dispositions of her previous and current employers in giving her the freedom to promote environmental sustainability, one manager said:

I had to get quite hardline and professionalised about sustainability and only ever talk about facts and figures … I came into this job thinking: 'Well, I've honed myself down to be just a machine now, and I'll come into this hardline, fixed environment.' But it's actually a very family-oriented, warm culture. Now they're saying: 'That's fine – let's engage people [on sustainability].'

Changes in identity are also manifest in the transition between work and home. One response to the burnout and fatigue engendered by ongoing activism in a corporate setting is to disconnect in private. The group sustainability manager at a property company told us how his earlier job at an environmental NGO had made him acutely conscious of the urgency of climate change, which he needed to distance himself from in his home life: 'The thing is that when you do it for a living all day you kind of switch off ... You look at the horror of it all, the actual factual information, the melting, the death, the species loss, and you have to get over that.'

This disengagement was also evident for many in the contradictions of trying to 'live sustainably' in a society based on excessive consumption. Some of our interviewees drew attention to their lifestyle choices – including paying a premium for 'green' power, using public transport and downsizing their homes – while also acknowledging the limits of the 'committed activist' identity. As one confessed:

I call myself 'Mr Sustainable' as a bit of a joke. But the house is quite big, and the pool is quite nice, and so everyone goes: 'You liar!' And that's true. I don't know ... I'm maybe more than a token green, but the way I look at it is I'm trying to challenge those bigger fundamental issues about systemic change – and you try and do your own little bit as well.

The heroic self: narrative genres of climate change

Although people often move from one identity to another in negotiating between their self-interpretations and the demands of diverse contexts (Ricœur, 1994), identity is not infinitely malleable. The potential to adopt different identities is likely to be constrained by one's sense of self and one's commitment to specific values. Identity work therefore reflects not only the subject positions offered by local discourses but also the temporal dimension of individuals' experiences and beliefs. The creation of a broader narrative identity allows for a relatively coherent sense of self that accommodates conflict and incongruity between values and actions (Ricœur, 1994).

A common theme in managerial and professional identity work is to recast the self within the 'heroic' (Gabriel, 2000; McAdams, 1996; Watson, 2009) or 'aspirational' (Thornborrow and Brown, 2009) frame, in which the individual, as a moral agent, battles against adversity for a noble cause (see also McAdams, 2006). Several genres of the heroic narrative appear in the identity work of managers in engaging with climate change (see Table 6.2).

One common narrative genre is that of *achievement*, in which individuals stress a personal story of success and progress based on skills and knowledge accrued over time. This theme provides space to explain changes in identity as part of a career trajectory. Rational managers can harness their skills as green change agents; committed activists can engage with the business world as rational managers; and so on.

For example, a sustainability manager at an airline told us how her wealth of expertise in implementing new technologies fitted her current job of deploying environmentally friendly practices. '[I]t's very personally satisfying to be involved in something so future-facing', she said. 'That's where my bias is – technology delivering a better world.' Similarly, the culture and reputation manager at an insurance company highlighted how her background as a political adviser, along with her interest in social equity, was now invaluable in advocating a strategic business response to climate change.

Personal change is even more pronounced in the genre of *transformation*. Here attitudes towards the climate crisis evolve as they are exposed to new information, the influence of mentors, and novel activities and tasks. Many of our interviewees linked this theme to that of 'maturation' – the gaining of wisdom and its impact in shaping their knowledge and character. Some of the managers who took part in our study couched their engagement with environmental issues in the more classical terms of a 'journey', a 'quest', and a search for meaning.

One manager described how he had left the NGO sector – in which he had spent many years fighting for environmental issues – in part because he believed he could affect greater change from within the business world. In other words, he had a 'mission'. In this case we see a committed activist accounting for the adoption of the alternative identities of green change agent and even rational manager: 'I think I've just formed a view that if I can make [this company] better then that's my piece. My mission is to make [this company] a greener company.

Table 6.2 *Narrative identity genres of sustainability specialists*

Narrative genre	Examples of temporal and situational coherence between identities
Achievement Narrative of career success and personal progress based on skills and expertise developed over time	Rational manager's strategic and/or technical insight leads to effectiveness in advocating environmental improvements Alternatively, committed activism and concern with environmental and social equity bring new insights to business and result in pro-environmental change
Transformation Personal change over time through exposure to new experiences, information, and mentors; career and life as a journey involving maturation and gaining of wisdom	Personal reinvention from climate sceptic to green change agent to environmental activist Contrasting transformation from committed activist to green change agent or rational manager based on desire to work for change 'from within' business world
Epiphany Major life changes or upheavals that prompt fundamental change in perception and discovery of higher purpose	Personal crisis or critical event leads to reassessment of priorities (e.g., death, divorce, retrenchment lead rational manager to seek to 'make a difference' or 'leave a legacy' as green change agent or committed activist) Alternatively, moving from government or NGO into corporate world results in new insights about business and how to effect change (from committed activist to green change agent or rational manager)
Sacrifice Forsaking material rewards for socially worthy outcome; alternatively, recognising the need to sacrifice some principles for greater good	Acceptance that working for environmental sustainability often lacks material rewards and involves risks (e.g., being green change agent invites lesser corporate status; being committed activist threatens organisational legitimacy and career) Achieving environmental gains requires pragmatism and some sacrifice of principles in short term (e.g., adopting discourse of sales and profits to sell environmental improvements – 'a work-around for the cause').

Table 6.2 (*cont.*)

Narrative genre	Examples of temporal and situational coherence between identities
Adversity Toiling against hardship and criticism; the individual as underdog who eventually triumphs through persistence and political skill	Green change agent and committed activist as someone 'swimming against the tide' and subject to criticism and rejection; need to be determined and clever to succeed Contrasting view that underdog status leads to burnout and need to 'switch off' from activism outside of work

And having [this company] being greener will have a big influence in the world, because they are pretty big.'

Another related theme is *epiphany*. We have already encountered this in Gary Warden's switch from corporate globetrotter to climate-change campaigner. As business journalist Joe Confino has noted: 'If you delve into the triggers for transformation among business leaders it is often an epiphany rather than greater knowledge that leads to the raising of consciousness, as well as concrete action.' The chairman of Puma, Jochen Zeitz, credits his conversion to the cause of better valuing nature to his experience in a Benedictine monastery, whereas the chief executive of Unilever, Paul Polman, says his 'came from looking into his children's eyes and recognising he would be failing them if he did not do all he could to ensure their future well-being' (Confino, 2012).

Many of the managers we spoke to revealed how their apprehensions about sustainability and climate change grew out of such critical events, major life changes, or upheavals that led them to reconsider their jobs and careers and look for a higher purpose. One told how he undertook a mid-life career transition from marketing to sustainability after the breakdown of his marriage: 'I thought I could convince people to buy my cheese more than someone else's cheese or my chocolate bar more than someone else's chocolate bar,' he reflected, 'and I struggled to find meaning in that.' Another manager explained how a personal tragedy led her to reassess her life and devote herself to a job that would make a difference: 'I started to realise how all-encompassing climate change was, and it took me one to two years to actually go: "Wow, this is everything." This is sort of so huge – it makes a lot of the other issues that we're dealing with on a day-to-day basis look really minor.'

An element of *sacrifice* is often implied in these depictions of career and life changes, as in the story of a senior financial analyst who became disillusioned with his well-paid job in global finance and decided to found his own sustainable funds management business to promote renewable energy start-ups. While conceding his family's increased financial vulnerability, he pointed out the satisfaction he gained from the realisation that he could use his skills for a more socially worthy outcome.

Sacrifice also relates to issues of organisational status and legitimacy. Many of our interviewees faced difficulties in attempting to establish themselves within their organisations, often suffering rebuffs and rejections. One sustainability manager at an insurance company recalled that even when her superiors detected merit in her initiatives they would be sure to undermine her overall stance on environmental matters:

He said, 'This is fantastic, this is great!' And then he turns around and says to me: 'You know I don't believe in it [climate change]. You know I haven't changed my mind. I think it's all still crap.' He literally looked me in the eye, and I went: 'Yeah Keith I do. That's fine. I don't care.'

While these accounts hint at the scope for the underdog to triumph in influencing change through political skill, such 'face-work' also involves substantial emotional labour as individuals juggle corporate performance with personal concern. As a sustainability adviser in the property sector lamented in analysing his own situation and that of his colleagues: 'A lot of it is that they're becoming exhausted, because the consequence of being very reactive to sustainability is you're always going against the tide … It's only sustainable for a limited time. People burn out.'

In some cases the changes in identity we have discussed are explicitly acknowledged and even celebrated. Other genres accommodate movement between identities in terms of the superior skills of the micro-political agent. 'Transformation', 'epiphany', and 'sacrifice' highlight the development of character over time within a favourable and heroic narrative arc; 'achievement' and 'adversity' revolve around astute use of influence and an ability to react to shifts in contextual dynamics.

Together, all of these narrative genres provide the syntax within which sustainability managers and consultants are able to explain different activities, incidents, experiences, and roles. They give a coherent and positive aura to these individuals' life stories. They supply the various plots that bond the temporal and situational aspects of identity within a narrative time. As such, they fashion an edited past, a preferred present, and a desired future.

Climate change and managerial identity

Personal concern about climate change has become an accepted position in the sphere of business – albeit one that must often align with pro-market and profit-making agendas. This much is plain from public examples of corporate environmentalism. Corporations play a central role in prescribing identities that accord with their own underlying wishes and motivations, but there is also space for individual agency in responding to the social and political discourses surrounding the climate crisis.

As we have seen, this is particularly evident among those charged with spearheading corporate sustainability initiatives. They are frequently highly aware of climate change and the enormous threats it poses, but at the same time they must act in the best interests of the organisations that employ them. As 'outsiders within', they face isolation and marginalisation if their ideas are sufficiently disruptive; equally, they face co-option if they subjugate their identities to better satisfy business imperatives.

This raises an acute problem for these individuals, who must find ways to cope with the multiple and conflicting discourses that construct their identities. The personas they adopt vary in their attachment to environmental considerations, ranging from a realistic recognition of business logics (e.g., the rational manager) to a less conciliatory standpoint (e.g., the green change agent or the committed activist). It is by enacting these different identities that sustainability managers bridge the tensions between their sense of self and divergent circumstances and audiences.

The construction of identities occurs both through interaction with others and in response to cultural and social contexts. Identities are thus *dialogical* and *situational* (McNay, 2008). It is through inter-action with others that one comes to know oneself – not just in terms of 'who I am' but in terms of 'who I am *not*' – which in turn allows one to maintain the all-important *sense* of self. Sustainability special-ists might enact being rational managers *and* green change agents while *not* viewing themselves as activists; and such enactments would depend not only on their interactions but also on the available dis-courses pertaining to specific contexts (Kuhn, 2006).

The limited number of discourses that can be used to understand oneself (Alvesson and Willmott, 2002) fosters a need for some con-formity in identity display. In effect, there is a promise to be consist-ent over time; and this is fulfilled through narrative identity (McNay, 2008; Ricœur, 1994). It is through the emplotment of narrative iden-tity that sundry experiences, relationships, and self-representations can be accommodated and a life story can be authored.

Narratives help to explain apparent disjunctures between beliefs and actions by providing a consistent storyline to lives and careers. They equip individuals with a precious impression of continuity 'between who they have been and who they are becoming' (Ibarra and Barbulascu, 2010: 136). Although they might still contain 'unre-solved antagonisms' (Clarke et al., 2009), they offer a feeling of unity, coherence, and purpose by bringing together 'the events of lived experience in the plot of the story a person tells about his or her life' (Ezzy, 1998: 239). They also have the capacity to 'link the past with the future by giving a sense of continuity to an ever-changing story of the self' (Rasmussen, 1996: 164).

We have already noted an overarching heroic theme within many of these narratives. However, as shown in Table 6.2, some also hold the potential for more nuanced explanations of behaviour.

The genre of *transformation*, for instance, was evident in the storylines of interviewees who described the journey from corporate executive to environmental activist. Yet it might also be used to explain the reverse – that is, how a committed activist could choose to work in a corpor-ate setting to effect change from within (see also Meyerson and Scully, 1995). Similarly, the genre of *sacrifice* could include not only the mater-ial costs of becoming an environmental advocate but also the act of dis-counting one's principles in the short term to make a longer-term gain. It might also relate to living somewhat unsustainably in order to make larger systemic changes – in essence, a 'work-around' for the cause.

These narratives, in accommodating conflicting identities, help to furnish individuals with a more coherent depiction of themselves, so highlighting a key feature of 'identity reconciliation' (Creed et al., 2010). That said, the process of resolving identity fragmentation through emplotment should not be confused with an essentialist idea of the self: there are limits to imposing a narrative structure on identities, and exceeding those limits might result in disjunction between experiences of the self (Ricœur, 1994).

Narrative identities are also 'political projects' that inform discourses and influence political ends. Identity work involves not just individual claims but collective struggle, in that 'power partially determines outcomes, and power relations are changed by the struggles' (Calhoun, 1994: 21). Identity politics suggests that ' "I act because of who I *am*", not because of a rational interest or set of learned values' (Somers, 1994: 608). The dialectics between the self and others provide a space for creativity or imagination; and the enactment of identities has the potential to challenge established thinking and to demonstrate alternative possibilities (Creed et al., 2010; Meyerson and Scully, 1995).

For example, Meyerson and Scully (1995) elucidate the explicitly political nature of identity work in their depiction of 'tempered radicals' – individuals who are committed to organisational and professional discourses (e.g., capitalism, profitability, individualism) but who also identify with possibly conflicting discourses (e.g., feminism, racial equality, and social justice). Such 'dual subjectivities' are seen as hard to maintain, yet they provide concordance between the self and others. In these cases the identity work extends beyond the internal crafting of the self to a potentially political role in which individuals come to personify particular change agendas by enacting identities (Creed et al., 2010; Watson, 2008). The tension between 'the horizon of expectations and the space of experience' implicit in identity work shows the scope for such political activities (McNay, 1999: 330).

As we have outlined, for some managers the micro-politics of climate change are central to their identities at work, at home, and socially. The managers who took part in our research gave us numerous examples of how these identities were linked to the political act of spreading knowledge about the climate crisis and influencing others. The politics of identity work was most obvious in the case of the green change agent and in the enactment of seemingly discordant identities such as the rational manager (e.g., when negotiating environmental 'wins' by promoting cost or efficiency improvements) and the committed activist (e.g., when disputing environmentally damaging proposals, so prizing the greater good over career prospects). It is safe to say, given the ideological and partisan interpretations the issue now attracts, that climate change provides an increasingly fractious setting for such identity work.

Conclusion

Climate change presents an unprecedented challenge to our collective future and to the conventional discourses of boundless economic growth and human progress. Our own identities are critical to shaping how we respond (Crompton and Kasser, 2009).

The corporate emphasis on creative self-destruction, as driven by market solutions and technological innovation, suggests defined identities for employees and citizens as ethical consumers, political constituents, and ecopreneurs. Yet there are opportunities to dispute such subject positions and instead invent identities of our own. Understanding how we create narratives of ourselves and our behaviour is central to theorising how humanity can engage with an emergency as utterly all-consuming as the climate crisis.

We have argued that climate change has become a touchstone for many managers and employees. Much of this attention can be explained by traditional business discourses, but there is also considerable personal concern about the world our children will inherit. As an existential threat to not only our economic, social, and physical well-being but also to our very identities, climate change questions our understanding of ourselves as individuals and as a species within a greater ecosystem.

While this can be welcomed as a positive sign, until the identity work of enough people is linked to this issue we are unlikely to witness the flourishing of a wider social movement agitating for the fundamental social and economic upheaval required. Like the civil rights movement in the United States, anti-colonial nationalist movements in the Third World, the women's movement, and the gay movement, all of which sought instrumental goals as well as the affirmation of excluded identities (Calhoun, 1994: 4), acting to curb climate change has to be associated with the broader identification of action as a public good.

Paradoxically, in exposing our own mortality and the limitations of our species, climate change encourages more narrative reflection about the purpose and meaning of our lives. For some this will lead to the adoption of identities based on social and political change; others, as we are now witnessing in the ever more partisan political battles over carbon regulation, will defer to a state of denial, re-emphasising established roles as employees, managers, consumers, and citizens (Norgaard, 2006). Our identities, as moulded by competing discourses at work and in society at large, are likely to become even more pivotal to our individual and shared decisions to engage or retreat as scientific projections of the crisis continue to worsen.

7 | Emotions, corporate environmentalism, and climate change

I guess I've always been a bit of an optimist, and you have to be in this game. I've got hope in terms of human ingenuity that we will trade our way out of this somehow.

(Interview, corporate sustainability manager, March 2010)

In the space of a decade, climate change has materialised within public discourse as both an existential threat and a topic of major political disagreement (Hoffman, 2012). Perhaps not surprisingly, future interpretations of a climate-shocked world prompt strong emotional responses, whether our concerns focus on the extinction of animal species, humanitarian disasters, geopolitical conflicts, or the well-being of our society, our local community, or our children (Hansen, 2009; Hulme, 2009).

A simple perusal of media coverage reveals how the issue has become increasingly polarised and emotion-laden for all, from those who promote urgent policy action to those who reject the climate crisis as a serious danger (Boykoff, 2011; McCright and Dunlap, 2010). Witness the ever more emotive statements from both sides, whether in the form of shock videos from NGOs such as Greenpeace, Plane Stupid, and 10:10 (Vaughan, 2010), heartfelt appeals from youth and community leaders during UN climate negotiations (Vidal, 2012), the anger of the denial movement at anti-government rallies, or the pronouncements of politicians, commentators, and businesspeople for and against the regulation of carbon emissions; and witness, too, the fervent responses evident in the social disengagement and disavowal of an issue that some think too large, too complex, and too much of a hazard to existing ideologies (Norgaard, 2006). In short, climate change discourses can be associated with new norms of emotional expression in which passion, rage, fear, and hostility, as well as apathy and ambivalence, are central features of social debate (Dörries, 2010; Moser, 2007).

In this chapter we explore how emotions are mobilised within corporate responses to climate change. The idea of emotionality is often downplayed in business settings, but emotions are as much a part of company life as they are any social setting. We argue that the promotion of corporate environmentalism is itself inherently emotional, given that firms must not only navigate the highly charged discourses on climate change but also try to create positive interpretations of a future in which their solutions are endorsed, embraced, and celebrated.

As discussed in the previous chapter, this is especially apparent for those managers tasked with leading sustainability initiatives by advising on new strategies and implementing novel practices, products, and services. A critical component of their role is the adaptation and management of standards of emotional expression within organisations – what we term 'emotionology work'. They must strive to harness employee and customer emotions around climate change in ways that contribute to profitability and value creation; they must manage their own emotions, calculating, championing, constraining, and compartmentalising them in a variety of contexts; and, as ever, they must balance their own interests, concerns, wishes, and goals with those of the organisations that employ them. The demands, as we will see, can be substantial.

Managers, emotions, and the climate crisis

In March 2007, John Doerr, a partner at venture capital firm Kleiner Perkins, walked on to the stage at the annual Technology, Entertainment, and Design conference in Monterey, California (TED, 2007). Doerr had led the financing of 'new economy' juggernauts such as Google, Amazon, and Netscape. He was renowned for his optimistic portrayals of the digital age. Most of the members of the packed audience expected a typically positive address.

It was not to be. Doerr began his presentation by confessing: 'I'm scared. I don't think we're going to make it.' Over the next 20 minutes he laid bare his fears about the climate catastrophe facing humanity and the chances of a 'green' economy saving the world. Weeping openly, he finally closed by reflecting: 'I really, really hope that we multiply all our energy, all of our talent and all of our influence to solve this problem ... because if we do I can look forward to the conversation I'm going to have with my daughter in 20 years.'

Stunned, those in attendance rose to their feet and gave Doerr a standing ovation. He hugged several people as he left the stage. It was a landmark illustration of climate change's ability to challenge comfortable assumptions of economic growth and social advance: the brilliant, fabulously successful Silicon Valley stalwart reduced to public tears by the environmental nightmare confronting humanity. The subsequent media reaction consisted in large part of business pundits voicing their unconfined surprise that the ever-confident tech sector had suddenly become so terribly serious and so ... well ... *emotional.* What was going on?

For many managers and executives it has been customary to view the idea of emotionality at work in a negative light. The heroic stereotype of the cool professional stresses the traits of objectivity and calculation based on data and facts and untainted by subjective perceptions and feelings (Putnam and Mumby, 1993; Watson, 1994). Expressing human emotion has been routinely regarded as the antithesis of the 'norm of rationality', and a performance such as Doerr's would long have been denounced as illegitimate and even dangerous (Ashforth and Humphrey, 1995; Fineman, 1999; Morgan, 1986).

However, the business organisation is far from an emotion-free zone. Consultants and business gurus have for some time advocated greater passion, charismatic leadership, and emotional intelligence (Fineman, 2004; 2010; Goleman, 1995). Emotions and 'affect' have become an increasingly popular focus for management research, although many such accounts lack a critical sociological understanding of emotionality in these settings (Fineman, 2010; Loseke and Kusenbach, 2008). The more critical study of emotions is evident in the work of researchers who identify organisations as made up of 'emotional cultures' (Gordon, 1990) and 'emotional zones' or 'arenas', with 'a local emotional order ... tacitly negotiated and distinct from adjacent zones' (Fineman, 1993; 2010: 28).

A vital issue in this regard is how standards of emotional expression are formed and maintained. Broader social conventions play an important role, with various 'emotionologies' that have been developed over time defining standards for different categories of people (Stearns and Stearns, 1985). Emotionologies delineate 'society's "take" on the way – and to whom – certain emotions are to be expressed', as well as 'local' norms of emotionality (Fineman, 2010: 27). As feminist scholars have highlighted, diverse emotional standards impact on the work-roles and expected behaviours of men and women and the types of jobs to which they have access (Acker, 1990; Hochschild, 1979); they also provide varying standards of 'appropriate' expression for disparate occupations (e.g., social workers, doctors, police officers) (Fineman, 2010; Rafaeli and Sutton, 1989; Van Maanen and Kunda, 1989).

Key actors in the construction of social emotionologies include the media, advertising, popular culture, religious organisations, political parties, social movements, and activist groups (Boltanski, 1999; Goodwin et al., 2001). As 'politico-ideological constructs', emotionologies are often 'shaped by prevailing currents of nationalism, ethnocentrism, racism or homophobia, as well as governmental, religious and party-political dogmas' (Fineman, 2010: 27); they are not static and frequently undergo rapid change because of economic, demographic, technological, and other shifts. Consider the emotionology surrounding terrorism, which, at least within the United States, altered markedly after the events of 9/11 (Loseke, 2009).

During the past 20 years, through the influence of opinion setters such as the media, business groups, think tanks, and political parties (Dunlap and McCright, 2011), emotional norms in relation to climate change have been transformed. To take one obvious example: bi-partisan support from US Republicans and Democrats for action on the issue was still apparent as recently as 2008 (Klein, 2014) but seems very distant today. What used to be a field of sombre study has descended into a veritable minefield of emotions, with researchers accused of producing 'junk' science and sometimes even branded public enemies (Oreskes and Conway, 2010).

Social emotionologies are also subject to contrary interpretations, which can prevail in spite of their conflict with wider social norms. This 'interplay between regnant emotionologies and local competing or "contra" emotionologies' (Fineman, 2010: 28) is particularly relevant when, as with the growth of corporate environmentalism, social issues of high emotional import become a source of business concern and lead to the allocation of resources and expertise. The inter-relationship between social and local emotionologies can be seen in the creation of new corporate sustainability functions, groups, and roles: the people who spearhead these 'green' initiatives essentially act as 'emotionology workers', 'boundary spanners', and, in their need to upset local norms of apathy and antipathy, even 'boundary shakers' (Balogun et al., 2005).

In addition, while their corporate duties involve managing local emotional norms (i.e., managing others), there is also a need for personal emotional engagement (i.e., managing the self). This is illustrated by the concept of the change agent as 'tempered radical' (Hoffman, 2010; Meyerson and Scully, 1995). Emotional self-management is critical not only in championing issues (Andersson and Bateman, 2000; Dutton and Ashford, 1993) but also in coping with tensions and contractions (Gabriel, 2010). Spanning emotional arenas – shaping and being shaped by sundry emotionologies – provides room for self-reflection and assessment (Holmes, 2010), which may bring about emotional (de-) integration (King, 2006). Consequently, various powerful emotions are likely to be pivotal to these individuals' work in dealing with the subjectivity of the self.

The emotionologies of climate change

Research on social attitudes to climate change identifies fear, anxiety, anger, concern, passion, and guilt as common kinds of emotional expression (Dörries, 2010; Moser, 2007). This is particularly so among individuals directly affected by the physical corollaries of the phenomenon. For instance, representatives of Pacific Island nations threatened with the destruction of their homes and cultures by the rising sea levels have expressed trepidation, rage, and grief in their appeals for international action to mitigate GHG emissions (Farbotko and McGregor, 2010).

More generally, extreme weather events present the public with strong emotional images linked to an uncertain future. The destruction of New Orleans by Hurricane Katrina in 2005, the Black Saturday bushfires in Victoria in 2009, the flooding of New York City following Superstorm Sandy in November 2012, and the devastating Typhoon Haiyan in the Philippines in 2013 are notable examples. Beyond specific events, researchers have also pinpointed the angst, stress, and depression ('solastalgia') that people experience as they observe longer-term environmental deterioration in their communities through resource extraction, deforestation, and drought (Albrecht et al., 2007).

As a result, one commonplace social emotionology stresses *climate change as threat*. Here the norms of emotional expression include fear, anxiety, concern, guilt, and sympathy, as habitually encapsulated in apocalyptic visions of the climate crisis in the mass media, popular culture, and environmental accounts (Levy and Spicer, 2013; O'Neill and Nicholson-Cole, 2009). Films such as *The Day After Tomorrow* (2004), *An Inconvenient Truth* (2006), and *The Age of Stupid* (2011), as well as books such as James Hansen's *Storms of My Grandchildren* (2009), Bill McKibben's *Eaarth* (2010), and Paul Gilding's *The Great Disruption* (2011), emphasise the cataclysmic implications of climate change, evoking emotions in response to existential peril.

Activist organisations endorse this emotionology through their use of iconic animal species as talismans for emotional engagement. The polar bear – featured by, among others, Greenpeace and Plane Stupid – has become an especially resonant symbol. As Slocum (2004: 428) has argued:

The polar bear charts a clear route into the imagination and the emotions of people who think of themselves as environmentalists in some sense of that word or as people who care about or live in the 'disappearing North'. Greenpeace Canada's strategy places the bear's body directly in the way of the warming that will melt its habitat. It makes climate change visible through the effects on a particular non-human life.

Feelings of sympathy, sorrow, and bereavement are thus aroused by the likelihood that climate change will bring about the extinction of such an evocative species. As Yusoff (2010: 76) has pointed out: 'Polar bears have become a prosthetic emotional device for testing the water of loss.'

Yet the reaction such messages engender is far from clear. Surveys of public opinion suggest the extent and nature of emotional engagement varies significantly between nations, regions, and communities. Pew Research Center's Global Attitudes Project (2013) found public concern about climate change to be high in Latin America, Europe, sub-Saharan Africa, and the Asia-Pacific region but far lower in the United States. In one survey around 12 per cent of the US population described themselves as 'alarmed' by the climate crisis, 27 per cent were 'concerned', and 35 per cent were 'disengaged', 'doubtful', or 'dismissive' (Leiserowitz et al., 2011). Political affiliation, ideologies, and values can play a huge part (Leviston et al., 2011; McCright and Dunlap, 2011a; 2011b; Wolf and Moser, 2011).

More generally, negative emotions of helplessness, guilt, loss, and grief can result in individuals attempting to distance themselves from climate change. This is a means of emotion management (Norgaard, 2006). One way people might try to control their internal fear and uncertainty is by regarding the phenomenon as something that will affect only future generations or peoples in far-off lands (Randall, 2009). Other responses include externalising responsibility and blame, fatalistic framings, and even complete rejection of global warming as a hoax or 'laughable' (O'Neill and Nicholson-Cole, 2009: 363).

Other emotionologies have become conspicuous amid climate change's politicisation and submergence into a broader 'culture war' (Hoffman, 2012). The discourse of climate change as an *ideological battleground* has encouraged anger, frustration, and hostility. Confrontational negative emotions have been manifest in the partisan public debate over climate politics and carbon regulation, as noted in Chapter 4. In Australia the government's proposed introduction of carbon pricing in 2010 sparked furious protests by 'climate sceptic' groups, hate-mail campaigns, death threats against climate scientists, and a patent schism among the population on the question of 'belief' in climate change (Wright and Nyberg, 2012); comparable vitriol has surfaced in the United States as climate-change denial has been promulgated by vested interests in the fossil fuel industries (Mann, 2012; McCright and Dunlap, 2011b).

The denial of climate change has even become a profoundly emblematic feature of far-right political groups such as the Tea Party, with patriotism linked to vehement anti-government populism. 'Belief' in climate change is seen as an attack on 'free markets' and personal liberty (Hoffman, 2011b; Klein, 2014; McCright and Dunlap, 2011a). Such identity politics are rich in the emotions of passion and anger, with the use of fossil fuels seen as a god-given right: 'You want clean air and a tiny carbon footprint? Well, screw you!' (Weigel, 2014). This emotionology has also been to the fore in media coverage in the United States, the United Kingdom, and Australia, further stoking a confrontational and combative social view of the issue (Painter, 2011).

Corporate environmentalism and positive emotionality

Corporations have sought to navigate a path through these wider social discourses in a way that preserves their legitimacy and interests.

As we noted in Chapter 3, this involves not only managing the regulatory, reputational, and market risks of climate change and its accompanying politics but also seizing potential opportunities. In particular, corporate enactments of emotion around climate change offer a third and far more positive emotional framing: *climate change as challenge and opportunity*.

In this framing the economic and social risks of climate change and the concomitant emotions of fear and uncertainty are countered by the upside potential of new markets, products, and technologies. The key emotions stressed include hope, enthusiasm, passion, and excitement. The emotional enactment of climate change thereby becomes a critical space for corporate marketing and branding and for internal policies, practices, and local emotionologies.

Creating a positive climate emotionology for external audiences

Corporate marketing and branding around sustainability and 'green' themes has undergone dynamic growth over the past decade as social concern over the environment and climate change has spiralled. Many major consumer brands – including Walmart, Ben & Jerry's, GE, Toyota, Patagonia, Frito-Lay, Timberland, Tesco, and even Shell – have embraced a 'green' message in their marketing. A principal aim has been to successfully tap into consumers' increased environmental awareness while avoiding allegations of duplicity or 'greenwashing' (Ottman, 2011). Pearse (2012) has documented that there is often a disconnect between the 'green' boasts of corporate advertising and the reality of environmental impact. A selective focus on specific products and activities is sometimes exposed, as are assertions that are simply inaccurate; but what remains unmistakable in all such activities is an emphasis on evoking positive emotions among consumers and the public in general as part of an alternative emotionology of challenge and opportunity.

One powerful emotional theme in 'green' advertising has been to draw attention to the hope and optimism that spring from technological innovation. The imagined possibilities of new technologies that harness the environment rather than exploit and destroy it are presented as satisfying fantasies. We have already looked at one classic example, GE's ecomagination marketing, which has showcased imagined futures of renewable energy and environmentally beneficial industrial activities. In one especially redolent ecomagination commercial a young girl pictures a future world of underwater tidal energy farms, jet planes with birds' wings, and trains that move in unison with swaying trees. The audience is invited to greet this comforting, idealistic dream of technology married to nature with similarly child-like wonder, awe, and curiosity as the girl describes her mother's work:

My Mom, she makes underwater fans that are powered by the moon. My Mom makes airplane engines that can talk. My Mom makes hospitals you can hold in your hand. My Mom can print amazing things right from her computer. My Mom makes trains that are friends with trees. My Mom works at GE. (GE, 2014)

The theme of technology and nature proceeding hand-in-hand is also prevalent in much recent 'green' car advertising, including:

- The marketing of the enormously successful Toyota Prius (Garland et al., 2013), as touched upon in Chapter 3.
- Ford's 'Why would you sit on a soybean?' advert, which shows female members of the company's R&D department working on soy-based car foam (Ford, 2008). Soy-based foam is lighter, more effective, and biodegradable; according to the advert, it is also a technology that Ford set out to perfect but which rival manufacturers dismissed. The narrator, identified as a mother of small children, underlines the need to protect future generations, saying: 'We need to preserve the environment now.' Emotions of pride, respect, and satisfaction predominate in such accounts of corporate innovation reducing the perceived environmental cost of consumption.
- Nissan's advert for its new electric model, which further ratchets up the positive emotionality with its tale of a lone polar bear undertaking an epic journey from the melting Arctic to a major city. There the animal embraces a man who is about to climb into his new Nissan (Nissan, 2010). The touching imagery and soundtrack engage the audience in empathy and sadness for the bear's plight but then reverse this in the penultimate scene with a message of hope and optimism: nature will thank us if we all buy 'green' cars.
- Audi's 'Green Police' advert, which debuted during the 2010 Super Bowl. This offers a humorous satire of a fictional green police force arresting various members of the public for energy and waste

offences. In the key scene a diesel-powered Audi SUV is waved through an 'eco-roadblock' after being passed as compliant with tough environmental codes. The tag line declares: 'Green has never felt so right!' (Audi, 2010).

The emotions of humour and positivity contained in adverts such as these stand in stark contrast to the negative and confronting emotions showcased in the likes of Greenpeace's 'Angry Kid' (Greenpeace, 2007) or Plane Stupid's depiction of polar bears plummeting from the sky (Plane Stupid, 2009).

Moreover, corporate promotion of such a positive emotionology around the environmental impact of the business world extends beyond the mere advertising of products. As discussed in Chapter 5, corporations also make public declarations of worthiness to meet criticism and rejuvenate their image.

Take Canada's exploitation of the tar sands, which has led to an extensive PR blitz intended to revamp the fossil fuel industry as a producer of 'ethical oil' (Levant, 2010). Here emotions of pride and admiration are linked to nationalism. The assumption is that Canada, as a liberal democracy, should be regarded as a more morally worthy context for fossil fuel extraction: 'Countries that produce Ethical Oil protect the rights of women, workers, indigenous peoples and other minorities, including gays and lesbians. Conflict Oil regimes, by contrast, oppress their citizens and operate in secret, with no accountability to voters, the press or independent judiciaries. Some Conflict Oil regimes even support terrorism' (Hickman, 2011).

Analogously, Peabody Energy's endorsement of coal as a solution to 'energy poverty' in the developing world is designed to underscore the laudable outcomes of the company's activities. Chevron's 'We Agree' campaign uses 'real people' to soften its corporate image and strengthen its claims regarding 'clean' fossil fuel use, with the public asked to share in the excitement and optimism of such sentiments by clicking the 'I agree' button on a dedicated website (www .chevron.com/weagree/). All of these PR efforts have much the same goal: to make consumers feel somehow proud and satisfied that they can consume fossil fuels – and, by extension, to make them avoid the guilt that stems from concern over the destruction of the planet.

Creating a positive emotionology within the firm

Developing a 'green' emotionology also encompasses attempts to manage corporate cultures. This parallels the view of ecological modernisation and is also in keeping with businesses' greater tendency to cast themselves as agents of social transformation. Repeatedly stressed is a vision of hope, enthusiasm, pride, and even excitement in the ability of the market and technology to resolve the climate crisis.

A fondness for 'greening' as part of corporate culture management has been a growing trend in many industries (Fineman, 1996; Harris and Crane, 2002; Renwick et al., 2013). This links to a more widespread recognition of the importance of corporate culture as a source of employee motivation and competitive success (Deal and Kennedy, 1982; Peters and Waterman, 1982), as well as a pervasive means of workplace control (Fleming, 2009; Willmott, 1993).

Sustainability managers and consultants are key agents in the corporate 'greening' process. They are charged with not only fashioning responses to the more far-reaching public discourse of climate change but also implementing internal practices of environmental sustainability, including managing how staff participate in such initiatives. The 'greening' schemes they oversee can take numerous forms, including:

- 'Green office' programmes that urge employees to reduce their printing, recycle their waste, and switch off their computers at the end of the working day
- Company weblogs and intranets that publicise 'green' initiatives
- The appointment of designated 'green champions'
- Competitions that reward carbon emissions reductions and innovations that enhance energy efficiency.

Here sustainability specialists act as 'boundary spanners' and intermediaries (Aldrich and Herker, 1977; Leifer and Delbecq, 1978), translating larger social emotionologies within local emotional arenas. The social emotionology of concern and anxiety surrounding climate change as threat is not just imported but harnessed in ways that can contribute to improved employee engagement, productivity, and corporate reputation through community, empathy, and compassion. As the sustainability strategist at a power utility stated in outlining how addressing climate change could create a sense of workforce pride: '[S]o making staff very proud of the organisation that they're working for ... I think particularly in call centres, they *love* hearing news from corporate. They like to be included. They like to know they're working for a good organisation.'

The theme of encouraging employees' emotional engagement around the environment and climate change was pronounced in many of our interviews with sustainability managers. Corporate sustainability initiatives were explicitly tied to employees' own personal fears over the climate crisis. As a strategist for an airline remarked: 'We have a Green Team, which is more than a thousand volunteers now, who can be mobilised for a whole bunch of things. They are probably the most passionate [about climate change], and they come from all levels of the organisation, too, which is very cool.'

An initiative by one of Australia's leading media companies offers a good example of the desire to span social and local emotional arenas. Following an initial rollout of a carbon-neutral programme, the firm's sustainability group instituted staff competitions to encourage further 'green' improvements in employees' work and personal lives. The scheme became the dominant theme in a subsequent rebranding exercise, with posters of staff and their families accompanied by tag lines such as 'Climate change is about all of us', 'Everyone can contribute by changing what we do, in lots of ways, every day', and 'How far would you go to save the planet?'. The apogee was a competition in which employees were required to document their attempts to reduce their carbon footprints, with laptop computers and even a Toyota Prius awarded to the best entries. Recalling the workforce's enthusiasm, the company's environment manager told us:

The guy that won, he filled in his swimming pool, grew vegetables, put a wind tower in his back yard. He was a pretty smart guy with pretty good engineering. He then decided he was going to change the way the neighbourhood did things, so he got a bag of low-energy lightbulbs and door-knocked all his neighbours. He wrote a little diary of their quotes of what they said when he door-knocked and stuff. They started to have street fairs and things on this topic in their community ... He sent me a note saying he just wanted to thank us for the competition. It's actually changed the way his family interacts with itself ... They feel the world is a better place. It was a really fantastic outcome.

Through 'green office' and culture-change programmes, as well as initiatives to improve efficiency and cut waste, sustainability specialists strive to affect attitudes about climate change and its relevance to daily business practice. Just as significantly, they strive to affect the emotional salience of the issue within the workplace.

Inculcating new emotionologies also involves challenging established local emotional norms. As change agents, sustainability specialists encounter resistance and scepticism, not least when managers and employees identify with rival messages that are more cynical about the climate crisis. As the sustainability manager at an insurance company said of her drive to raise awareness of the implications of global warming:

It got a lot of pushback ... If you look at the profile of people within that business it was predominantly male, overweight, 50-plus – sceptics probably most of them ... Nice guys, but they're just more interested in going out and boozing with the insurance brokers than really thinking fundamentally about what this [climate change] means to the business.

One popular approach to creating a new corporate emotionology of climate change is to connect environmental sustainability with locally resonant practices. These might include the measurement and reporting of efficiency improvement – topics that many operational managers see both as central to their jobs and as sources of meaning and satisfaction. A number of our interviewees spoke of the excitement of production managers determined to raise productivity or slash waste. One environment manager at a global food manufacturer explained how he regularly set about linking his personal environmental concerns with his factory managers' enthusiasm for efficiency: 'To me', he said, 'that's absolutely a "win–win" for everybody.' A partner at an auditing practice told us: 'I've a strong passion in efficiency and how you use resources, because I think waste is the worst thing.' The focus on efficiency and cost is particularly meaningful, in that 'being rational is also being emotional' (Sturdy, 2003: 94).

New local emotionologies of corporate environmentalism also serve to differentiate companies from their competitors. This is achieved through distinctive 'green' branding and the portrayal of a firm as not only concerned about climate change but also active in addressing it. The local emotionology of climate change as challenge and opportunity duly feeds into the more expansive 'green' marketing of a corporation.

Inevitably, creating a positive emotionology around climate change is not without its contradictions. Senior managers at several of the consulting firms we studied reported that employees could sometimes become 'too emotional' around the issue and question a company's environmental record, forcing their employers to hold staff meetings or set up committees to allow such anxieties to be given voice. As one consultancy director told us:

We've got an ethical committee that helps us think through what work we take on ... One of the directors chairs that committee. Basically, there's a set of criteria, you score it, and that gives you the first decision-making tool. What's the implication of that? And then you sit down and just use good thinking about whether we want to do this and then make a call.

A simpler response is to prohibit the expression of personal environmental concerns during client interactions. As a senior manager at another advisory firm admitted: 'We have some people who have got distinct views, who are very passionate on this subject [climate change] ... That's nice, but if a client doesn't want to hear it they're *not* allowed to say it.'

However, attempting to control the local emotionology of climate change through meetings, committees, and rules is by no means easy. One manager revealed how some companies were perceived so negatively by staff, even despite efforts to corral emotional exchanges around client work within an 'ethics committee', that appeals to 'rational debate' frequently fell on deaf ears: '[One company] has got such a bad reputation that they won't even bother to understand what the rationale of the business case for it is – especially some of the younger staff.'

Some managers also noted how promoting emotions in response to climate change could have the unintended upshot of raising employee expectations of their companies' performance beyond levels originally envisaged. In these circumstances the positive emotionality of passion, commitment, and motivation could quickly turn to frustration, disillusion, and anger if organisations failed to live up to their professed environmental values. Recalling the ramifications of a decision to switch to a more 'environmentally-friendly' model of company car, the sustainability manager at a financial services company said:

We converted our fleet cars to Prius and caused all manner of outrage on the intranet blog – that it wasn't green enough or it was the car that you buy when you seem to be green, not when you really are … So, yes, they [employees] definitely hold us to account. They're our toughest critics by far.

In addition, the fluctuating nature of social debate around climate change can pose problems for these emotionologies. A recurring theme in our discussions with sustainability specialists was the way in which public opinion of the climate crisis has become more and more incredulous and/or fatigued, prompting senior management within some companies to query the wisdom of pursuing 'green' branding. 'It is annoying', said one interviewee whose firm's customer base was fiercely divided on climate change, 'because this is our carbon-neutral year – and, frankly, I don't think you could run a campaign celebrating it right now!'

Emotionology work and emotional labour

As we have seen, the emotionology work of sustainability specialists and managers can result in tensions, unmet expectations, and criticism. As organisational boundary spanners, these professionals find themselves operating within a liminal space (Beech, 2011) – betwixt and between the social emotionologies of climate change as a threat and an ideological battleground and the local corporate emotionologies of climate change as a challenge and an opportunity for business growth.

The managers who took part in our research spoke of how they needed to moderate and contain their own emotions to gain acceptance of their initiatives. They also spoke of the conflicting feelings they had about not only their work but, more widely, their lives and identities. Some switched from optimism to pessimism and vice versa, in light of confrontations with colleagues who protested 'it was all crap', thoughts about their children and whether they would be able to 'still see birds flying', news bulletins, meetings, and myriad other triggers. Emotionality provided them with a mechanism for self-reflection but also required them to confront contradictions and to function within different situations. More deeply, they had to consider their sense of self and deal with the potential disharmony between public displays of emotion and their own beliefs regarding the climate crisis. As outlined

Table 7.1 *Managing emotions in emotionology work*

Calculative emotionality	Adopting locally relevant emotions in selling new practices (rationality and 'fact-based' analysis or passion directed at conventional and accepted goals); 'inauthentic' emotionality justified as a necessary strategy to achieve pro-environmental outcomes and improve local legitimacy and status
Constraining emotionality	Hiding or downplaying one's own concerns and emotions; justified as necessary in light of the problem of articulating negative emotionality that questions the organisational emotionology of climate change as a challenge and an opportunity
Compartmentalising emotionality	Distinguishing between one's emotional expressions in different arenas (e.g., work vs. home, public vs. private); justification of separate emotional arenas where the private allows for genuine or 'authentic' emotionality
Championing emotionality	Explicit expression of personal emotions, irrespective of local cultures and norms; justification of being true to one's feelings or an issue that is too important not to speak out on; personifying the change message through emotional expression

in Table 7.1, they identified several approaches they adopted in handling the dissonance between social and local emotionologies.

One favoured approach among our interviewees was a *calculative* use of emotionality in casting environmental sustainability initiatives. Many told of the need to tailor their style of presentation in dealing with sceptical or disengaged managers and employees. Enacting the rational manager – the appearance of being 'professional' and outlining a clear 'business case' for action – was a familiar emotional refrain. Echoing the broader literature on 'issue-selling' (Andersson and Bateman, 2000; Dutton and Ashford, 1993), sustainability managers recognised that to be effective in shaping the perceptions of their more operationally focused counterparts they had to frame proposals within appropriate language and time-honoured business metrics (e.g., increased efficiency or market share). As one interviewee said: 'That's the other challenge: how do you have passion without being seen as too passionate?'

Essentially, fervour for the environment must be tempered; in tandem, impressions of zealotry must be guarded against. Some of our interviewees acknowledged the strategic adoption of 'professionalism' and 'objectivity' as somewhat 'inauthentic', yet they justified such actions as necessary to achieve pro-environmental outcomes and augment local legitimacy and status. The chief climate-change consultant at a global resource company neatly captured this manner of calculative emotionality in describing the care with which he would expound the merits of various proposals for organisational change: 'If you can demonstrate to peers and superiors that you're not arguing ideology, that you're arguing from a position of rigorous analysis, perhaps you last a bit longer in the debate.'

Relatedly, other managers told how their work sometimes involved the *constraining* of their own emotionality. This was particularly the case when their own negative emotions contrasted with the positive corporate emotionology of climate change as a challenge. One sustainability manager at a sizeable property development company revealed how he had to suppress his strong personal feelings for the environment to flourish within a 'bottom-line-focused' firm, instead couching initiatives in the emotionality surrounding the business's keenness for cost-cutting energy efficiency: 'If you could save $50 million from this ... There's nothing [in the discussion] about climate change and the stuff they can't get hold of. You can't talk about drought and floods. We looked at this stuff, but they can't get hold of it.'

Our research found this sort of strategy predictably routine among individuals working in organisational contexts in which the environment was traditionally seldom contemplated or even largely ignored. Yet it was also used in corporations where the new local emotionology of climate change as an opportunity was embedded: here, too, sustainability specialists had to bury their negative emotions and doubts and exhibit passion, excitement, and pride for their firms' environmental achievements – however meagre some of those achievements might be.

For some of our interviewees, though, the calculated and constrained use of emotion proved too unpalatable. Many spoke of their 'sense of mission' in fostering pro-environmental behaviour in corporate settings. 'It's part of why I *love* my job so much,' one told us, 'because it [environmental sustainability] is something that I feel is really important, and it's *great* to be able to work on it.' Rather than concealing their feelings about climate change, these managers saw explicitly articulating their emotions as advantageous in influencing others. In short, they preferred to *champion* their emotionality. To quote two sustainability specialists who viewed their own interest in climate change as infectious within organisational milieux:

[It] inspires others and gets things done. It's a fantastic tool. It's how behavioural change happens.

I come across with a great deal of passion when I talk, and I back it up with a lot of my personal story ... because I think people find it very hard to actually question what you've done personally.

Moreover, as we explored in Chapter 6, managers' own concerns about climate change often reach beyond their organisational roles and are a defining aspect of their personal and family lives. Some of our interviewees stated that, although risky, giving vent to their emotions supplied both a source of motivation for their responsibilities as change agents and a powerful signal to others in diffusing pro-environmental behaviour. In line with Meyerson and Scully's (1995: 596) concept of 'spontaneous, authentic action', the expression of emotions that are sincerely felt can have a persuasive impact on others by personifying the change message and advocating alternatives (Creed et al., 2010; Moser, 2007).

Unsurprisingly, the conflict between personal concerns and organisational and social emotionologies can lead to more negative emotions. Although keenly felt, these might remain hidden. This represents a fourth pattern of emotion work: *compartmentalising* emotionality.

For instance, many of our interviewees voiced their frustration – and, indeed, their anger – over companies, media, and politicians held to be at the vanguard of the cause of climate-change scepticism. One senior manager at a resource company said of a high-profile 'climate denier': 'I wonder what motivates him. Where is he coming from? Is he truly evil? Does he know he's deliberately peddling bullshit or is he incompetent? It's one or the other.'

Others told of the emotional toll of organisational decisions that undercut their advocacy and initiatives to enhance environmental sustainability. One complained of '10 years of work just gone up in smoke', lamenting: 'I'm angry about that, because I just think that was a waste, because now we've got to rebuild that all again.' Some pointed to the deep-rooted contradiction of fighting to ameliorate the environmental effects of a system that insists on ever-greater economic growth, with one sustainability adviser suggesting:

I would say that most businesses' efforts, probably with a genuine intent, are more about appearing to be environmental and reducing impact where possible where there's a business case for doing so ... because the best thing a business could do for the environment would be to shut down, (pause) but that's clearly not a viable option.

Such negative emotionality, while rarely aired at work, also stretches to individuals' home and family lives – usually because working in environmental sustainability accentuates the practical problems of living 'sustainably' in a modern economy. This can lead to guilt and frustration, as exemplified by one of our interviewees when he contemplated his own contribution to environmental well-being:

I try and do what I can, which is not having a car. I haven't owned a car since I was 23. I try and use public transport as much as possible. I try and minimise what I can. But I haven't gone to the extent of cutting down all my travel by plane.

The perceived shortcomings of wider social action on climate change and the everyday reminders of expanding consumption and environmental degradation led to feelings of disappointment, disillusionment, and sometimes even despair for many of those who participated in our study. One sustainability manager at an insurance corporation told us: 'I oscillate. I hear those things, and then you just look at everything else and just go: "It's all doomed."' For some the desolation was almost crushing. Maybe the ultimate concession of noble futility, of raging against the dying of the light, came from the manager who confided: 'Well, personally, I think it's the end of the world. I get the whole story, and I have got to just paralyse my fear about the whole thing. I have no doubt about what's going to happen.'

Conclusion

Climate change has become personally and emotionally resonant for many business leaders, managers, and employees. Our interviews with sustainability specialists made plain that many share John Doerr's dread that 'we're not going to make it'. While corporate activities are often characterised in terms of making logical decisions and controlling risk, coping with a concept as all-pervading as the climate crisis lays bare the fundamental emotionality that underlies the rational veneer of organisational life.

Navigating between rival social emotionologies of *climate change as threat* and *climate change as ideological battleground*, many global businesses have developed an alternative and far more positive emotionology. Here, in accordance with the discourses of ecological modernisation and corporate environmentalism (Hoffman, 2001; Jermier et al., 2006), emotions of fear, anxiety, anger, and hostility are deftly supplanted by emotions of pride, enthusiasm, and passion – which, conveniently enough, can easily be linked to business considerations such as lowering costs, enhancing efficiency, and cutting waste.

As we have seen, this positive emotionology is writ large in an abundance of 'green' corporate marketing, with adverts and PR campaigns trading on emotions of hope, wonder, and excitement. A near-child-like fascination is begged in response to novel products and imagined corporate futures in which innovation and the environment burgeon in perfect, awe-inspiring harmony. Such public interventions also aim to answer social criticism of corporate activities and to enrich companies' legitimacy as leaders in addressing climate change.

In addition, emotionologies like these are vital to cultivating 'green' corporate cultures intended to motivate employees and give them a higher purpose in their work. This demands that sustainability managers and consultants assist in achieving organisational objectives, which in turn allows them to undertake what we have labelled 'emotionology work' – the translation, reconfiguration, and creation of an organisational emotionology of climate change as a challenge and an opportunity for expansion. Unlike more quotidian corporate matters, the climate crisis enables sustainability professionals to marry personal concerns with wider business goals, and for many this brings satisfaction and 'emotional harmony' (Rafaeli and Sutton, 1987); and yet managing others' emotions also involves managing one's *own* emotions, the consequent tensions of which can be substantial.

As we observed in Chapter 6, many sustainability managers are acutely conscious of the contradictions inherent in their activities and the compromises that might be entailed. Reflecting the politics of 'dirty hands' (Walzer, 1973), they know complicity in the transformation of climate change into a business opportunity might generate its own emotional discordance. The very nature of sustainability work in endeavouring to make capitalism 'sustainable' underpins the basic paradox of their situation. As we have already seen, the bitter irony is that it is very often the people who cherish the environment most dearly who customarily find themselves mired in the furtherance of its ruination.

Emotionology work is likely to become much more testing as the physical reality of climate change grows increasingly obvious. Social and organisational responses to the crisis will therefore not only alter human behaviour and practice – what we do and how and why we do it – but the accepted norms of emotional expression. This is liable to be the case in society generally but in organisational life in particular. The inescapable inference: emotional dissonance is already a part of the job – and we can only expect that part to become larger and larger.

8 | Political myths and pathways forward

One of the penalties of an ecological education is that one lives alone in a world of wounds. Much of the damage inflicted on land is quite invisible to laymen. An ecologist must either harden his shell and make believe that the consequences of science are none of his business ... or he must be the doctor who sees the marks of death in a community that believes itself well and does not want to be told otherwise.

(Leopold, 1966: 183)

As Aldo Leopold has argued, those of us attuned to environmental degradation do, indeed, live in a 'world of wounds'. The relentless expansion of global capitalism has accentuated humanity's ecological impact to the extent that we are now fundamentally reshaping eco-systems and the very climate of the planet in disastrous ways. For those aware of the worsening climate crisis there is a sense of unreality about the situation as people go on with their busy lives, apparently oblivious to the looming catastrophe.

In the prosperous 'First World' a bevy of advertising encourages us to pursue our dreams of rewarding careers, affluent lifestyles, and the insatiable consumption of 'necessities'. We think nothing of hopping on a plane to travel to a remote holiday destination, eating gourmet food, possessing the latest smartphone or technical gadget, or aspiring to a luxury car or designer home. Yet this model of economic normal-ity comes at an astronomical environmental cost. The 'marks of death' are searingly evident in ever-escalating GHG emissions, deforestation, polluted waterways, species extinction and acidifying oceans. Political, media, and business discourses proclaim all is well and turn a deaf ear to the scientists and activists who highlight the folly of our madness. Denial of a very basic kind lies at the heart of our engagement with climate change.

In 2008, when we embarked on our research, there appeared some hope that the world's political leaders had at last recognised the need for a coordinated response to mitigating GHG emissions. Nicholas Stern (2007) had produced his influential economic analysis, emphasising the urgency of tackling the greatest market failure of all time. Political and business momentum seemed directed towards collective global action. There was a genuine expectation that the following year's Copenhagen climate talks would culminate in a game-changing global agreement and an acceleration towards low-carbon economic reinvention.

As we now know, such hopes were to prove forlorn. Despite recent agreement between China and the United States on emissions reduction (Landler, 2014), climate scientists have calculated that meeting the defined carbon budget to avoid more than 2°C of global warming this century will require emissions to peak in a matter of years and then fall on a scale far beyond the imagining of current political discussion. Some commentators have warned that economic 'de-growth' in developed economies will be necessary if we are to have any credible chance of averting environmental cataclysm (Anderson and Bows, 2011; 2012).

In this chapter we ponder why the response to the climate crisis has been so limited. We suggest that three political myths have been central to the maintenance of the prevailing 'business as usual' ethos and the obfuscation of the nightmare whose unfolding has been obvious for the better part of 40 years.

As we remarked at the end of Chapter 1, the status quo is liable to endure until we appreciate how effectively these myths accomplish their purpose and protect the interests of those who propagate them. They uphold a certain capitalist imaginary with ready-made narratives of how to make sense of climate change, and they do so extraordinarily well; however, the visions they offer are simply not sustainable. While our objective in this book has been to explore the role of corporations and neoliberal capitalism as drivers of climate change, we now point towards some alternatives to our present trajectory in the renewed hope that these myths might finally be exploded and that other imaginaries and stories – ones more radical, rooted in sincere optimism, and potentially beneficial for all – may at last take their place.

Corporate engagement with climate change as political myth

Understanding the construction of various political myths sheds an informative and much-needed light on the corporate response to climate change. These myths are common narratives that address the particular political conditions or criticisms facing a society by answering 'a need for significance' (Bottici, 2007: 133 and 136). They assist in coping with complicated problems by reducing complexity and acting as sense-making devices. They provide narratives that mould political experiences and activities. In the case of climate change they justify the furtherance of creative self-destruction.

Three principal myths are evident in our analysis. Each encapsulates recurrent and powerful narratives that bolster a capitalist imaginary. They are:

- The myth of corporate environmentalism
- The myth of corporate citizenship
- The myth of corporate omnipotence.

These myths work as blinders. They limit our imagination, preventing us from seeing not just where we are heading but the roads we have neglected to take. They are by no means the only political myths or narratives through which to comprehend the climate crisis (see, for instance, Hulme, 2009: 340–58), but within the business world they are the dominant framings for preserving corporate legitimacy and reacting to critique.

The myth of corporate environmentalism

As we have seen in previous chapters, the myth of *corporate environmentalism* presents corporations as active participants in the mitigation of environmental damage. Above all, it promotes their role in 'solving' climate change through technological innovation and the production and consumption of 'green' products and services. Underpinning this myth is a broad range of practices, from eco-efficiency, waste reduction, and recycling to 'green' branding, environmental reporting, and the adoption of more 'sustainable' approaches.

Corporate environmentalism has developed over the past 40 years in the face of mounting criticism of businesses' ecological impact and amid government regulation of industrial pollution (Hoffman, 2001; Jermier et al., 2006). As discussed in Chapter 2, it advances the notion that economic growth and environmental well-being are mutually supportive – in essence, that corporations can 'do well by doing good' (Falck and Heblich, 2007; see also Porter and van der Linde,

1995) – and that external interference is therefore unnecessary. The myth is palpable not only in corporate practices but also in new standards of voluntary reporting (e.g., the Carbon Disclosure Project, the Dow Jones Sustainability Index, and the Global Reporting Initiative) (Knox-Hayes and Levy, 2011), more investor focus on companies' environmental performance, and the creation of specialist sustainability functions within major firms (Wright et al., 2012).

Corporate environmentalism fits within the wider concept of ecological modernisation, which offers a buoyant vision of human ingenuity and adaptive capacity in dealing with environmental degradation. Even as the enormity and scale of the climate crisis have been laid bare, novel strains of such thinking have emerged under the labels of 'new environmentalism' and 'ecopragmatism'. Groups such as the Breakthrough Institute, a California-based think tank, have called for environmentalism to be reinvented for the twenty-first century through a conviction that new technologies – among them genetic engineering and nuclear power – can be harnessed to the advantage of both humanity and the environment (Shellenberger and Nordhaus, 2004; 2011).

Some ecological modernists have gone as far as to proclaim a so-called Good Anthropocene, in which humans continue to manipulate the environment to suit an ever-distending population. Here, it seems, nothing can constrain our existence. As one proponent asserts: 'The only limits to creating a planet that future generations will be proud of are our imaginations and our social systems. In moving toward a better Anthropocene, the environment will be what we make it' (Ellis, 2013). Such a stance appears to reject the notion that extant economic and social structures need to be rethought: enterprise and corporate capitalism are championed as the optimum means of delivering the innovation that will guarantee our lasting prosperity. Critics have noted the familiar convenience of such a refrain. As Clive Hamilton (2014) has said: '[This] argument absolves us all of the need to change our ways, which is music to the ears of political conservatives. The Anthropocene is system-compatible.'

The significance of corporate environmentalism as a political myth is profound. With corporate responses to climate change persistently acclaimed – and, by extension, their non-corporate counterparts perpetually downplayed – the 'business as usual' credo becomes ingrained. We find ourselves accustomed to it. We take it for granted. It is the norm. We are first persuaded and then repeatedly reminded that our own retort to the climate crisis should not be to question the underlying logic of our economic system: rather, we should do more of what we already do as 'green' employees and consumers.

The myth even gives meaning to our unremitting consumption. Consumer choice is depicted as a democratic ideal; freedom is equated with private ownership. Corporate environmentalism narrows the cognitive dissonance between our concerns and our conduct. By suggesting that individual choices are the solution to a collective problem (Hamilton, 2010), it squares our fears over climate change with our contributions to GHG emissions. Corporations are value-neutral providers, and whether we use their wares to do good or to do harm is entirely a matter for us.

This is how the myth of corporate environmentalism invites the human race to consume its way out of a crisis brought about by overconsumption. This, however, misses the point that it is not enough to politicise these actions – for example, choosing between 'brown' versus 'green' consumption – rather we need to politicise the solutions, both individual and collective. As we note later, this suggests the need to highlight a range of alternative concepts (such as humanity, community, future generations, Earth, biodiversity) in order to face the gap between our beliefs and behaviour and the ecological violence we have unleashed.

The myth of corporate citizenship

The myth of corporate environmentalism trumpets apparent solutions to climate change. In tandem, the myth of *corporate citizenship* equips businesses with a recognised and moral role in addressing the issue.

The 'good' corporate citizen is writ large in twenty-first-century life. It has come to the fore against a backdrop of neoliberal economic reform (Crouch, 2011) and is manifest in the business world's ever-growing involvement in education, health, sanitation, security, and other kinds of social provision. In the developing world, where the state's capacity to act is often seen to be lacking, corporations are regarded as the prime movers in solving social problems (Scherer and Palazzo, 2011; Valente and Crane, 2010). Closely aligned with 'corporate social responsibility' and other associated conceits, corporate citizenship has become a common mode of discourse in annual reports and on websites, with many sizeable companies participating in initiatives such as the United Nations Global Compact and the World Economic Forum (Crane et al., 2008).

Crucial to all of these endeavours, the myth of corporate citizenship affords legitimacy for expanding the scope of businesses' political activity. As Barley (2007) has observed, this has included the espousing of self-serving legislation, the intrusion into and 'capture' of regulatory agencies, and the privatisation of governmental functions across all levels of society.

As we saw in Chapter 4, corporations increasingly present themselves as the key civil actors best placed to shape political agendas and satisfy social and environmental needs. They achieve this by campaigning in ways that are compliant with their objectives and by exemplifying their contributions to society's well-being. Such efforts go beyond the normal ambit of corporate activity and into the world of politics (Shamir, 2008), the formative goal being to give the impression that businesses are acting not purely in their own interests and those of their shareholders but with employees, customers, suppliers, communities, and even humanity as a whole in mind. Witness, for example, how corporations – and, revealingly, governments – now routinely defend the ongoing exploitation of fossil fuels as the only moral way of defeating energy poverty in developing countries (Peabody Energy, 2013).

That 'corporate citizenship' is a dead metaphor only underscores the strength of the myth, which is further reworked and reinforced by the debate over whether companies actually can or should act as 'good' citizens (Porter and Kramer, 2011; Valente and Crane, 2010) and, conversely, by claims that they are really 'bad' citizens (Banerjee, 2008b; Barley, 2007). The personification of businesses as moral citizens committed to the betterment of civil society not only neatly obscures executives' fiduciary obligation to serve their shareholders above all others: it has come to be seen as the natural state of affairs. Corporations are perceived as moral entities that speak for 'the people' and are allied with social identities.

Accordingly, the myth of corporate citizenship offers an interpretive lens through which individuals and groups can make sense of climate change and exercise their right either to endorse the phenomenon as a 'scientific fact' or to denounce it as a 'scam'. 'The people' are afforded political recognition and a voice – even without speaking – via consumption, which itself is granted a political identity. This is how citizenship itself is subverted and relegated to a surrogate for profit and shareholder value. As critics have pointed out (Barley, 2007; Crouch, 2004), the result is a rising imbalance in political power between corporations and other groups and a decline in democracy as businesses' ability to influence legislative and social outcomes intensifies. This allows the creative self-destruction of our environment and ecology to be justified on the basis that what is good for corporations is good for all.

The myth of corporate omnipotence

The third myth central to how the sphere of business responds to climate change is that of *corporate omnipotence*. The narratives that support this myth paint corporate capitalism as an ineluctable and superior form of economic organisation – one founded on managerial tools and practices that are not only commendably rational but also highly effectual – and as the sole, supremely inevitable rejoinder to the climate crisis both now and in the future.

Since it must supply both an explanation for the success of corporate capitalism's development and an answer for its failures, this myth adopts many guises. One has been the focus on expanding capitalism through the pricing of so-called externalities, including GHG emissions (Newell and Paterson, 2010; Spaargaren and Mol, 2013); more generally we have experienced the emergence of 'natural capitalism' (Hawken et al., 1999). A predictable repercussion of framing climate change as 'the biggest market failure the world has seen' (Stern, 2008: 1) has been the predilection for a 'market solution' in which the private sector is insistently touted as holding all the curative aces.

Given that we live in an era in which neoliberalism has become the dominant political ideology, it is perhaps unsurprising that policy initiatives around the climate crisis have concentrated on 'the market'. Maybe we should not be unduly shocked, too, that these initiatives have been supplemented by monetary subsidies to encourage businesses to be less environmentally harmful. It has become customary for governments to attend only to the general architecture of such policies, leaving the specifics of cutting emissions to corporations (Newell and Paterson, 2010: 25–29). This is how climate change has been commodified – fictitiously – into 'carbons' that can be measured and traded; and it is how climate change has been repackaged as an enterprising opportunity. Such solutions suggest any unintended consequences should be dealt with as 'market failures' rather than as failures of the 'market society' (Polanyi, 1957).

At the very heart of the myth of corporate omnipotence is the claim that the rational expertise businesses have at their disposal is somehow capable of taming nature. The direct government regulation of GHG emissions, mandated restrictions on the extraction and combustion of fossil fuels, and other approaches are thereby marginalised: they cannot – and, indeed, are not permitted to – compete. The state is not sidestepped per se but is instead demoted, its remit confined to the co-creation and ratification of schemes in which the bottom line is the top priority (Castree, 2011).

The logic of this myth dictates that any action in response to climate change must first demonstrate a 'business case'; moreover, any action that threatens profitability must be rejected. Corporations are transformed into mythical creatures, assuming god-like qualities through their unfettered ability to craft social value and affect social reorganisation. In keeping with Cassirer's contention that prophecy would be an essential component of a 'new technique of rulership' (1946: 289), with the most improbable or even impossible promises made, business elites are hailed as nothing less than prophets. Ultimately, only corporate solutions are viable – both now and during the years ahead.

Taken together, these three myths serve to buttress the modern hierarchy of human mastery over the natural world. They fashion a future in which we avoid sacrifice. With the 'rational' corporation as a model, they deepen the bifurcation between culture and nature, as symbolised in the oft-cited 'triple bottom line' of economy, society, and environment – with the economy firmly first and the environment resolutely last (Norman and MacDonald, 2004). The hierarchy endures as the practical methods corporations can allegedly muster – carbon capture and storage, solar radiation management, ocean fertilisation, and other forms of geoengineering – are used to justify further climate change as a stepping-stone towards addressing the crisis (Szerszynski, 2010). The idea that we can manage or stabilise nature diverts energy from more radical responses (Boykoff et al., 2010), and instead of questioning the division between culture and nature we determinedly reproduce it – despite the incontrovertible observation that without an environment there can be no society, let alone an economy.

These myths therefore shield us from the spectre of catastrophe as we search for ever more innovative ways of exhausting our ecosystem. They equip us with justifications and identities as the process of creative self-destruction rolls on. They show the 'symbolic power' of political myths in their almost hegemonic ability to sculpt attitudes and behaviour as common-sense assumptions. To doubt the myths of corporate environmentalism, corporate citizenship, and corporate omnipotence is tantamount to sacrilege and the most treacherous of thinking. Small wonder, then, that the most vehement opposition to even minimal forms of emissions mitigation are led by those who promote the mythologies of 'free-enterprise' capitalism (Jacques et al., 2008). Environmentalists, in questioning the narrative of capitalist growth and the global consumer economy, have become the new communists – green on the outside, red on the inside (Potter, 2011).

Alternative narratives and imaginings

The myths of corporate environmentalism, corporate citizenship, and corporate omnipotence support a particular capitalist social imaginary of how we collectively make sense of and act in the world (Castoriadis, 1987). This imaginary gives meaning to and shapes our experiences with climate change (Wright et al., 2013). The significance of this imaginary motivates more corporate involvement and dissuades us from radical engagement with an issue that threatens the very existence of life on our planet. Given that the present course leads to oblivion, what are our alternative narratives, imaginings, and possible futures? In short, if not 'business as usual' then what?

In previous periods of extreme peril some societies have been able to quickly fashion new political myths and galvanise rapid changes in organisation and governance. As a species, we are capable of acting in quite revolutionary ways once a 'Great Disruption' becomes plain. For example, Paul Gilding (2011) cites Britain's reaction to the prospect of invasion by Germany during the Second World War as a situation with potential parallels to the need to transfigure our response to the climate crisis.

Clearly the consequences of ecological collapse are far greater and more complex than those of a foreign incursion; and yet this 'Great

Disruption' has yet to be met with an organisational and governmental revolution even remotely comparable to that which saved Britain from Nazi occupation. Where are the new myths in this instance? In the following section we briefly examine four alternative narratives that are currently emerging in the battle over climate politics and business: renewable reinvention; regulatory and legal intervention; steady-state economics and collapse; and social mobilisation and divestment.

Renewable reinvention

An obvious alternative narrative, one we have touched on throughout this book, is the potential for a shift from fossil-fuel-based energy to the large-scale adoption of 'renewables'. This is a vision that implies a positive future for humanity based on the market success of increasingly cheap and efficient solar, wind, and other renewable sources of energy. Cases in point include the dramatic reduction in the cost of solar photovoltaic technologies for producing electricity (Parkinson, 2014b) and the innovations of companies such as Tesla Motors, which is now building huge factories to mass-produce less expensive and more effective lithium-ion batteries as storage devices. Many energy industry analysts foresee traditional electricity grids ceding to local energy production and petrol-fuelled cars yielding to electric vehicles (St John, 2014; Woody, 2013). This brave new world appeals to entrepreneurs and others who believe the market, as prescribed by the myth of corporate environmentalism, offers a way out of the climate crisis.

For some this imaginary extends to the development of shale and coal seam gas as a transitional fossil fuel or a 'bridge' towards renewable energy (DECC, 2014). As we have seen, however, the 'gas rush' expands narratives that place economic growth above environmental destruction; and critics are sceptical about the supposed emissions benefits from such a switch, arguing that the tax rebates and government funding would be more wisely invested in renewables (Davis and Shearer, 2014).

For others nuclear energy is a vital and faster means of cutting fossil fuel emissions, and even environmentalists traditionally opposed to nuclear energy have reconsidered their position in the face of the climate crisis (Monbiot, 2011). Theoretically, a dramatic rise in nuclear power would help deliver the required reductions. Yet whether nuclear plants could be built fast enough to make a meaningful difference over the next 20 years is a moot point. Moreover, as underlined by the 2011 Fukushima accident, precipitous investment in nuclear power is innately contentious in an age likely to be characterised by increasingly extreme weather events and social and geopolitical conflict (Diesendorf, 2014; Kopytko and Perkins, 2011).

More importantly, the scale and speed of decarbonisation necessary to avoid hazardous climate change is frequently ignored in optimistic interpretations of the future 'green' economy. Although the cost of solar-based and wind-based technologies continues to drop – often exceeding projections – renewables still constitute only a small proportion of our overall energy needs (EIA, 2014), and the escalation of GHG emissions persists even at a time when substantial diminution is needed in a relatively short period. This is a point to which we will return.

In addition, much of the advocacy for renewable energy underestimates the political might of the fossil fuel industry in resisting change. In Australia this has become especially apparent since a new government reversed not only previously agreed targets for renewables growth but also the carbon pricing mechanism that helped mitigate emissions and make decarbonisation a far more attractive financial investment. As we noted in Chapter 4, climate change is foremost a political phenomenon, and the politics are critical in deciding how much – if at all – we will divert from our current trajectory.

Finally, the variations of the renewable reinvention narrative do not acknowledge the contradictory element of the crisis. For many in the business community much of this narrative is folded within the wider political myth of corporate environmentalism, in which long-standing business goals of competition, innovation, and profit are seen to propel both corporate and social well-being; but climate change is a collective problem that demands collective solutions – many of which depart from the narrow objective of making money. We would need something akin to a perpetual-motion machine to keep pace with spiralling consumption by continuously producing new renewable technology on a massive and industrial scale. The atomistic advances of a few innovative corporations will not suffice: the climate crisis merits a genuinely systemic response.

The fact is that any narrative that embraces the ongoing consumption of the Earth's resources fails to overturn the essential paradox of corporate capitalism as it stands today. It is not enough to push the 'right' technologies. We need to pursue alternative narratives of how we make sense of human society within the limits of our planet – how we organise work, how we define success and well-being, and how we are represented in the decision-making process. This most common and persuasive alternative narrative is post-political, in that the 'problem' of climate change can be handed over to technocratic management and consensual policymaking (Swyngedouw, 2010).

Regulatory and legal intervention

State intervention has long been a stock response to market failure and corporate indulgence. As evident in the Great Depression and the Second World War, government regulation of economic behaviour has been crucial to the development of modern capitalism, saving it from its own excesses, recuperating it from crisis, and passing laws that protect its legitimacy (Polanyi, 1957).

During the late 1960s and the 1970s, as we saw in Chapter 2, the harm caused by industrial pollution resulted in laws that prohibited or at least limited such activities. Often strong state regulation followed a lengthy spell of social and community protest and some level of political mobilisation, as happened with the prohibition and subsequent eradication and replacement of DDT and CFCs (Kinkela, 2011; Sunstein, 2007). Soon enough, however, business groups countered the regulatory threat by adopting a more accommodating stance, insisting that they could be relied on to avoid environmental damage. Corporate environmentalism portrayed companies as concerned environmental stewards, and the tenor of regulation moved towards a more availing position marked by industry self-regulation and business–government collaboration.

For critics this illustrates a more wide-ranging trend. The ascendancy of neoliberalism as a political and economic doctrine since the 1970s has coincided with governments edging away from a focus on strict market regulation. Government has come to be regarded as impeding value creation and economic prosperity, and its role in economic management has therefore steadily drifted to the formulation of labour, product, and financial markets that facilitate profit maximisation. Governments have become enmeshed within the interests of global capital, with financially powerful corporations able to buy into the political apparatus through party lobbying and funding. Established representative political structures have been rendered increasingly ineffectual in curtailing corporate power and market abuse (e.g., Barley, 2010).

As we outlined in Chapter 4, fierce opposition to regulatory restrictions on GHG emissions has been central to corporate political engagement on climate change. For the fossil fuel industry this has involved the funding of climate-change denial, preaching doubt about climate science and acclaiming the benefits that purportedly flow from fossil-fuel-based energy in terms of wealth generation and national well-being. Even many progressive businesses have rebuffed mandatory limitations on fossil fuel use in favour of voluntary action or state assemblage of market mechanisms such as emissions trading schemes. Parties on both sides of the political spectrum have accepted the preferred corporate agenda, not least since the global financial crisis of 2008 focused concerns on economic growth and employment.

The political rejection of regulatory curbs on the continued expansion of fossil fuel extraction and use has become pronounced in recent years as the charge to exploit reserves for an energy-hungry world gathers momentum. In the United States, despite a recognition of the need to cut GHG emissions, President Obama has endorsed an 'all of the above' energy policy, much to the delight of the ever-burgeoning oil and shale gas industries; the United States is now the world's leading producer of oil (Smith, 2014). Canadian prime minister Stephen Harper has been a prominent champion of the tar sands industry, both in opposing local communities' objections and in the construction of pipelines to facilitate processing and export (Nikiforuk, 2010). In Australia the conservative Abbott government has dismantled policies mitigating carbon emissions, with the prime minister declaring that 'coal is good for humanity' and the 'foundation of prosperity … for now and the foreseeable future' (Bourke, 2014). In the United Kingdom the Tory government has encouraged fracking as a short-to-medium-term contribution to the fight against climate change (DECC, 2014). A pivotal question, particularly since the state itself has become usurped within a model of market rationalism (Boltanski, 2011), is whether this ceaseless, quasi-ubiquitous distension of the market can be met with a counter-movement of legislative protection and conservation (see Polanyi, 1957).

An early taste of this philosophy is to be found in *Should Trees Have Standing* (1974), in which Christopher Stone argued that entities such as forests, oceans, and rivers, along with 'the natural environment as a whole', should be safeguarded through inclusion in the civic sphere by being granted legal rights similar to those of citizens. These rights, Stone suggested, could be represented in court like those of another silent yet clearly heard subject: the corporation. The claim failed because of a lack of 'grounded' understanding in the community – 'rights for natural objects proved too strange (unnatural?)' (Jasanoff, 2010: 246) – yet the quest to accord nature a measure of legal standing goes on.

In New Zealand, for instance, a tribunal recently recognised a river as a legal entity in an agreement signed between the Whanganui River *iwi* and the Crown. The river was seen to have the same rights and interests as a company (Shuttleworth, 2012). This echoes analogous initiatives in Bolivia and Ecuador, where constitutional amendments have included specific rights for the environment (Burdon, 2011). Irrespective of their practical impact, such schemes are testament to intensifying social awareness of environmental destruction and the need for civic control over market capitalism's extremes.

Even so, the bleak prospect of more authoritarian and draconian forms of state involvement in the climate crisis should not be overlooked. We remarked at the end of Chapter 4 that the redesigning of international trade law has lately been based in large apart around the notion of removing national restrictions on corporations in areas such as environmental regulation. As currently negotiated, the Trans-Pacific and Trans-Atlantic Partnerships bestow more opportunities for corporations to sue governments that hamper access to resources or constrict businesses' profit-making activities (Monbiot, 2013; Rimmer and Wood, 2014).

As the physical realities of climate change become more profound, it seems likely that the conflict between the market and the environment will be a space of more friction, criticism, and compromise; concomitantly, state regulation might be aimed less at protecting our ecosystems and more at disciplining groups and individuals opposed to economic development judged to be in the national economic interest. As Naomi Klein (2014) vividly documents, the use of police and security forces to uphold the interests of multinational corporations over those of local communities is already commonplace. The 'war on terror' and the attendant fervour for the official surveillance of populations could soon routinely encompass the monitoring of environmental activists hostile to the further exploitation of fossil fuels (Ahmed, 2014; Potter, 2011).

Ironically, it is authoritarian state control, the very path against which corporations and 'free market' campaigners fight so vigorously, that may yet come to dominate in the decades ahead (Oreskes and Conway, 2014). As infrastructure and social and economic constructs buckle and break under the weight of devastating weather events, rising sea levels, and ocean acidification, governments could be called upon to intervene in much more direct and totalitarian ways as they struggle to maintain order. It seems reasonable to assume that such a wartime-like mobilisation will lack many of the democratic norms that we currently take for granted (Delina and Diesendorf, 2013).

Steady-state economics and collapse

While the switch to renewable energy and increased regulation of fossil fuel emissions offer two alternative narratives to the 'fossil fuels forever' imaginary (Levy and Spicer, 2013), other visions focus on more substantial critiques of the climate crisis. For instance, for many observers the promotion of the 'green' economy and market innovation around renewable energy ignores the broader issue of our reliance on compound economic growth. Although growing population and affluence have brought us to the point at which our material impacts on the planet can no longer be ignored, politicians and economists are all but unanimous in cheering economic growth as the definitive gauge of success and the worthiest of ambitions. To even question the benefits of increasing Gross Domestic Product (GDP) is tantamount to treason in this age of economic rationalism.

For critics of economic growth, a range of alternative visions are presented. One is that of the 'steady-state economy'. This is an economy that does not exceed ecological limits and has 'stable (or mildly fluctuating) levels of population, consumption and therefore GDP' (Czech, 2013: 119). Pioneered by ecological economists such as Herman Daly (1977), it entails a human economy that fits within the ecological confines of Earth's ecosystems and a more equitable distribution of wealth both nationally and globally. Realising such a vision would involve significant economic change, of course, and advocates acknowledge that its implementation would necessitate the 'de-growth' of wealthy nations – which, needless to say, would be politically unpalatable. Although based upon a noble goal, the advocacy of a steady-state economy is less clear on how such an agenda can be implemented, particularly in an era in which economic growth is seen as one of the most critical measures of political success.

As we have seen, for many proponents of climate action the idea that responding to the climate crisis might involve challenging economic growth is steadfastly rejected. So the recent study *The New Climate Economy* by the Global Commission on Economy and Climate, an elite group of senior politicians, businesspeople, and economists, was widely received as evidence that responding to climate change need not upset the economic growth model (Global Commission on the Economy and Climate, 2014). According to economist Paul Krugman (2014), it demonstrated that 'strong measures to limit carbon emissions would have hardly any negative effect on economic growth and might actually lead to faster growth'. Critics responded that while major reductions in emissions can result from carbon pricing and the deployment of renewable technologies, little thought has been given to the quantum and pace of cuts needed to prevent dangerous levels of climate change (Heinberg, 2014).

For instance, Kevin Anderson from the Tyndall Centre for Climate Change Research has attempted to quantify the economic transformation required to limit global warming to the politically agreed maximum of 2°C this century. Based on a defined budget of carbon emissions, his calculations indicate that industrialised nations would immediately have to slash their emissions by more than 10 per cent per annum – a reduction that, as he and Alice Bows have stressed, has never before been attained and is 'not compatible with economic growth' (Anderson and Bows, 2011: 40). 'De-growth' of a sort more dramatic than was witnessed during the collapse of the former Eastern Bloc economies in the early 1990s would be needed (Anderson and Bows, 2008). To maintain economic growth while simultaneously reducing emissions to stay within the 2°C maximum would necessitate an absolute decoupling of GDP from CO_2 emissions, which, even in light of improvements in energy efficiency, is a feat we have never come close to achieving (Jackson, 2009). Auditing firm PricewaterhouseCoopers

(2014) has estimated that the global economy would have to lower its carbon intensity by 6.2 per cent a year – five times faster than the present rate – till 2100 to meet the 2°C target.

While proponents of the 'steady-state economy' and even 'de-growth' emphasise visions that could thwart or lessen environmental disaster, others say collapse of some kind is now inevitable and creative self-destruction will lead to a momentous correction of human folly. In this narrative it is already too late to evade punishment for our impudent belief that we can master nature: catastrophe is not only imminent but also inescapable. Examples include computer scientist Stephen Emmott's *Ten Billion* (2013), science historian Naomi Oreskes' fictional account of the future in *The Decline of Western Civilisation* (Oreskes and Conway, 2014), and evolutionary biologist Guy McPherson's *Going Dark* (2013).

Here the idea of 'near-term extinction' and 'human die-back' is treated as an inexorable corollary of climate disruptions playing out over the coming decades (Gripp, 2013). Even 'optimistic' variants of the genre, which foretell a rejuvenation of civilisation from the ashes of collapse, predict massive human mortality. Paul Gilding (2011: 53), in envisaging the 'Great Disruption', reflects: 'In the geopolitical, economic and climate chaos involved I expect we'll tragically lose a few billion people.' Some groups, like the Dark Mountain Project, accept collapse and immerse themselves in cultural responses that echo the reality of ecological breakdown (Kingsnorth and Hine, 2009). Given the existential nature of the climate crisis, how we gaze into the abyss has been likened to the fall of previous civilisations, which used dreaming as a means of trying to make sense of extinction (Gosling and Case, 2013).

Social mobilisation and divestment

The fourth and final alternative narrative encapsulates a far more grass-roots response to the climate crisis – one that is sprouting spontaneously from within local communities that are rising up and directly opposing the expansion of fossil fuel extraction. Naomi Klein (2014: 293–336) has characterised this phenomena as 'Blockadia'. It is evident in the Greek villagers protesting the destruction of their forests by a Canadian gold-mining company, running battles between police and anti-fracking protesters in Romania and England, indigenous communities fighting oil extraction in the Amazon, blockades against huge new mines in Australia, outrage over proposed pipelines to transport Canadian tar sands bitumen to processing plants in the southern United States, and export terminals in British Columbia. Across different continents, often in the most diverse locations imaginable, companies accustomed to buying consent with the promise of jobs, economic renaissance, and government royalties are facing concerted resistance that goes beyond traditional localism. As Klein (2014: 335) notes:

More and more, these communities are simply saying 'No.' No to the pipeline. No to Arctic drilling. No to the coal and oil trains. No to the heavy hauls. No to the export terminal. No to fracking. And not just 'Not in My Backyard' but, as the French anti-fracking activists say: *Ni ici, ni ailleurs* – neither here, nor elsewhere. In other words: no new carbon frontiers.

Although critics have noted that many established environmental NGOs – so-called Big Green – appear to have been co-opted within the corporate environmental agenda (Dauvergne and LeBaron, 2014), new patterns of activism are also emerging based around earlier traditions of civil disobedience which challenge the very basis of 'business as usual'. Key players and events have included:

- Greenpeace, which has spearheaded campaigns against oil extraction in the Arctic, the development of new mines in Australia, and deforestation for palm oil in Asia (www.greenpeace.org/australia/en/what-we-do/climate/)
- Plane Stupid, which has condemned the climate impact of the airline industry and the expansion of facilities such as London's Heathrow Airport (www.planestupid.com/aboutus)
- 350.org, which has led protest action that has successfully delayed the US government's approval of Keystone XL, a controversial pipeline that would transport Canadian bitumen to American refineries and further boost the exploitation of tar sands (Greenfeld, 2013; McKibben, 2013c)
- The People's Climate March, held in New York City in September 2014, which attracted an attendance of more than 300,000 (Foderaro, 2014).

Underpinning much of this protest has been greater civil awareness of the climate dilemma that now confronts us. As 350.org founder

Bill McKibben (2012) set out in a widely read *Rolling Stone* op-ed, the mathematics are simple. We have a set carbon budget if global warming is not to exceed 2°C; we have already burned two-thirds of this budget, and the remainder is exceeded more than fivefold by the remaining reserves of fossil fuel; ergo around 80 per cent of known fossil fuel resources must stay in the ground – a proposition that raises fundamental economic and moral arguments.

Economically, an ever-louder chorus within the investment community has warned of the likelihood of a 'carbon bubble' and 'stranded assets' if governments hinder the continued exploitation of fossil fuels (Carbon Tracker Initiative, 2012). Oil majors such as ExxonMobil and Shell have explicitly dismissed the notion of stranded assets (Lamb and Litterman, 2014; Nichols, 2014), but this view is far from universally shared. Financial analysts have stated that we are entering a phase of structural decline in the global coal industry, driven in part by investment in renewable energy, the plummeting cost of solar photovoltaic technologies, and the expected production of low-cost lithium-ion batteries (Buckley, 2014).

Morally, climate change's 'terrifying new math' has generated another compelling and fast-moving narrative in the shape of fossil fuel divestment. Inspired by the success of the 1980s anti-apartheid divestment campaign, this movement urges individuals and groups to sell their shares in fossil-fuel-related investments. Popularised by 350.org through a programme directed at US colleges and local government, it has swiftly gained international traction and earned backing from many high-profile organisations. As McKibben (2013b) has explained:

The logic of divestment couldn't be simpler: if it's wrong to wreck the climate then it's wrong to profit from that wreckage. The fossil fuel industry … has five times as much carbon in its reserves as even the most conservative governments on Earth say is safe to burn – but on the current course it will be burned, tanking the planet. The hope is that divestment is one way to weaken those companies – financially but even more politically. If institutions like colleges and churches turn them into pariahs then their two-decades-old chokehold on politics in DC and other capitals will start to slip.

While critics have sought to downplay the direct financial impact that divestment will have on stocks of fossil fuel (Welch, 2014), its real power revolves around disputing the industry's legitimacy and social licence to operate. The involvement of church and religious organisations and the support of prominent figures such as UN Secretary General Ban Ki-Moon, Archbishop Desmond Tutu and former Irish President Mary Robinson highlights a moral dimension lacking in much of the political debate surrounding climate change (Galbraith, 2014). In particular, by stigmatising companies and highlighting their contribution to global warming, it has created a new 'sin industry', perhaps clearing the way for much tougher regulatory intervention and diminishing perceptions of long-term financial viability.

The authors of a recent analysis of the divestment movement (Ansar et al., 2013) have posited that there is scope for such social campaigning to transition beyond civil society groups and affect broader market norms, closing off previous channels of finance and adding to downward pressure on the stock prices of fossil fuel companies. This could further hasten the advent of the 'carbon bubble' and stranded assets. The emergence of ethical investment and pension funds that exempt fossil fuel stocks are indicative of this shift (Saunders, 2014).

So far around 180 organisations, most of them from civil society, have committed to divest from fossil fuels. Stanford University, the cities of Seattle, San Francisco, and Portland, the World Council of Churches, Glasgow University, the British Medical Association, and maybe most symbolically, the Rockefeller Foundation – which owes its $860 million in wealth to the founder of the US oil industry, John D. Rockefeller (Schwartz, 2014) – are among those to have joined the cause. While still far from the type of market and regulatory disruption needed to trigger a wholesale move from fossil fuels to renewable energy, divestment is undoubtedly an alternative narrative to the mainstream model of 'business as usual'.

Indeed, one indication of the impact of this emergent political narrative has been the vehemence of the response from the fossil fuel industry itself. Major oil companies have responded frostily to claims that they may be holding 'stranded assets' in the near future (ExxonMobil, 2014). Australian National University's announcement that it would be divesting from an array of resource stocks promoted a caustic retort from the industry body, the Minerals Council, as well as a stern rebuke from the conservative prime minister and scathing editorials in business-oriented media (Cox, 2014b). These are early days, but the movement shows signs of reinventing social attitudes towards fossil fuels – and the eventual ramifications could be significant.

Conclusion

To varying extents, the above alternative narratives challenge the corporate capitalist social imaginary. Those that help us to make sense of the climate crisis while obviating the all-consuming continuation of corporate capitalism are especially deserving of attention.

Unfortunately, for many politicians, business leaders, journalists, and other stakeholders – even those whose familiarity with the debate surrounding climate change is modest or downright ephemeral – they have no appeal. They are unduly pessimistic. They are naïve. They are unhelpful. They are unrealistic. Such is the strength of the extant capitalist imaginary: any alternative is easily disdained, scorned, laughed off as utopian or dystopian. And in many ways this is our most crushing tragedy: not content with hastening our planet's ruination, we can now barely countenance an alternative path.

So is our fate sealed? Is our slide towards the abyss unstoppable? Whether there is really any hope left, whether society can ever be engaged in alternative imaginings of our climate future, is the topic we turn to in our final chapter.

9 | *Imagining alternatives*

It may seem impossible to imagine that a technologically advanced society could choose, in essence, to destroy itself, but that is what we are now in the process of doing.

(Kolbert, 2006: 189)

In this book we have argued that anthropogenic climate change is not only a result of humanity's addiction to fossil fuels but also, more fundamentally, a consequence of the global economic system. We see the climate crisis as revealing perhaps the ultimate contradiction of corporate capitalism: its reliance on the consumption of nature for its own development. On the basis of established climate science, our examination of the corporate world's responses to the most serious and all-encompassing threat of our age paints a grim picture of humanity staggering towards the point of no return. The political myths of corporate environmentalism, corporate citizenship, and corporate omnipotence make it highly likely that our collective efforts to deal with climate change will remain wedded to the perpetuation of the 'business as usual' philosophy and the relentless, blinkered pursuit of creative self-destruction.

And yet, as we outlined in the previous chapter, there exists a range of alternative imaginaries to corporate capitalism. Mirroring the analysis in the previous chapters, we suggest there are arguably six possible movements to further engage people's imagination in demanding a change to how things are. These six movements revolve around:

- How we see our relationship to nature
- The disruption of language
- The promotion of greater democracy in climate politics
- Understanding the worth of the environment beyond a market commodity
- Developing a 'green' identity beyond consumption
- Championing the positive emotionality of climate action.

185

By way of conclusion, we briefly summarise our analysis before discussing how these alternative imaginaries might take hold and whether there is genuine hope that they can engage people sufficiently to unsettle, upset, and overturn the status quo.

The argument restated

Despite their central role as engines of the global economy, corporations are often missing in the public discussion surrounding climate change. This is in part because of how fossil fuels such as oil, coal, and gas are intimately ingrained in our daily lives as sources of energy: they are the carotid arteries sustaining a complex global economy that relies on ever-increasing output, activity, and consumption.

By way of example, consider the 2010 BP Deepwater Horizon disaster, which saw five million barrels of oil leak into the Gulf of Mexico. Although public attention was galvanised, the reality of the far larger environmental calamity stemming from such facilities' 'normal' extraction of oil and other fossil fuels and their subsequent combustion went utterly unremarked. Ultimately, it was a classic instance of 'business as usual'. This may be where climate change differs from traditional forms of environmental damage: escalating GHG emissions and deforestation are now such familiar cornerstones of our economic system that it is hard to envisage any alternative.

We crave fossil fuels. They give us energy. They deliver compound economic growth. We revel in the magic of consumption and technology. Yet science tells us that if we keep progressing as we have, if we carry on feeding our addiction, humanity will face devastation from dangerous climate change by the middle of this century or even earlier (Mann, 2014).

Any adequate response to the climate crisis must therefore address the very basis of our economic system and our understanding of ourselves as human beings in the twenty-first century. This, of course, represents no small task. Indeed, it could well be the near-overwhelming scale of problem and solution alike that compels so many to reject the scientific message.

For their part, corporations have been adept at deflecting critical analysis of their actions and impacts. After all, are they not merely the agents of broader public wants and needs? As we are constantly informed, global warming is due to all of us. We are the ones who want the convenience and comfort that fossil fuels bring us, whether in the form of the cars we fill with petrol, the planes we fly in, or the myriad technological gadgets on which we have come to rely. A common refrain is that we should not blame corporations for the mess in which we find ourselves: they are simply doing what we, the citizenry, demand (Shapinker, 2014). Such is the hegemony of business in capitalist society that for many commentators critiquing corporations is tantamount to heresy. As we have pointed out, however, corporations play numerous roles with regard to climate change; and this is clear when we investigate the political and economic drivers of this issue.

While rising GHG emissions have been especially evident ever since the adoption of fossil fuel energy during the Industrial Revolution, the pace and extent of exploitation have reached new levels since the 1950s. As we saw in Chapters 1 and 2, we are now exceeding the planetary boundaries that underpin our well-being as a species. The globalisation of the capitalist economy, increasing economic growth, and dramatic upsurges in the world's population have precipitated the climate crisis. It is no coincidence that many of the largest and most profitable companies on Earth are fossil fuel corporations.

We have suggested, in seeking to comprehend this process theoretically, that our economic system is mired in what we have termed 'creative self-destruction' – a ruthless quest for ever more imaginative ways to extract and exhaust the planet's finite resources. Climate change therefore brings to the foreground the most appalling contradiction: that capitalism's very existence, dynamism, and expansion hinge on the ongoing consumption of the natural world that we depend on for survival.

Of course, such a scenario stands in marked contrast to the convenient assumptions that have long dominated Western economies. For decades the conventional wisdom has been that economic and technological progress reduces environmental destruction (Grossman and Krueger, 1995; Mol and Sonnenfeld, 2000). Ecological modernisation places great faith in our ability to manage the world through our inventiveness and our regulation of economic behaviour. There are undoubtedly benefits from promoting innovation directed towards activities less harmful to the environment (e.g., a switch from fossil fuels to renewable energy sources), but such analyses seem to have not only overestimated our ability to change our economic trajectory but

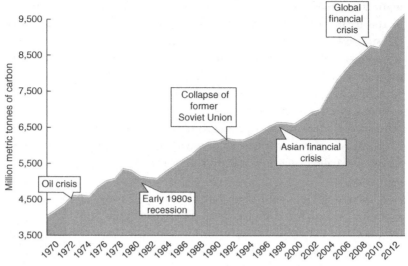

Figure 9.1 Global carbon emissions and economic crisis, 1970–2012.
Source: Based on data from Boden, T. A., Marland, G. and Andres, R. J. (2013) *Global, Regional, and National Fossil-Fuel CO$_2$ Emissions*. Oak Ridge, TN: Carbon Dioxide Information Analysis Center, Oak Ridge National Laboratory, U.S. Department of Energy, http://cdiac.ornl.gov/trends/emis/tre_glob_2010.html

also underestimated the political power of vested interests focused on protecting accepted patterns of capital accumulation.

In tandem, there is a failure to acknowledge the difficulties of practically decoupling economic growth from its material effects on our climate (Czech, 2013; Daly, 1996; Jackson, 2009). Global warming has now attracted political and economic attention for the better part of four decades, yet the rise in GHG emissions has not been halted. As demonstrated in Figure 9.1, in recent years emissions have actually accelerated and it has only been during periods of dramatic economic contraction – the recent financial crisis, for example – that there has been any sort of pause in emissions growth (Peters et al., 2012; Van Noorden, 2011).

As detailed in Chapter 2, a more cogent explanation for the climate crisis can be found in corporate capitalism's reliance on the unending exploitation of nature – the so-called treadmill of production perspective (Schnaiberg, 1980). The current obliteration of the environment is not so much an unfortunate by-product of industrialisation as an essential feature of our ceaseless and ever-intensifying consumption (Schnaiberg and Gould, 1994; York, 2004). There was a time when the basic conflict between capitalism and the environment could be papered over, but climate change has rendered the cracks far too wide to conceal.

The alarmingly limited scope of humanity's response gives us the title of this book. Instead of pausing to question our suicidal trajectory, we plough on. Having gambled almost everything, we up the ante. To challenge the existing state of affairs is viewed as economic lunacy. Obfuscation is the weapon of choice, allowing the climate crisis to be managed in a way that ensures 'nothing really has to change' (Swyngedouw, 2010: 219).

Thus environmental criticism is incorporated within capitalist value creation. As Boltanksi and Chiapello (2005) have pointed out, capitalism uses critique as a source of reinvention and to preserve its social legitimacy. Accordingly, the climate crisis provides opportunities for new business and profit-making. Witness the rush to find new, 'unconventional' sources of fossil fuels, among them shale and coal seam gas, deepwater and Arctic oil drilling and the processing of tar sands for oil – all initiatives that only exacerbate our addiction.

The marketisation of climate change is also obvious in the moves worldwide towards 'carbon pricing' as a dominant policy response (Neuhoff, 2011; Newell and Paterson, 2010). The creation of a 'market solution' invites claims that the 'externalities' of GHG emissions can be better valued within the economic system, so promoting a shift towards alternative, renewable energy technologies. Emerging efforts to geoengineer solutions – including spraying sulphate particles into the stratosphere and fertilising oceans – further demonstrate our seemingly boundless creativity in undermining the natural environment (Hamilton, 2013; Wagner and Weitzman, 2012).

In Chapter 3 we explored how businesses have constructed climate change as a space for business risk and opportunity rather than as an area of uncertainty. Risk constructions are performative and political, in that they justify and produce particular corporate activities and practices. The risk framings that companies apply to the crisis are rooted in visions of self-regulation, local innovation, and market-based drivers of economic transformation. Moreover, the consequences of these risk constructions unequally affect those at the fringes of economic activity.

In Chapter 4 we extended this line of reasoning by examining how corporations influence the political debate over climate change. We looked at how practices such as astroturfing, lobbying, campaign funding, and marketing encourage discussions and policies that favour market solutions and industry self-regulation; and we looked at how these practices reshape more general understandings of citizenship by incorporating individuals in a 'war of positions' over climate politics and policy. Through these political activities, the world is increasingly seen through the prism of corporate capitalism.

In Chapter 5 we saw how corporations and managers make appeals to justify their actions over climate change based on rival social goods, including 'the market', industrial efficiency, civic interest, the worlds of opinion and inspiration and the good of the environment. We discussed how businesses use these justifications and how competing justifications for corporate actions are internally resolved. Making these 'orders of worth' commensurate involves converting the environment into a commodity, thereby corrupting its intrinsic value in deference to a market logic.

In our last two empirical chapters we turned our attention to how managers and employees within corporations make sense of the climate crisis. In Chapter 6 we investigated how sustainability professionals endeavour to balance their personal environmental concerns with their professional duties by narrating coherent identities that maintain their integrity. In Chapter 7 we delved further into the ways in which these individuals make sense of climate change and how corporations have attempted to generate a more positive emotionology – one centred on challenge and opportunity.

Finally, in Chapter 8 we brought together these strands and highlighted how specific political myths have tied us firmly to the credo of creative self-destruction. We outlined how the narratives of corporate environmentalism, corporate citizenship and corporate omnipotence have framed climate change and humanity's response within the prevailing ethos of neoliberal market capitalism. We identified alternative political myths and narratives but conceded that these remain tangential to mainstream policy debate.

As we have argued, the myths that dominate at present work extraordinarily well. They fulfil their purpose all too effectively. It is first important to understand *how* and *why* they function so sublimely;

then it is vital to dislodge and replace them. In the following section we ponder the movements required for alternative, non-corporate paths to be forged.

Imagining alternative climate futures

When we present our research we frequently face comments that we are too negative. We are told a more constructive outlook would better engage and mobilise people. Martin Luther King Jr's 1963 'I have a dream' speech, in which he roused support for the civil rights campaign by delivering a vision of a utopia of freedom and racial equality, is often cited as an example of positive political motivation (see, e.g., Nordhaus and Shellenberger, 2007).

We need to acknowledge, though, the difference between the plight of black Americans in the 1960s and twenty-first-century climate politics. King contrasted a bright future with the horrors of racial segregation and discrimination, whereas today the prosperous citizens of developed economies are living the dream while fashioning a nightmare that is still to come. In short, King was preaching to people who had little to lose and much to gain; our message, at least in the eyes of many, cannot be so conveniently clear-cut.

Of course, confronting affluent Western consumers with the realities of climate change necessitates an uncomfortable conversation. Who wants to hear about declining living standards and a blighted Earth? As Elizabeth Kolbert has recently highlighted: 'When you tell people what it would actually take to radically reduce carbon emissions, they turn away. They don't want to give up air travel or air-conditioning or HDTV or trips to the mall or the family car or the myriad other things that go along with consuming 5,000 or 8,000 or 12,000 watts' (Kolbert, 2014a). How, then, can we build a wider social discussion that enables collectively imagined alternative futures to 'business as usual'?

As stated at the start of this chapter, we suggest there are six possible movements. Let us examine each in turn.

Biocentrism and our relationship to nature

The current anthropocentric view of humanity puts nature squarely below both the economy and society in an entrenched hierarchy. Our assumed mastery of the environment, our belief that we can manipulate and manage the Earth as we see fit, is at this stage being further perverted to fit narrow capitalist interests.

Any movement towards greater wealth distribution (e.g., Occupy) has only limited value if it does not dispute the commodification of nature. This being the case, the next movement will be about equality of burden rather than wealth. The revolt of nature requires challenging the privatisation, monetisation, and commercialisation of all aspects of the natural world (Harvey, 2014). A biocentric outlook demands that the Earth alone should set the boundaries for our living (Devall and Sessions, 1985; Naess, 1973). We neither intend nor endorse the idolisation of nature, which is an anthropocentric movement of creating new gods; rather, we urge a broadening of our thinking in terms of humanity's position in the universe. There should be no distinction between culture and nature.

Biosemiotics and the disruption of language

We need a different account of climate change – one wholly at odds with the dominant narrative of risk and opportunity. Our relationship to the environment necessitates new conditions of meaning. Given the performative effect of language, the narratives we employ will form our response to and, in turn, the consequences of climate change.

It is outside the current economic and business discourses that we can expect to find a language that denies the stability of the climate we have grown used to, disrupts the possibility to calculate and predict the future and resists any independence from nature (Szerszynski, 2010). Possibilities already exist in the imagery of Gaia, 'spaceship Earth' and economic growth as cancer (Boulding, 1966; Harré et al., 1999; Lovelock, 2000). Climate change will ask us increasingly harsh questions about our relationship with the natural world, and in doing so it will force us to express and make sense of it in fresh and more fruitful ways.

Promoting carbon democracy

The corporate capture of politics, as seen in lobbying, public campaigns against legislation, political donations and the support of think tanks and super-PACs, is hindering alternative narratives. The realm of corporate climate politics has diverse agendas, both for and against pricing mechanisms, but is determinedly underpinned by self-interest. Introducing more transparency to lobbying – for example, through detailed registers – and the reigning in of corporate political activities through legislation might offer hope, but the fact is that donating time and money to make one's voice heard is how representative democracy works today.

What is needed, then, is a more direct and radical kind of democracy. The global movement of dissent requires local democratic initiatives that puncture the hegemonic consensus of the capitalist imaginary. Alternatives should be debated and consequences acknowledged. This might take the form of deliberative democracy and citizen involvement (Dryzek, 2013) or the more embryonic and emergent strains of local democracy. The corollaries of climate change provide the possibility to engage democratically with the inegalitarian outcomes of the present imaginary (see, for instance, the political discussion following Hurricane Katrina). A single imaginary cannot capture the diverse experiences of climate change's effects.

Environmental values rather than 'value'

With the valuation of nature in monetary terms, as seen in carbon markets and 'green' capitalism, the environment itself has been converted into *a* value. This singularity makes it comparable and exchangeable. Defying this corruption of the environment means refusing such a simplistic evaluation of the planet.

One example, as we alluded to earlier, is to give nature legal standing. However, rather than changing the status of the environment from a market to a civic worth, we need to augment our appreciation of the planet. This movement suggests folding the market *within the environment* – rather than vice versa, as is the case now – and recognising the environmental plurality of values. All goods and values are dependent on an ecological relationship, which is why a 'green' order of worth should be taken seriously and regarded as more than just a construct of human utility (Thévenot et al., 2000).

Beyond the green consumer

The consumption of 'green' products and services allows for the narrating of positive self-images. We can quite literally shop ourselves out of individual and collective cognitive dissonance, fashioning identities for ourselves through the products and services we buy and consume. But by opening up the disjuncture between beliefs and actions, so revealing the inconsistency of our lives and disturbing the comfortable emplotment of coherent identity narratives, it could be possible to engage with wider political movements.

The process of resolving identity fragmentation requires work, and this can be channelled towards political agency. The enactments of identities are important political resources for alternative narratives to take hold. Refusing the smugness of 'green' consumption is a springboard for fashioning new constructions of how we make sense of ourselves as citizens in a climate-changed world.

Championing climate change emotionally

As we have seen, climate change exists within a volatile emotional milieu. We contemplate our future and feel fear, despair, anxiety, and anger. Rather than denying them, we can use these emotions to champion alternative narratives.

It might be argued that the emotional charges from climate change routinely come from acknowledging a lack of fairness or justice. It is also these emotions that make us extend a hand to strangers, offer hospitality to the displaced, and give succour to the faceless and the stateless. Both Mahatma Gandhi and Martin Luther King Jr taught us that it is love that interrupts institutionalised social imaginaries (Caygill, 2013). Positivity is powerful.

These six movements are clearly not 'solutions' to climate change. As climate scientists have made plain, the processes of a warming planet are already in train. Extreme weather events, record heat, the melting Arctic, and acidifying oceans lay bare the folly of advocating 'solutions' in the strictest sense. There will be no silver bullet. There will be no heroic, cure-all act of salvation. Our only hope is damage limitation.

We said at the outset that the future looks bleak. We not only stand by that assertion; we sincerely question the motives – if not the sanity – of anyone who insists otherwise. But this is not to say that we cannot make the future *less* bleak; and it is certainly not to say that we should not try.

Taken together, the movements outlined above might just help us to accept alternative narratives to the capitalist imaginary in making sense of climate change. They might just help us to reverse and separate modernity's siblings of capitalism and democracy; and they might just allow the latter to determine the former's role in responding to the present as well as the future. Let us hope so, for one thing is certain in this horribly uncertain world: we cannot go on as we have.

Appendix

Our research into business responses to climate change began in late 2008 as an area of emerging organisational change in major corporations. Climate change had become the subject of increasing political debate in the lead-up to the 2007 federal election in Australia, and following that, in proposals by the then Labor government for the introduction of an Emissions Trading System (ETS). Corporations, business associations, the media, and political parties placed increasing emphasis on the issue of climate change and GHG emissions regulation during this period, and as we have outlined in the book this policy debate has driven significant corporate activity.

During 2009 we undertook extensive background research on this topic by reviewing media coverage of business responses to climate policy and initiating background interviews with key industry informants. In early 2010, we applied for Australia Research Council (ARC) Discovery Grant funding to investigate this topic with a focus on its organisational change implications. We were successful in gaining funding for the period 2011–2013 (ARC Discovery Grant DP110104066).

Data collection

In gathering data about business responses to climate change, we sought to access both documentary and interview data. We began by undertaking a systematic review of publicly-available sustainability reports, webpages, and presentations from large corporations operating within Australia. This included companies from a broad range of industry sectors including manufacturing, transport, retail, communications, construction, energy, resources, and financial and professional business services. Many of these organisations were subsidiaries of large multinational corporations allowing us to link our analysis of their stated strategies and practices with broader global initiatives.

A secondary stage of data collection focused on semi-structured interviews with senior sustainability specialists in a selection of these organisations. We identified these individuals through their profiles on corporate websites and through networks of sustainability professionals. Our initial stage of interviewing resulted in a total of 36 interviews with a broad range of such sustainability specialists. Beyond descriptions of sustainability practices, we asked individuals about their work and career history and their personal attitudes to the environment and climate change. We concluded each interview by asking respondents about the challenges they faced in their jobs and how they dealt with potential contradictions between their values and work activities. Each interview lasted between 50 and 120 minutes and was recorded and fully transcribed. This provided a rich source of qualitative data (amounting to over a thousand pages of transcript). Interviews were supplemented with documentation from the respondents' organisations, including sustainability strategy documents, internal communications, submissions to government inquiries, press releases, and media coverage. These texts allowed us to gain a more detailed understanding of the broader organisational context and the dominant discourses that respondents interacted with.

We then identified five organisations as case studies for more detailed data gathering and analysis (see Tables A.1 and A.2). As we noted in Chapter 1 this included:

- A leading energy producer that was supplementing fossil fuel generation with renewable energy sources
- A large insurer that was measuring the financial risks of extreme weather events
- A major financial services company that was factoring a 'price on carbon' into its lending to corporate clients
- A global manufacturer that was reinventing itself as a 'green' company producing more efficient industrial equipment and renewable energy technologies
- A global media company that had embarked on a major eco-efficiency drive to become 'carbon-neutral'.

Here we broadened our interview sample beyond just sustainability specialists and also interviewed a range of operational and senior managers about specific strategies and practices that each organisation

Table A.1 *Interview respondents*

Organisation	Title	Age	Gender
Accounting practice A	Associate Director, Sustainability and Climate Change Services	40–45	F
Accounting practice B	Partner, Climate Change and Sustainability Services	45–50	M
Airline A	Manager, Climate Change Strategy	35–40	F
	Head of Environment and Climate Change	40–45	M
Airline B	Environment Manager	40–45	M
Banking and financial services	Adviser, Group Sustainability	35–40	F
	Director, Emissions and Environment	35–40	F
	Director, Carbon and Energy Project Finance	40–45	M
	Director, Government and Industry Affairs	35–40	M
	Director, Carbon and Corporate Banking	45–50	M
	Director, Infrastructure and Utilities	45–50	M
	Head of Agribusiness	35–40	M
Car manufacturer A	Energy and Environment Director	40–45	M
Car manufacturer B	Manager, Environmental Policy	45–50	M
Construction and mining	Group Sustainability Manager	50–55	M
Energy utility	Manager, Sustainability Strategy	30–35	F
	Head of Sustainability	40–45	M
	Carbon Price Implementation Manager	35–40	M
	Group Head, Corporate Affairs	45–50	M
	Commercial Business Manager	40–45	M
	Business Partner, People and Culture	35–40	F

Organization	Role	Age	Gender
-	National Sales Manager	40–45	M
-	Lead, Electricity Workstream	35–40	F
Engineering consultancy	Manager, Sustainability and Climate Change	35–40	M
-	Senior Sustainability Consultant	25–30	F
Environmental consultancy	Leader, Climate Change Practice	30–35	F
-	Senior Associate	30–35	F
-	Director	50–55	M
-	Director	45–50	M
Food manufacturer	Environment Manager	40–45	M
Funds management	Principal, Sustainable Funds Management	35–40	M
Industrial manufacturer A (global MNC)	Sustainability Director	40–45	M
	CEO (ANZ)	50–55	M
	Vice President, Operations	45–50	M
	Corporate Communications Director	35–40	F
	Business Development Leader	35–40	M
Industrial manufacturer B	Manager, Sustainability Programmes	30–35	F
Industrial services A	Environment Manager	25–30	F
Industrial services B	Head of Strategy	40–45	M
Infrastructure company	Sustainability Research Manager	40–45	M
Insurance company A	Culture and Reputation Executive	40–45	F
-	Head of Strategy	40–45	M
-	Adviser, External Relations	50–55	M

Table A.1 (*cont.*)

Organisation	Title	Age	Gender
–	Senior Manager, Reinsurance	45–50	M
–	Senior Manager, Business Sustainability	35–40	F
–	Chief Risk Officer	50–55	M
Insurance company B (global MNC)	Sustainability Manager	40–45	F
Management training organisation	Programme Director	35–40	F
Media company	Manager, Environment and Climate Change	50–55	M
–	Sustainability Manager	30–35	F
–	Creative Director	50–55	M
–	Human Resources Director	30–35	F
–	Group Organisational Development Manager	40–45	F
–	Human Resource Manager	45–50	M
–	Director, Corporate Affairs	40–45	M
–	Editor in Chief	45–50	M
–	General Manager	50–55	M
–	Communications Manager	30–35	M
–	Procurement Manager	45–50	M
–	Supervisor	40–45	M
Property and commercial building A	Sustainability Manager	45–50	F

Property and commercial building B	Group Sustainability Manager	40–45	M
Property and commercial building C	Sustainability Manager	40–45	F
Property and real estate (global MNC)	Head of Sustainability	35–40	M
Resource and mining A (global MNC)	Business Improvement Director	40–45	M
–	Vice President, Environment and Climate Change	45–50	M
Resource and mining B	Manager, Climate and Energy Efficiency	50–55	M
Resource and mining C (global MNC)	Sustainability Adviser	30–35	M
Resource and mining D (global MNC)	Climate Change Adviser	45–50	M
Resource and mining E	Executive Director	50–55	M
Retailer	Group Manager, Corporate Responsibility and Sustainability	40–45	F

Table A.2 *Case study organisations*

Case	Description	Interviews	Climate change practices	Indicative documents
BankCo	Financial services (36,000 employees)	11	Advocacy for carbon pricing; changes to institutional lending based on government pricing of carbon emissions; reducing organisational carbon emissions.	Sustainability reports 2008–2012; Carbon updates 2009–2012; 'BankCo' Climate Change Policy; Position Statement on Sustainable Finance and Energy; Carbon Disclosure Project 2009 Response.
EnergyCo	Electricity and gas production and retail (1,500 employees)	18	Investing in a range of renewable energy supply options (e.g., wind, hydro, biomass); redesign of company processes to implement a government-mandated carbon emissions price; alliance with environmental NGOs.	Sustainability reports 2008–2012; 'EnergyCo' Carbon Pollution Reduction Scheme Submission 2008; Carbon Policy Briefing Notes; Emissions Trading presentation notes 2010; 'EnergyCo' Environmental Principles.

GlobalCo	Global manufacturer (5,600 employees)	9	Manufacture of more sustainable industrial products including renewable energy and efficient industrial equipment; branding as a 'green' company.	GlobalCo Annual reports 2008–2012; press releases 2010–2012; Vice President's sustainability presentation 2011.
InsureCo	National insurer (12,700 employees)	10	Early advocacy for carbon pricing; development of extreme weather risk analysis; pricing insurance policies with reference to future climate change impacts; liaising with government regarding regional climate adaptation.	Sustainability reports 2009–2012; 'Climate change and the insurance industry' presentation 2010; Environmental sustainability report.
MediaCo	Media company (8,000 employees)	15	Improved efficiency and achievement of 'carbon-neutral' status; culture-change initiative for employees aimed at GHG emissions reduction.	Annual reports 2010–2012; Environment at MediaCo, 2010–2012; Energy Reduction Plan 2011; media releases on environment plan; presentations on emissions reduction plans.

had developed in responding to climate change as a business issue. In building up each case study, we also accessed an extensive range of documentation including corporate policy documents, PowerPoint presentations, communications and training documents, submissions to government on proposed carbon regulation, and attendance at a number of corporate functions and internal meetings.

Data analysis

Data analysis for this project comprised a number of stages. The first stage involved a detailed reading of the textual material (interview transcripts and documents). Using the qualitative data analysis software *QSR NVivo* we openly coded relevant 'nodal points' around which practices, strategies, narratives, and discourses in the text were identified. This resulted in the classification of over 115 'nodes', each of which illustrated the relationship between climate change, local discourses, the organisation, and individual actors.

From this initial coding we then undertook a process of more targeted coding based around emergent concepts that we identified from our earlier analysis of the data and our reading of critical organisational and sociological literature. This abductive approach (Van Maanen et al., 2007) involved iteration between a detailed reading and interpretation of our data and a broad range of theoretical literature from a range of disciplines.

For instance, early on in our analysis we focused on the individual role of sustainability specialists and the way in which responding to climate change often promoted strong statements around identity and emotions (outlined in Chapters 6 and 7). The analysis focused on managers' identity work and the stories they told about their education and careers, their work activities, and their personal and home life.

Later, we broadened our analysis to consider how individual engagement with climate change interacted with organisational practices and policies through the concepts of justification and compromise (see Chapter 5). Our analysis here focused on the identification of different orders of worth as forms of justification for various actions and inactions on climate-related issues.

Our focus on how corporations interacted with broader political and social discourses on climate change also led us to explore corporate political activity in regard to climate change (Chapter 4), and later the discourse of risk (Chapter 3). Here our data analysis focused on identifying discourses and the processes through which these discourses were constructed both within corporations and in their public representations.

Broadening our analysis further, in later work we sought to locate our earlier analysis of corporate responses to climate change into a broader theoretical framing. Here we engaged with the concepts of the 'spirit of capitalism' (Boltanski and Chiapello, 2005), political myth (Bottici, 2007), and the idea of 'creative self-destruction' which forms the argument of our book (Chapters 2 and 8).

Each of these cases involved an extensive process of qualitative data analysis in which we re-analysed our initial coding and developed new coding based around key themes and categories from the data (Miles and Huberman, 1994; Strauss and Corbin, 1998). Further details on the specific data analysis processes used in each of these areas can be found in the journal articles that resulted from this earlier research (Nyberg et al., 2013; Nyberg and Wright, 2012; Nyberg and Wright, 2013; Wright and Nyberg, 2012; 2014; Wright et al., 2012).

Global comparison

Many of the major corporations in the study operate on a global scale. Even so, to ensure that the empirical claims have global reach, we expanded the collection of secondary sources. For each of the chapters, we looked at similar empirical cases and claims in different contexts. This included corporate and governmental reports as well as other academic and consultancy studies. While the jurisdictions differ, we found similar corporate discourses in relation to climate change across the globe. The win–win scenario defending business as usual is the dominant discourse in all different varieties of capitalism.

The global comparison also confirmed the strategies and tactics used by different industry sectors in a range of national contexts. For example, the fossil fuel industry's approach to influencing climate change regulation operates according to the same blue print in Australia, Canada, the United States, and the United Kingdom. Partly, this is because of their multinational operations. However, it is also a result of the institutional and industry-specific pressures fossil fuel companies face. Similar isomorphism can also be found in other, perhaps less obvious, industries, such as consumer goods, banking, and insurance. While our focus is on large and often multi-national corporations, small and medium-sized businesses appear to toe the line and so do most major political parties. Voices against business as usual operate at the fringes of international and local politics.

Finally, the individual stories and emotions expressed by our participants are stories and emotions shared across the planet. The respondents in our study were all, to varying degrees, concerned, and often scared, of the future consequences of a changed climate. They all related their existence in some form to climate change. Identity projects and emotional work that everyone sooner or later engages in.

References

ABC. (2011a) *Background Briefing: The Lord Monckton Roadshow*, www .abc.net.au/rn/backgroundbriefing/stories/2011/3268730.htm.

ABC. (2011b) 'The Carbon War', *4 Corners*, 19 September, www.abc.net .au/4corners/stories/2011/09/15/3318364.htm.

ACA. (2009) 'Proposed Emissions Trading Scheme Amendments Will Sacrifice Regional Jobs but Not Cut Emissions', *Australian Coal Association Media Release*, 24 November.

ACA. (2010) 'Climate Change Is a Real Problem. NewGenCoal Is All About Solutions', 27 April, www.youtube.com/watch?v=lyEt3lGQVWw.

Acker, J. (1990) 'Hierarchies, Jobs, Bodies', *Gender & Society* 4(2): 139–58.

Adger, W., Dessai, S., Goulden, M., Hulme, M., Lorenzoni, I., Nelson, D., Naess, L., Wolf, J., and Wreford, A. (2009) 'Are There Social Limits to Adaptation to Climate Change?', *Climatic Change* 93(3): 335–54.

Ahmed, N. (2014) 'Defence Officials Prepare to Fight the Poor, Activists and Minorities (and Commies)', *The Guardian*, 13 June, www.the guardian.com/environment/earth-insight/2014/jun/13/uk-defence-fight -poor-activists-minorities-marxists-commies.

Ailon, G. (2012) 'The Discursive Management of Financial Risk Scandals: The Case of *Wall Street Journal* Commentaries on LTCM and Enron', *Qualitative Sociology* 35(3): 251–70.

Albrecht, G., Sartore, G.-M., Connor, L., Higginbotham, N., Freeman, S., Kelly, B., Stain, H., Tonna, A., and Pollard, G. (2007) 'Solastalgia: The Distress Caused by Environmental Change', *Australasian Psychiatry* 15(s1): S95–S98.

Aldrich, H. and Herker, D. (1977) 'Boundary Spanning Roles and Organization Structure', *The Academy of Management Review* 2(2): 217–30.

Alvesson, M. and Willmott, H. (2002) 'Producing the Appropriate Individual: Identity Regulation as Organizational Control', *Journal of Management Studies* 39(5): 619–44.

Andersen, T. J. and Schrøder, P. W. (2010) *Strategic Risk Management Practice*. Cambridge: Cambridge University Press.

Anderson, K. and Bows, A. (2008) 'Reframing the Climate Change Challenge in Light of Post-2000 Emission Trends', *Philosophical Transactions of the Royal Society A: Mathematical, Physical and Engineering Sciences* 366(1882): 3863–82.

(2011) 'Beyond "Dangerous" Climate Change: Emission Scenarios for a New World', *Philosophical Transactions of the Royal Society A: Mathematical, Physical and Engineering Sciences* 369(1934): 20–44.

(2012) 'A New Paradigm for Climate Change', *Nature Climate Change* 2: 639–40.

Andersson, L. M. and Bateman, T. S. (2000) 'Individual Environmental Initiative: Championing Natural Environmental Issues in US Business Organizations', *Academy of Management Journal* 43(4): 548–70.

Andresen, S. and Agrawala, S. (2002) 'Leaders, Pushers and Laggards in the Making of the Climate Regime', *Global Environmental Change* 12(1): 41–51.

Annan, K. (2014) 'A United Call for Action on Climate Change', *Washington Post*, 22 January, www.washingtonpost.com/opinions/kofi-annan-a-united-call-for-action-on-climate-change/2014/01/22/3694fa0c-82c1-11e3-9dd4-e7278db80d86_story.html.

Ansar, A., Caldecott, B., and Tilbury, J. (2013) *Stranded Assets and the Fossil Fuel Divestment Campaign: What Does Divestment Mean for the Valuation of Fossil Fuel Assets?* Oxford: Smith School of Enterprise and Environment, University of Oxford, www.qualenergia.it/sites/default/files/articolo-doc/01416%20Divestment%20and%20fossil%20fuel%20assets%20report%20-%20web.pdf.

Archer, D. and Rahmstorf, S. (2010) *The Climate Crisis: An Introductory Guide to Climate Change*. Cambridge: Cambridge University Press.

Arts, B. (2002) '"Green Alliances" of Business and NGOs. New Styles of Self-Regulation or "Dead-End Roads"?', *Corporate Social Responsibility and Environmental Management* 9(1): 26–36.

Asdal, K. (2008) 'Enacting Things through Numbers: Taking Nature into Account/ing', *Geoforum* 39(1): 123–32.

Ashforth, B. E. and Humphrey, R. H. (1995) 'Emotion in the Workplace: A Reappraisal', *Human Relations* 48(2): 97–125.

Associated Press. (2014) 'Exxon Mobil Says Climate Change Unlikely to Stop It Selling Fossil Fuels', *The Guardian*, 2 April, www.theguardian.com/environment/2014/apr/01/exxon-mobil-climate-change-fossil-fuels-oil.

Audi. (2010) 'Green Police: Audi Super Bowl Ad', 5 February, www.youtube.com/watch?v=Ml54UuAoLSo.

Austin, J. L. (1962) *How to Do Things with Words*. Cambridge, MA: Harvard University Press.

Bakan, J. (2004) *The Corporation: The Pathological Pursuit of Profit and Power*. London: Constable.

Balogun, J., Gleadle, P., Hope-Hailey, V., and Willmott, H. (2005) 'Managing Change across Boundaries: Boundary-Shaking Practices', *British Journal of Management* 16(4): 261–78.

Banerjee, B. (2008a) 'Necrocapitalism', *Organization Studies* 29(12): 1541–63.

Banerjee, S. B. (2008b) 'Corporate Social Responsibility: The Good, the Bad and the Ugly', *Critical Sociology* 34(1): 51–79.

Barley, S. R. (2007) 'Corporations, Democracy, and the Public Good', *Journal of Management Inquiry* 16(3): 201–15.

(2010) 'Building an Institutional Field to Corral a Government: A Case to Set an Agenda for Organization Studies', *Organization Studies* 31(6): 777–805.

Barrett, P. M. (2012) 'It's Global Warming, Stupid', *Bloomberg Businessweek*, 1 November, www.businessweek.com/articles/2012-11-01/its-global-warming-stupid#r=hp-ls.

Bartel, C. and Dutton, J. (2001) 'Ambiguous Organizational Memberships: Constructing Orgnizational Identities in Interactions with Others', in M. A. Hogg and D. J. Terry (eds) *Social Identity Processes in Organizational Contexts*, pp. 115–30. Philadelphia, PA: Psychology Press.

Baxter, C. (2011) 'Koch Industries: Still Fueling Climate Denial', *Greenpeace*, 6 May, www.greenpeace.org/usa/en/news-and-blogs/campaign-blog/koch-industries-still-fueling-climate-denial/blog/34609/.

Beavis, S. (2011) 'HSBC – Partnering with Earthwatch to Educate Staff', *The Guardian*, 26 May, www.theguardian.com/sustainable-business/hsbc-earthwatch-partnership-educate-staff.

Bebbington, J., Larrinaga, C., and Moneva, J. M. (2008) 'Corporate Social Reporting and Reputation Risk Management', *Accounting, Auditing & Accountability Journal* 21(3): 337–61.

Beck, U. (1992) *Risk Society: Towards a New Modernity*. London: Sage.

Beder, S. (2002a) 'Bp: Beyond Petroleum?', in E. Lubbers (ed) *Battling Big Business: Countering Greenwash, Infiltration and Other Forms of Corporate Bullying*, pp. 26–32. Totnes: Green Books.

(2002b)'Environmentalists Help Manage Corporate Reputation:Changing Perceptions Not Behaviour', *Ecopolitics* 1(4): 60–72.

(2011) 'Corporate Discourse on Climate Change', in G. Sussman (ed) *The Propaganda Society: Promotional Culture and Politics in Global Context*, pp. 113–29. New York: Peter Lang.

Beech, N. (2011) 'Liminality and the Practices of Identity Reconstruction', *Human Relations* 64(2): 285–302.

Beinhocker, E., Oppenheim, J., Irons, B., Lahti, M., Farrell, D., Nyquist, S., Remes, J., Nauclér, T., and Enkvist, P. A. (2008) *The Carbon Productivity Challenge: Curbing Climate Change and Sustaining Economic Growth*. New York: McKinsey & Company, www.mckinsey.com/insights/energy_resources_materials/the_carbon_productivity_challenge.

Bell, S. and Warhurst, J. (1993) 'Business Political Activism and Government Relations in Large Companies in Australia', *Australian Journal of Political Science* 28(2): 201–20.

Berman, M. (1982) *All That Is Solid Melts into Air: The Experience of Modernity*. New York: Simon and Schuster.

Biggart, N. W. and Beamish, T. D. (2003) 'The Economic Sociology of Conventions: Habit, Custom, Practice, and Routine in Market Order', *Annual Review of Sociology* 29: 443–64.

Blackburne, A. (2013) 'Unilever, John Lewis and M&S in Top 10 Most Sought-after Employers', *Blue & Green Tomorrow*, 4 November, blueandgreentomorrow.com/2013/11/04/unilever-john-lewis-and-ms-in-top-10-most-sought-after-employers/.

Blok, A. (2013) 'Pragmatic Sociology as Political Ecology on the Many Worths of Nature(s)', *European Journal of Social Theory* 16(4): 492–510.

Boden, T. A., Marland, G., and Andres, R. J. (2013) *Global, Regional, and National Fossil-Fuel CO_2 Emissions*. Oak Ridge, TN: Carbon Dioxide Information Analysis Center, Oak Ridge National Laboratory, U.S. Department of Energy, http://cdiac.ornl.gov/trends/emis/tre_glob_2010.html.

Bogardi, J. and Warner, K. (2008) 'Here Comes the Flood', *Nature Reports Climate Change*, 11 December, www.nature.com/climate/2009/0901/full/climate.2008.138.html.

Bogle, A. and Oremus, W. (2014) 'The Saudi Arabia of the South Pacific', *Slate*, 24 September, www.slate.com/articles/technology/future_tense/2014/09/australia_s_environmental_movement_has_been_overthrown.html.

Böhm, S., Misoczky, M. C., and Moog, S. (2012) 'Greening Capitalism? A Marxist Critique of Carbon Markets', *Organization Studies* 33(11): 1617–38.

Boltanski, L. (1999) *Distant Suffering: Morality, Media and Politics*. Cambridge: Cambridge University Press.

(2011) *On Critique: A Sociology of Emancipation*. Cambridge: Polity Press.

Boltanski, L. and Chiapello, E. (2005) *The New Spirit of Capitalism*. London: Verso.

Boltanski, L. and Thévenot, L. (1999) 'The Sociology of Critical Capacity', *European Journal of Social Theory* 2(3): 359–77.

(2000) 'The Reality of Moral Expectations: A Sociology of Situated Judgement', *Philosophical Explorations* 3(3): 208–31.

(2006) *On Justification: Economies of Worth*. Princeton: Princeton University Press.

Bonini, S. and Oppenheim, J. (2008) 'Cultivating the Green Consumer', *Stanford Social Innovation Review* 6(4): 56–61.

Bottici, C. (2007) *A Philosophy of Political Myth*. Cambridge: Cambridge University Press.

Boulding, K. E. (1966) 'The Economics of the Coming Spaceship Earth', in H. Jarrett (ed) *Environmental Quality in a Growing Economy*, pp. 3–14. Baltimore, MD: Johns Hopkins University Press.

Bourke, L. (2014) 'Coal Is "the Foundation of Prosperity" for Foreseeable Future, Says Prime Minister Tony Abbott', *Sydney Morning Herald*, 4 November, www.smh.com.au/federal-politics/political-news/coal-is-the-foundation-of-prosperity-for-foreseeable-future-says-prime-minister-tony-abbott-20141104-11gh7k.html.

Boyd, J. and Banzhaf, S.(2007) 'What Are Ecosystem Services? The Need for Standardized Environmental Accounting Units', *Ecological Economics* 63(2–3): 616–26.

Boykoff, M. T. (2011) *Who Speaks for the Climate? Making Sense of Media Reporting on Climate Change*. Cambridge: Cambridge University Press.

Boykoff, M. T., Frame, D. and Randalls, S. (2010) 'Discursive Stability Meets Climate Instability: A Critical Exploration of the Concept of "Climate Stabilization" in Contemporary Climate Policy', *Global Environmental Change* 20(1): 53–64.

BP. (2009) 'Bp – Beyond Petroleum [US 2000 Re-Launch Commercial]', www.youtube.com/watch?v=thXeYv-Zxr4.

BP. (2014) 'BP Brand and Logo', www.bp.com/en/global/corporate/about-bp/our-history/history-of-bp/special-subject-histories/bp-brand-and-logo.html.

Brulle, R., Carmichael, J., and Jenkins, J. C. (2012) 'Shifting Public Opinion on Climate Change: An Empirical Assessment of Factors Influencing Concern over Climate Change in the U.S., 2002–2010', *Climatic Change* 114(2): 169–88.

Brulle, R. J. (2014) 'Institutionalizing Delay: Foundation Funding and the Creation of US Climate Change Counter-Movement Organizations', *Climatic Change* 122(4): 681–94.

Brysse, K., Oreskes, N., O'Reilly, J., and Oppenheimer, M. (2013) 'Climate Change Prediction: Erring on the Side of Least Drama?', *Global Environmental Change* 23(1): 327–37.

Buckley, T. (2014) 'Oz Coal at Risk as Major Economies Turn on Fossil Fuels', *RenewEconomy*, 6 June, http://reneweconomy.com.au/2014/australian-coal-industry-unprecedented-risk-major-powers-act-fossil-fuels-25814.

Burawoy, M. (1979) *Manufacturing Consent: Changes in the Labour Process under Monopoly Capitalism*. Chicago: University of Chicago Press.

Burdon, P. D. (2011) 'Earth Rights: The Theory', *IUCN Academy of Environmental Law e-Journal*, http://ssrn.com/abstract=1765386.

Busch, T. (2011) 'Organizational Adaptation to Disruptions in the Natural Environment: The Case of Climate Change', *Scandinavian Journal of Management* 27(4): 389–404.

Butler, J. (2010) 'Performative Agency', *Journal of Cultural Economy* 3(2): 147–61.

Calhoun, C. (1994) 'Social Theory and the Politics of Identity', in C. Calhoun (ed) *Social Theory and the Politics of Identity*, pp. 9–36. Cambridge, MA: Blackwell.

Callon, M. (2009) 'Civilizing Markets: Carbon Trading between in Vitro and in Vivo Experiments', *Accounting, Organizations and Society* 34(3): 535–48.

Cambone, D. (2014) 'Climate Change Is Single Biggest Risk to Global Economy – Paulson at CGI2014', *Forbes*, 22 September, www.forbes.com/sites/kitconews/2014/09/22/climate-change-is-single-biggest-risk-to-global-economy-paulson-at-cgi2014/.

Campbell, K. M. (ed). (2009) *Climatic Cataclysm: The Foreign Policy and National Security Implications of Climate Change*. Washington, DC: Brookings Institution Press.

Carbon Tracker Initiative. (2012) *Unburnable Carbon: Are the World's Financial Markets Carrying a Carbon Bubble?* London: CTI.

Carrington, D. (2011) 'Climate Change Concern Tumbles in US and China', *The Guardian*, www.theguardian.com/environment/damian-carrington-blog/2011/aug/30/climate-change-opinion-skeptic.

(2013) 'Global Carbon Dioxide in Atmosphere Passes Milestone Level', *The Guardian*, 11 May, www.theguardian.com/environment/2013/may/10/carbon-dioxide-highest-level-greenhouse-gas.

Carson, R. (1962) *Silent Spring*. Boston: Houghton Mifflin.

Cassirer, E. (1946) *The Myth of the State*. New Haven, CT: Yale University Press.

Castoriadis, C. (1987) *The Imaginary Institution of Society*. Cambridge: Polity.

(1997) *World in Fragments: Writings on Politics, Society, Psychoanalysis, and the Imagination*. Stanford, CA: Stanford University Press.

Castree, N. (2011) 'Neoliberalism and the Biophysical Environment 3: Putting Theory into Practice', *Geography Compass* 5(1): 35–49.

Cave, T. and Rowell, A. (2014) *A Quiet Word: Lobbying, Crony Capitalism and Broken Politics in Britain*. London: Bodley Head.

Caygill, H. (2013) *On Resistance: A Philosophy of Defiance*. London: Bloomsbury.

Chan, G. (2014) 'Tony Abbott Says "Coal Is Good for Humanity" While Opening Mine', *The Guardian*, 13 October, www.theguardian.com/world/2014/oct/13/tony-abbott-says-coal-is-good-for-humanity-while-opening-mine.

Chesbrough, H. (2012) 'GE's Ecomagination Challenge: An Experiment in Open Innovation', *California Management Review* 54(3): 140–54.

Chiapello, E. (2013) 'Capitalism and Its Criticisms', in P. du Gay and G. Morgan (eds) *New Spirits of Capitalism? Crises, Justifications, and Dynamics*, pp. 60–81. Oxford: Oxford University Press.

Cho, C., Martens, M., Kim, H., and Rodrigue, M. (2011) 'Astroturfing Global Warming: It Isn't Always Greener on the Other Side of the Fence', *Journal Of Business Ethics* 104(4): 571–87.

Clark, D. (2013) 'Which Companies Caused Global Warming?', *The Guardian*, 21 November, www.theguardian.com/environment/interactive/2013/nov/20/which-fossil-fuel-companies-responsible-climate-change-interactive.

Clark, D. and Berners-Lee, M. (2013) *The Burning Question: We Can't T Burn Half the World's Oil, Coal and Gas. So How Do We Quit?* London: Profile Books.

Clark, N. (2014) 'Geo-Politics and the Disaster of the Anthropocene', *The Sociological Review* 62: 19–37.

Clarke, C. A., Brown, A. D., and Hope-Hailey, V. (2009) 'Working Identities? Antagonistic Discursive Resources and Managerial Identity', *Human Relations* 62(3): 323–52.

Clarke, J. (2011) 'Carbon Complex', *BOSS Magazine (Australian Financial Review)* 12: 20–24.

Climate Commission. (2013) *The Critical Decade: Global Action Building on Climate Change*. Canberra: Comonwealth of Australia.

CNA Military Advisory Board. (2014) *National Security and the Accelerating Risks of Climate Change*. Alexandria, VA: CNA Corporation.

Coady, C. A. J. (2008) *Messy Morality: The Challenge of Politics*. Oxford: Clarendon Press.

Coll, S. (2012) *Private Empire: Exxonmobil and American Power*. New York: Penguin.

Commonwealth of Australia. (2011) *Securing a Clean Energy Future: The Australian Government's Climate Change Plan*. Canberra: Commonwealth of Australia.

Confino, J. (2012) 'Moments of Revelation Trigger the Biggest Transformations', *The Guardian*, 9 November, www.theguardian.com/sustainable-business/epiphany-transform-corporate-sustainability.

Connolly, W. E. (2012) 'Steps toward an Ecology of Late Capitalism', *Theory & Event* 15(1): N_A.

Cook, I. R. and Swyngedouw, E. (2012) 'Cities, Social Cohesion and the Environment: Towards a Future Research Agenda', *Urban Studies* 49(9): 1959–79.

Cook, J., Nuccitelli, D., Green, S. A., Richardson, M., Winkler, B., Painting, R., Way, R., Jacobs, P., and Skuce, A. (2013) 'Quantifying the Consensus on Anthropogenic Global Warming in the Scientific Literature', *Environmental Research Letters* 8(2): 1–7.

Cooley, S. R. and Doney, S. C. (2009) 'Anticipating Ocean Acidification's Economic Consequences for Commercial Fisheries', *Environmental Research Letters* 4(2): 024007.

Cooper, M. (2010) 'Turbulent Worlds: Financial Markets and Environmental Crisis', *Theory, Culture & Society* 27(2/3): 167–90.

Coumou, D. and Rahmstorf, S. (2012) 'A Decade of Weather Extremes', *Nature Climate Change* 2(7): 491–96.

Cox, L. (2014a) 'Carbon Tax Is Gone: Repeal Bills Pass the Senate', *Sydney Morning Herald*, 17 July, www.smh.com.au/federal-politics/political-news/carbon-tax-is-gone-repeal-bills-pass-the-senate-20140717-3c2he.html.

(2014b) 'Tony Abbott Attacks ANU's "Stupid Decision" to Dump Fossil Fuel Investments', *Sydney Morning Herald*, 15 October, www.smh.com.au/federal-politics/political-news/tony-abbott-attacks-anus-stupid-decision-to-dump-fossil-fuel-investments-2014 10 15-116a0y.html.

Crane, A., Matten, D., and Moon, J. (2008) 'The Emergence of Corporate Citizenship: Historical Development and Alternative Perspectives', in A. G. Scherer and G. Palazzo (eds) *Handbook of Research on Global Corporate Citizenship*, pp. 25–49. Cheltenham: Edward Elgar.

Creed, W. E. D., DeJordy, R., and Lok, J. (2010) 'Being the Change: Resolving Institutional Contradiction through Identity Work', *Academy of Management Journal* 53(6): 1336–64.

Crompton, T. and Kasser, T. (2009) *Meeting Environmental Challenges: The Role of Human Identity*. Godalming: WWF-UK.

Crouch, C. (2004) *Post-Democracy*. Cambridge: Polity.

(2011) *The Strange Non-Death of Neoliberalism*. Cambridge: Polity.

Crowley, K. (2007) 'Is Australia Faking It? The Kyoto Protocol and the Greenhouse Policy Challenge', *Global Environmental Politics* 7(4): 118–39.

(2013) 'Irresistible Force? Achieving Carbon Pricing in Australia', *Australian Journal of Politics & History* 59(3): 368–81.

Crutzen, P. J. (2002) 'Geology of Mankind: The Anthropocene', *Nature* 415(6867): 23.

CSIRO. (2011) *Flight Path to Sustainable Aviation*. Melbourne: CSIRO.

Cubby, B. and Lawes, A. (2010) 'The Benefit of the Doubt', *Sydney Morning Herald*, 8 May: www.smh.com.au/environment/climate-change/the-benefit-of-the-doubt-20100507-ujof.html.

Czech, B. (2013) *Supply Shock: Economic Growth at the Crossroads and the Steady State Solution*. Gabriola Island, BC: New Society.

Daily, G. (1997) *Nature's Services: Societal Dependence on Natural Ecosystems*. Washington, DC: Island Press.

Daly, H. (1977) *Steady State Economics*. San Francisco: W.H. Freeman.

Daly, H. E. (1996) *Beyond Growth: The Economics of Sustainable Development*. Boston, MA: Beacon Press.

Dauvergne, P. and LeBaron, G. (2014) *Protest Inc.: The Corporatization of Activism*. Cambridge: Polity Press.

Dauvergne, P. and Lister, J. (2013) *Eco-Business: A Big-Brand Takeover of Sustainability*. Cambridge, MA: MIT Press.

Davis, S. J. and Shearer, C. (2014) 'Climate Change: A Crack in the Natural-Gas Bridge', *Nature* 514(7523): 436–37.

Deal, T. and Kennedy, A. (1982) *Corporate Cultures: The Rites and Rituals of Corporate Life*. Reading MA: Addison-Wesley.

DECC. (2014) *The Government's Response to the Mackay-Stone Report: Potential Greenhouse Gas Emissions Associated with Shale Gas Extraction and Use*. London: Department of Energy & Climate Change.

DEFRA. (2012) *Ecosystem Markets Task Force*, www.defra.gov.uk/ecosystem-markets/.

Delina, L. L. and Diesendorf, M. (2013) 'Is Wartime Mobilisation a Suitable Policy Model for Rapid National Climate Mitigation?', *Energy Policy* 58: 371–80.

Derrida, J. (2003) 'Autoimmunity: Real and Symbolic Suicides – A Dialogue with Jacques Derrida', in G. Borradi (ed) *Philosophy in a Time of Terror: Dialogues with Jurgen Habermas and Jacques Derrida*, pp. 85–136. Chicago: Chicago University Press.

Devall, B. and Sessions, G. (1985) *Deep Ecology: Living as If Nature Mattered*. Salt Lake City, UT: Gibbs Smith.

Dickinson, T. (2014) 'Inside the Koch Brothers' Toxic Empire', *Rolling Stone*, 24 September, www.rollingstone.com/politics/news/inside-the-koch-brothers-toxic-empire-20140924.

Diesendorf, M. (2014) *Sustainable Energy Solutions for Climate Change*. Sydney: UNSW Press.

Dörries, M. (2010) 'Climate Catastrophes and Fear', *Wiley Interdisciplinary Reviews: Climate Change* 1(6): 885–90.

Dryzek, J. S. (2013) *The Politics of the Earth: Environmental Discourses*. Oxford: Oxford University Press.

du Gay, P. and Morgan, G. (2013) 'Understanding Capitalism: Crises, Legitimacy, and Change through the Prism of *The New Spirit of Capitalism*', in P. du Gay and G. Morgan (eds) *New Spirits of Capitalism? Crises, Justifications, and Dynamics*, pp. 1–39. Oxford: Oxford University Press.

Dunlap, R. E. and McCright, A. M. (2011) 'Organized Climate Change Denial', in J. S. Dryzek, R. B. Norgaard, and D. Schlosberg (eds)

The Oxford Handbook of Climate Change and Society, pp. 144–60. Oxford: Oxford University Press.

Dunlap, R. E. and Mertig, A. G. (1992) *American Environmentalism: The US Environmental Movement, 1970–1990*. Washington DC: Taylor & Francis.

Dutton, J. E. and Ashford, S. J. (1993) 'Selling Issues to Top Management', *Academy of Management Review* 18(3): 397–428.

Dyer, G. (2010) *Climate Wars: The Fight for Survival as the World Overheats*. Oxford: Oneworld.

Ecofys and World Bank. (2014) *State and Trends of Carbon Pricing*. Washington, DC: World Bank Group.

Economic Intelligence Unit. (2011) *Adapting to an Uncertain Climate: A World of Commercial Opportunities*. London: UK Trade and Investment.

Edwards, P. N. (2010) *A Vast Machine: Computer Models, Climate Data and the Politics of Global Warming*. Cambridge, MA: MIT Press.

Ehrenfeld, J. R. and Hoffman, A. J. (2013) *Flourishing: A Frank Conversation about Sustainability*. Stanford, CA: Greenleaf Publishing.

EIA. (2014) *International Energy Outlook 2014*. Washington, DC: US Energy Information Administration.

Elgin, B. (2014) 'Chevron Backpedals Again on Renewable Energy', *Bloomberg Businessweek*, 9 June, www.businessweek.com/articles /2014-06-09/chevron-backpedals-again-on-renewable-energy.

Ellis, E. (2013) 'Overpopulation Is Not the Problem', *New York Times*, 13 September, www.nytimes.com/2013/09/14/opinion/overpopulation-is-not-the-problem.html.

Emmerich, R. (2004) *The Day after Tomorrow*, 20th Century Fox.

Emmott, S. (2013) *Ten Billion*. New York: Vintage Books.

Environmental Defence Fund. (2014) *Achieve Green: Grow Your Sustainability Goals ... And Your Bottom Line*, http://business.edf.org/.

Ernst & Young. (2012) *How Should Business Approach Carbon Neutrality? The Solutions and Benefits*. London: Ernst & Young, www.ey.com/ Publication/vwLUAssets/Informe_carbon/$FILE/Carbon_Neutrality_ v16.pdf.

Espeland, W. N. and Stevens, M. L. (1998) 'Commensuration as a Social Process', *Annual Review of Sociology* 24: 313–43.

Esposito, E. (2013) 'The Structures of Uncertainty: Performativity and Unpredictability in Economic Operations', *Economy and Society* 42(1): 102–29.

Esty, D. C. and Winston, A. S. (2006) *Green to Gold: How Smart Companies Use Environmental Strategy to Innovate, Create Value, and Build Competitive Advantage*. Hoboken, NJ: John Wiley & Sons.

Etzion, D. and Ferraro, F. (2010) 'The Role of Analogy in the Institutionalization of Sustainability Reporting', *Organization Science* 21(5): 1092–107.

Ewald, F. (1991) 'Insurance and Risk', in G. Burchell, C. Gordon, and P. Miller (eds) *The Foucault Effect*, pp. 197–210. London: Harvester/Wheatsheaf.

ExxonMobil. (2014) 'Energy and Carbon – Managing the Risks', 31 March, http://cdn.exxonmobil.com/~/media/global/files/other/2014/report--energy-and-carbon---managing-the-risks.pdf.

Ezzy, D. (1998) 'Theorizing Narrative Identity', *Sociological Quarterly* 39(2): 239–52.

Fairley, P. (2011) 'Will Electric Vehicles Finally Succeed?', *Technology Review* 114(1): 58–63.

Falck, O. and Heblich, S. (2007) 'Corporate Social Responsibility: Doing Well by Doing Good', *Business Horizons* 50(3): 247–54.

Farber, S. C., Costanza, R., and Wilson, M. A. (2002) 'Economic and Ecological Concepts for Valuing Ecosystem Services', *Ecological Economics* 41(3): 375–92.

Farbotko, C. and McGregor, H. V. (2010) 'Copenhagen, Climate Science and the Emotional Geographies of Climate Change', *Australian Geographer* 41(2): 159–66.

Feldman, D., Barbose, G., Margolis, R., Wiser, R., Darghouth, N., and Goodrich, A. (2012) *Photovoltaic (PV) Pricing Trends: Historical, Recent and Near-Term Projections*. Berkeley, CA: Lawrence Berkeley National Laboratory.

Feldman, L., Maibach, E. W., Roser-Renouf, C., and Leiserowitz, A. (2012) 'Climate on Cable: The Nature and Impact of Global Warming Coverage on Fox News, CNN, and MSNBC', *The International Journal of Press/Politics* 17(1): 3–31.

Fineman, S. (1993) 'Organizations as Emotional Arenas', in S. Fineman (ed) *Emotion in Organizations*, pp. 9–35. London: Sage.

(1996) 'Emotional Subtexts in Corporate Greening', *Organization Studies* 17(3): 479–500.

(1997) 'Constructing the Green Manager', *British Journal of Management* 8(1): 31–38.

(1999) 'Emotion and Organizing', in S. Clegg, C. Hardy, and W. Nord (eds) *Studying Organizations*, pp. 289–310. London: Sage.

(2004) 'Getting the Measure of Emotion– And the Cautionary Tale of Emotional Intelligence', *Human Relations* 57(6): 719–40.

(2010) 'Emotion in Organizations – A Critical Turn', in B. Sieben and Å. Wettergren (eds) *Emotionalizing Organizations and Organizing Emotions*, pp. 23–41. Basingstoke: Palgrave Macmillan.

Fleming, P. (2009) *Authenticity and the Cultural Politics of Work: New Forms of Informal Control*. Oxford: Oxford University Press.

Fleming, P. and Jones, M. T. (2013) *The End of Corporate Social Responsibility: Crisis and Critique*. London: Sage.

Fletcher, R. (2013) 'How I Learned to Stop Worrying and Love the Market: Virtualism, Disavowal, and Public Secrecy in Neoliberal Environmental Conservation', *Environment and Planning D: Society and Space* 31(5): 796–812.

Foderaro, L. W. (2014) 'Taking a Call for Climate Change to the Streets', *New York Times*, 21 September, www.nytimes.com/2014/09/22/nyregion/new-york-city-climate-change-march.html.

Ford. (2008) 'Why Would You Sit on a Soybean?', 18 November, www.youtube.com/watch?v=KelsWWnrua8.

Foster, J. B. (2000) *Marx's Ecology: Materialism and Nature*. New York: Monthly Review Press.

Foster, J. B., Clark, B., and York, R. (2010) *The Ecological Rift: Capitalism's War on the Earth*. New York: Monthly Review Press.

Foucault, M. (1991) 'Questions of Method', in G. Burchell, C. Gordon, and P. Miller (eds) *The Foucault Effect: Studies in Governmentality*, pp. 73–86. Chicago: University of Chicago Press.

   (2008) *The Birth of Biopolitics*. New York: Palgrave Macmillan.

Fourcade, M. (2011) 'Cents and Sensibility: Economic Valuation and the Nature of "Nature"', *American Journal of Sociology* 116(6): 1721–77.

Fox, N. J. (1999) 'Postmodern Reflections on "Risk", "Hazards" and Life Choices', in D. Lupton (ed) *Risk and Sociocultural Theory: New Directions and Perspectives*, pp. 12–33. Cambridge: Cambridge University Press.

Frankel, D., Ostrowski, K., and Pinner, D. (2014) 'The Disruptive Potential of Solar Power', *McKinsey Quarterly* (April): 50–55.

Fraser, N. (2013) 'A Triple Movement? Parsing the Politics of Crisis after Polanyi', *New Left Review* 81: 119–32.

   (2014) 'Behind Marx's Hidden Abode: For and Expanded Conception of Capitalism', *New Left Review* 86: 55–72.

Freed, J. (2012) 'BHP Acts on Climate Change', *Australian Financial Review*, 4 December: 16.

Friedman, M. (1970) 'The Social Responsibility of Business Is to Increase Its Profits', *New York Times Magazine*, 13 September: 33.

Funk, M. (2014) *Windfall: The Booming Business of Global Warming*. New York: Penguin.

Fuss, S., Canadell, J. G., Peters, G. P., Tavoni, M., Andrew, R. M., Ciais, P., Jackson, R. B., Jones, C. D., Kraxner, F., Nakicenovic, N., Le Quere, C., Raupach, M. R., Sharifi, A., Smith, P., and Yamagata, Y. (2014) 'Betting on Negative Emissions', *Nature Climate. Change* 4(10): 850–53.

Gaard, G. (1993) *Ecofeminism: Women, Animals, and Nature*. Philadelphia, PA: Temple University Press.

Gabriel, Y. (2000) *Storytelling in Organizations: Facts, Fictions, and Fantasies*. Oxford: Oxford University Press.

(2010) 'Beyond Scripts and Rules: Emotion Fantasy and Care in Contemporary Service Work', in B. Sieben and Å. Wettergren (eds) *Emotionalizing Organizations and Organizing Emotions*, pp. 23–41. Basingstoke: Palgrave Macmillan.

Galbraith, K. (2014) 'Churches Go Green by Shedding Fossil Fuel Holdings', *New York Times*, 15 October, www.nytimes.com/2014/10/16/business/international/churches-go-green-by-shedding-holdings-of-carbon-emitters.html.

Garland, J., Huising, R., and Struben, J. (2013) '"What If Technology Worked in Harmony with Nature?" Imagining Climate Change through Prius Advertisements', *Organization* 20(5): 679–704.

Garnaut, R. (2008) *The Garnaut Climate Change Review: Final Report*. Melbourne: Cambridge University Press.

GE. (2005) 'GE Launches Ecomagination to Develop Environmental Technologies', *BusinessWire*, 9 May, www.businesswire.com/news/home/20050509005663/en#.U_vpu_mSzTo.

GE. (2014) 'Childlike Imagination – What My Mom Does at GE', GE Channel, 5 February, www.youtube.com/watch?v=Co0qkWRqTdM.

Gerken, J. (2014) 'Utility-Sponsored Teacher Training at Mizzou Brings Climate Skepticism and Anti-EPA Message', *Huffington Post*, 28 August, www.huffingtonpost.com/2014/08/28/climate-change-teacher-training_n_5709357.html.

Giddens, A. (2009) *The Politics of Climate Change*. Cambridge: Polity Press.

Gilding, P. (2011) *The Great Disruption: Why the Climate Crisis Will Bring on the End of Shopping and the Birth of a New World*. New York: Bloomsbury Press.

Global Carbon Project. (2014) *Global Carbon Budget 2014*, www.globalcarbonproject.org/carbonbudget/14/hl-full.htm.

Global Commission on the Economy and Climate. (2014) *Better Growth, Better Climate: The New Climate Economy Report*. New York: GCEC, http://newclimateeconomy.report/.

Godfrey, M. and Tranter, C. (2011) 'Thousands Demonstrate for and against Carbon Tax', *Sydney Morning Herald*, 2 April: www.smh.com.au/environment/climate-change/thousands-demonstrate-for-and-against-carbon-tax-20110402-1cs36.html.

Goleman, D. (1995) *Emotional Intelligence: Why It Can Matter More Than IQ*. New York: Bantam.

Goodman, A. (2011) 'Entrepreneur: Capitalism Will Save World from Climate Crisis to Preserve Markets for ipads, Coke', *Democracy*

Now!, 8 December, www.democracynow.org/2011/12/8/entrepreneur
_capitalism_will_save_world_from.

Goodwin, J., Jasper, J. M., and Polletta, F. (eds). (2001) *Passionate
Politics: Emotions and Social Movements*. Chicago: University of
Chicago Press.

Gordon, K. (2014) *Risky Business: The Economic Risks of Climate Change
in the United States*. New York: RiskyBusiness.org.

Gordon, S. L. (1990) 'Social Structural Effects on Emotions', in T. D. Kemper
(ed) *Research Agendas in the Sociology of Emotions*, pp. 134–79.
Albany: State University of New York Press.

Gosling, J. and Case, P. (2013) 'Social Dreaming and Ecocentric
Ethics: Sources of Non-Rational Insight in the Face of Climate Change
Catastrophe', *Organization* 20(5): 705–21.

Gould, K. A., Pellow, D. N., and Schnaiberg, A. (2004) 'Interrogating the
Treadmill of Production: Everything You Wanted to Know about the
Treadmill but Were Afraid to Ask', *Organization & Environment*
17(3): 296–316.

Gramsci, A. (1971) *Selections from the Prison Notebooks*. New York:
International Publishers.

Greenfeld, K. T. (2013) 'Bill McKibben's Battle against the Keystone XL
Pipeline', *Bloomberg Businessweek*, 28 February, www.businessweek.com/
articles/2013-02-28/bill-mckibbens-battle-against-the-keystone-xl-pipeline.

Greenpeace. (2007) 'Angry Kid', 8 February, www.youtube.com/
watch?v=BY7875_rv1s.

Griffin, D. and Anchukaitis, K. J. (2014) 'How Unusual Is the 2012–2014
California Drought?', *Geophysical Research Letters* 41(24):
9017–23.

Griffiths, A., Haigh, N., and Rassias, J. (2007) 'A Framework of Understanding
Institutional Governance Systems and Climate Change: The Case of
Australia', *European Management Journal* 25(6): 415–27.

Grim, R. (2011) 'Rupert Murdoch: News Corp Is Carbon Neutral',
Huffington Post, 1 March, www.huffingtonpost.com/2011/03/01/
rupert-murdoch-news-corp-carbon-neutral_n_829640.html.

Gripp, G. (2013) 'On the Acceptance of Near-Term Extinction', *Nature Bats
Last*, 11 May, http://guymcpherson.com/2013/05/on-the-acceptance
-of-near-term-extinction/.

Grossman, G. M. and Krueger, A. B. (1995) 'Economic Growth and the
Environment', *The Quarterly Journal of Economics* 110(2): 353–77.

Guggenheim, D. (2006) *An Inconvenient Truth*. Paramount Classics.

Guha, R. (2000) *Environmentalism: A Global History*. New York:
Longman.

Gunther, M. (2014) 'General Mills Joins Climate Change Fight and Requires Pledges from Suppliers Too', *The Guardian*, 29 July, www.theguardian .com/sustainable-business/2014/jul/28/general-mills-climate-change -lobbying-suppliers-kelloggs-oxfam.

Haigh, N. and Griffiths, A. (2012) 'Surprise as a Catalyst for Including Climatic Change in the Strategic Environment', *Business & Society* 51(1): 89–120.

Hajer, M. (1995) *The Politics of Environmental Discourse: Ecological Modernization and the Policy Process*. Oxford: Oxford University Press.

Hamilton, C. (2010) *Requiem for a Species: Why We Resist the Truth about Climate Change*. London: Earthscan.

  (2013) *Earthmasters: Playing God with the Climate*. Sydney: Allen & Unwin.

  (2014) 'The New Environmentalism Will Lead Us to Disaster', *Scientific American*, 19 June, www.scientificamerican.com/article/the -new-environmentalism-will-lead-us-to-disaster/.

Hamilton, C. and Denniss, R. (2005) *Affluenza: When Too Much Is Never Enough*. Sydney: Allen & Unwin.

Hannam, P. (2007) 'Rupert Goes Green and Walks to Work', *Sydney Morning Herald*, 14 May, www.smh.com.au/news/business/rupert -goes-green-and-walks-to-work/2007/05/13/1178994998743.html.

Hansen, J. (2009) *Storms of My Grandchildren: The Truth about the Coming Climate Catastrophe and Our Last Chance to Save Humanity*. New York: Bloomsbury.

Hansen, J., Sato, M., Kharecha, P., Russell, G., Lea, D. W., and Siddall, M. (2007) 'Climate Change and Trace Gases', *Philosophical Transactions of the Royal Society A* 365(1856): 1925–54.

Hansen, J. E. and Sato, M. (2012) 'Paleoclimate Implications for Human-Made Climate Change', in A. Berger, F. Mesinger, and D. Sijacki (eds) *Climate Change*, pp. 21–47. Springer Vienna.

Harré, R., Brockmeier, J., and Mühlhäusler, P. (1999) *Greenspeak: A Study of Environmental Discourse*. Thousand Oaks, CA: Sage.

Harris, L. C. and Crane, A. (2002) 'The Greening of Organizational Culture: Management Views on the Depth, Degree and Diffusion of Change', *Journal of Organizational Change Management* 15(3): 214–34.

Hart, S. L. (2010) *Capitalism at the Crossroads: Next Generation Business Strategies for a Post-Crisis World*. Upper Saddle River, NJ: Wharton School Publishing.

Harvey, D. (1982) *The Limits to Capital*. London: Basil Blackwell.

(2005) *A Brief History of Neoliberalism*. Oxford: Oxford University Press.

(2007) 'Neoliberalism as Creative Destruction', *The ANNALS of the American Academy of Political and Social Science* 610(1): 21–44.

(2014) *Seventeen Contradictions and the End of Capitalism*. Oxford: Oxford University Press.

Hassard, J., McCann, L., and Morris, J. (2011) 'Employment Relations and Managerial Work: An International Perspective', in K. Townsend and A. Wilkinson (eds) *Research Handbook on the Future of Work and Employment Relations*, pp. 150–66. Cheltenham: Edward Elgar.

Hawken, P., Lovins, A., and Lovins, L. H. (1999) *Natural Capitalism: Creating the Next Industrial Revolution*. Boston: Little Brown & Co.

Hawker, M. (2007) 'Climate Change and the Global Insurance Industry', *Geneva Papers on Risk & Insurance – Issues & Practice* 32(1): 22–28.

Heede, R. (2014) 'Tracing Anthropogenic Carbon Dioxide and Methane Emissions to Fossil Fuel and Cement Producers, 1854–2010', *Climatic Change* 122(1–2): 229–41.

Heinberg, R. (2014) 'Paul Krugman's Errors and Omissions', *Post Carbon Institute*, 22 September, www.postcarbon.org/paul-krugmans-errors-and-omissions/.

Hickman, L. (2011) 'Canadian Campaign Puts the Spin on "Ethical Oil"', *The Guardian*, 28 July, www.theguardian.com/environment/blog/2011/jul/28/oil-tar-sands-canada-ethical.

Hillman, A. J., Keim, G. D., and Schuler, D. (2004) 'Corporate Political Activity: A Review and Research Agenda', *Journal of Management* 30(6): 837–57.

Hochschild, A. R. (1979) 'Emotion Work, Feeling Rules, and Social Structure', *The American Journal of Sociology* 85(3): 551–75.

Hodgkinson, J. H., Littleboy, A., Howden, M., Moffat, K., and Loechel, B. (2010) 'Climate Adaptation in the Australian Mining and Exploration Industries', CSIRO Climate Adaptation Flagship Working Paper No. 5, www.csiro.au/resources/CAF-working-papers.html.

Hoffman, A. J. (2001) *From Heresy to Dogma: An Institutional History of Corporate Environmentalism*. Stanford, CA: Stanford University Press.

(2005) 'Climate Change Strategy: The Business Logic behind Voluntary Greenhouse Gas Reductions', *California Management Review* 47(3): 21–46.

(2007) *Carbon Strategies: How Leading Companies Are Reducing Their Climate Change Footprint*. Ann Arbor, MI: University of Michigan Press.

(2010) 'Reconciling Professional and Personal Value Systems: The Spiritually Motivated Manager as Organizational Entrepreneur', in R. A. Giacalone and C. L. Jurkiewicz (eds) *Handbook of Workplace Spirituality and Organizational Performance*, pp. 155–70. Armonk, NY: M.E. Sharp.

(2011a) 'The Culture and Discourse of Climate Skepticism', *Strategic Organization* 9(1): 1–8.

(2011b) 'Talking Past Each Other? Cultural Framing under Climate Skeptical and Climate Convinced Logics', *Organization & Environment* 24(1): 3–33.

(2012) 'Climate Science as Culture War', *Stanford Social Innovation Review* 10(4): 30–37.

Hoffman, A. J. and Devereaux Jennings, P. (2011) 'The BP Oil Spill as a Cultural Anomaly? Institutional Context, Conflict, and Change', *Journal of Management Inquiry* 20(2): 100–12.

Hoffman, A. J. and Woody, J. G. (2008) *Climate Change: What's Your Business Strategy?* Boston, MA: Harvard Business School Publishing Corporation.

Holliday, C. O., Schmidheiny, S., and Watts, P. (2002) *Walking the Talk: The Business Case for Sustainable Development*. Aizlewood's Mill: Greenleaf Publishing.

Holmes, M. (2010) 'The Emotionalization of Reflexivity', *Sociology* 44(1): 139–54.

Howarth, R. W., Ingraffea, A., and Engelder, T. (2011a) 'Natural Gas: Should Fracking Stop?', *Nature* 477(7364): 271–75.

Howarth, R. W., Santoro, R., and Ingraffea, A. (2011b) 'Methane and the Greenhouse-Gas Footprint of Natural Gas from Shale Formations', *Climatic Change* 106(4): 679–90.

Hughes, L. (2011) 'Climate Change and Australia: Key Vulnerable Regions', *Regional Environmental Change* 11(1): 189–95.

Hulme, M. (2009) *Why We Disagree about Climate Change: Understanding Controversy, Inaction and Opportunity*. Cambridge: Cambridge University Press.

Humes, E. (2011) *Force of Nature: The Unlikely Story of Wal-Mart's Green Revolution*. New York: Harper-Collins.

Ibarra, H. and Barbulascu, R. (2010) 'Identity as Narrative: Prevalence, Effectiveness, and Consequences of Narrative Identity Work in Macro Work Role Transitions', *Academy of Management Review* 35(1): 135–54.

IEA. (2013) *Resources to Reserves 2013: Oil, Gas and Coal Technologies for the Energy Markets of the Future*. Paris: International Energy Agency.

Inez Ward, J. (2014) 'Missed Targets: When Companies Fail to Keep Their Key Sustainability Promises', *The Guardian*, 21 July, www.the-guardian.com/sustainable-business/blog/2014/jul/21/sustainability-goals-promise-broken-failure-target-walmart-disney.

IPCC. (2012) *Managing the Risks of Extreme Events and Disasters to Advance Climate Change Adaptation: Special Report of Working Groups I and II of the Intergovernmental Panel on Climate Change*. Cambridge: Cambridge University Press.

IPCC. (2013) *Climate Change 2013: The Physical Science Basis. Working Group I Contribution to the Fifth Assessment Report of the Intergovernmental Panel on Climate Change*. Cambridge: Cambridge University Press.

IPCC. (2014a) *Climate Change 2014: Impacts, Adaptation, and Vulnerability. Part A: Global and Sectoral Aspects. Contribution of Working Group II to the Fifth Assessment Report of the Intergovernmental Panel on Climate Change*. Cambridge: Cambridge University Press.

IPCC. (2014b) *Climate Change 2014: Mitigation of Climate Change. Contribution of Working Group III to the Fifth Assessment Report of the Intergovernmental Panel on Climate Change*. Cambridge: Cambridge University Press.

IPCC. (2014c) *Climate Change 2014 Synthesis Report: Summary for Policymakers*. www.ipcc.ch/pdf/assessment-report/ar5/syr/AR5_SYR_FINAL_SPM.pdf.

Jackson, T. (2009) *Prosperity without Growth: Economics for a Finite Planet*. London: Earthscan.

Jacques, P. J., Dunlap, R. E., and Freeman, M. (2008) 'The Organisation of Denial: Conservative Think Tanks and Environmental Scepticism', *Environmental Politics* 17(3): 349–85.

Jagd, S. (2007) 'Economics of Convention and New Economic Sociology: Mutual Inspiration and Dialogue', *Current Sociology* 55(1): 75–91.

   (2011) 'Pragmatic Sociology and Competing Orders of Worth in Organizations', *European Journal of Social Theory* 14(3): 343–59.

Jameson, F. (2003) 'Future City', *New Left Review* 21 (May–June): 65–80.

Jamison, A. (2001) *The Making of Green Knowledge: Environmental Politics and Cultural Transformation*. Cambridge: Cambridge University Press.

Jasanoff, S. (2010) 'A New Climate for Society', *Theory, Culture & Society* 27(2–3): 233–53.

Jermier, J. M., Forbes, L. C., Benn, S., and Orsato, R. J. (2006) 'The New Corporate Environmentalism and Green Politics', in S. R. Clegg, C. Hardy, T. B. Lawrence, and W. R. Nord (eds) *The Sage Handbook of Organization Studies*, pp. 618–50. London: Sage.

Jessop, B. (2001) 'Regulationist and Autopoieticist Reflections on Polanyi's Account of Market Economies and the Market Society', *New Political Economy* 6(2): 213–32.

Kahn, J. and Yardley, J. (2007) 'As China Roars, Pollution Reaches Deadly Extremes', *New York Times*, 26 August: 1.

Keith, D. W. (2000) 'Geoengineering the Climate: History and Prospect 1', *Annual Review of Energy and the Environment* 25(1): 245–84.

Keller, D. P., Feng, E. Y., and Oschlies, A. (2014) 'Potential Climate Engineering Effectiveness and Side Effects during a High Carbon Dioxide-Emission Scenario', *Nature Communications* 5: 3304.

Kenis, A. and Lievens, M. (2014) 'Searching for 'the Political' in Environmental Politics', *Environmental Politics* 23(4): 531–48.

Keys, T. S., Malnight, T. W., and Stoklund, C. K. (2013) *Corporate Clout 2013: Time for Responsible Capitalism*. Rivaz: Strategy Dynamics Global SA.

King, D. S. (2006) 'Activists and Emotional Reflexivity: Toward Touraine's Subject as Social Movement', *Sociology* 40(5): 873–91.

Kingsnorth, P. and Hine, D. (2009) *Uncivilisation: The Dark Mountain Manifesto*. http://dark-mountain.net/about/manifesto/.

Kinkela, D. (2011) *DDT and the American Century: Global Health, Environmental Politics, and the Pesticide That Changed the World*. Chapel Hill, NC: University of North Carolina Press.

Klein, N. (2007) *The Shock Doctrine: The Rise of Disaster Capitalism*. New York: Picador.

(2014) *This Changes Everything: Capitalism vs. The Climate*. New York: Simon & Schuster.

Knox-Hayes, J. and Levy, D. L. (2011) 'The Politics of Carbon Disclosure as Climate Governance', *Strategic Organization* 9(1): 91–99.

Kolbert, E. (2006) *Field Notes from a Catastrophe: Man, Nature, and Climate Change*. New York: Bloomsbury.

(2014a) 'Can Climate Change Cure Capitalism?', *The New York Review of Books*, 4 December, www.nybooks.com/articles/archives/2014/dec/04/can-climate-change-cure-capitalism/.

(2014b) *The Sixth Extinction: An Unnatural History*. New York: Henry Holt.

Kolk, A. and Levy, D. (2001) 'Winds of Change: Corporate Strategy, Climate Change and Oil Multinationals', *European Management Journal* 19(5): 501–9.

Kolk, A. and Pinkse, J. (2004) 'Market Strategies for Climate Change', *European Management Journal* 22(3): 304–14.

(2005) 'Business Responses to Climate Change: Identifying Emergent Strategies', *California Management Review* 47(3): 6–20.

(2007) 'Multinationals' Political Activities on Climate Change', *Business & Society* 46(2): 201–28.

Kopytko, N. and Perkins, J. (2011) 'Climate Change, Nuclear Power, and the Adaptation–Mitigation Dilemma', *Energy Policy* 39(1): 318–33.

Kosich, D. (2007) 'Defying Mining's Global Warming Skeptics', *Mineweb*, 11 September, www.mineweb.com/archive/defying-minings-global-warming-skeptics-rio-tinto-joins-u-s-climate-change-coalition.

Kristol, I. (1977) 'On Corporate Philanthropy', *Wall Street Journal*, 21 March: 18.

Krugman, P. (2014) 'Errors and Emissions', *New York Times*, 18 September, www.nytimes.com/2014/09/19/opinion/paul-krugman-co uld-fighting-global-warming-be-cheap-and-free.html.

Kuhn, T. (2006) 'A "Demented Work Ethic" and a "Lifestyle Firm": Discourse, Identity, and Workplace Time Commitments', *Organization Studies* 27(9): 1339–58.

Kurucz, E. C., Colbert, B. A., and Wheeler, D. (2008) 'The Business Case for Corporate Social Responsibility', in A. Crane, A. McWilliams, D. Matten, J. Moon, and D. S. Siegel (eds) *The Oxford Handbook of Corporate Social Responsibility*, pp. 83–112. Oxford: Oxford University Press.

Laclau, E. (2005) *On Populist Reason*. London: Verso.

Laclau, E. and Mouffe, C. (2001) *Hegemony and Socialist Strategy: Towards a Radical Democratic Politics*. London: Verso.

Lamb, N. and Litterman, B. (2014) 'Really? Exxonmobil Left the Risk out of Its Climate Risk Report', *GreenBiz.com*, 28 May, www.greenbiz.com/blog/2014/05/28/exxonmobil-left-risk-out-climate-risk-report.

Landler, M. (2014) 'U.S. And China Reach Climate Accord after Months of Talks', *New York Times*, 11 November, www.nytimes.com/2014/11/12/world/asia/china-us-xi-obama-apec.html.

Lash, J. and Wellington, F. (2007) 'Competitive Advantage on a Warming Planet', *Harvard Business Review* 85(3): 94–102.

Lê, J. K. (2013) 'How Constructions of the Future Shape Organizational Responses: Climate Change and the Canadian Oil Sands', *Organization* 20(5): 722–42.

Lefsrud, L. M. and Meyer, R. E. (2012) 'Science or Science Fiction? Professionals' Discursive Construction of Climate Change', *Organization Studies* 33(11): 1477–506.

Leifer, R. and Delbecq, A. (1978) 'Organizational/Environmental Interchange: A Model of Boundary Spanning Activity', *Academy of Management Review* 3(1): 40–50.

Leiserowitz, A., Maibach, E., Roser-Renouf, C., and Smith, N. (2011) *Global Warming's Six Americas, May 2011*. New Haven, CT: Yale Project on Climate Change Communication, http://environment.yale.edu/climate/files/SixAmericasMay2011.pdf.

Leopold, A. (1966) *A Sand County Almanac: With Other Essays on Conservation from Round River*. New York: Oxford University Press.

Levant, E. (2010) *Ethical Oil: The Case for Canada's Oil Sands*. Toronto: McClelland & Stewart.

Leviston, Z., Leitch, A., Greenhill, M., Leonard, R., and Walker, I. (2011) *Australians' Views of Climate Change*. Canberra: CSIRO.

Levy, D. L. (2008) 'Political Contestation in Global Production Networks', *Academy of Management Review* 33(4): 943–62.

Levy, D. L. and Egan, D. (1998) 'Capital Contests: National and Transnational Channels of Corporate Influence on the Climate Change Negotiations', *Politics and Society* 26(3): 337–61.

(2003) 'A Neo-Gramscian Approach to Corporate Political Strategy: Conflict and Accommodation in the Climate Change Negotiations', *Journal of Management Studies* 40(4): 803–29.

Levy, D. L. and Kolk, A. (2002) 'Strategic Responses to Global Climate Change: Conflicting Pressures on Multinationals in the Oil Industry', *Business and Politics* 4(3): 275–300.

Levy, D. L. and Spicer, A. (2013) 'Contested Imaginaries and the Cultural Political Economy of Climate Change', *Organization* 20(5): 659–78.

Lewis, S. C. and Karoly, D. J. (2013) 'Anthropogenic Contributions to Australia's Record Summer Temperatures of 2013', *Geophysical Research Letters* 40(14): 3705–9.

Lin, B. and Sun, C. (2010) 'Evaluating Carbon Dioxide Emissions in International Trade of China', *Energy Policy* 38(1): 613–21.

Linnenluecke, M. and Griffiths, A. (2010) 'Beyond Adaptation: Resilience for Business in Light of Climate Change and Weather Extremes', *Business & Society* 49(3): 477–511.

Linnenluecke, M., Stathakis, A., and Griffiths, A. (2011) 'Firm Relocation as Adaptive Response to Climate Change and Weather Extremes', *Global Environmental Change* 21(1): 123–33.

Little, A. (2005) 'GE Kicks Off Ambitious Green Initiative', *Grist*, 11 May, http://grist.org/article/little-ge/.

Lohmann, L. (2006) 'Carbon Trading: A Critical Conversation on Climate Change, Privatisation and Power', *Development Dialogue* (48): 31–218.

(2009) 'Toward a Different Debate in Environmental Accounting: The Cases of Carbon and Cost-Benefit', *Accounting, Organizations and Society* 34(3–4): 499–534.

(2010) 'Uncertainty Markets and Carbon Markets: Variations on Polanyian Themes', *New Political Economy* 15(2): 225–54.

Loseke, D. R. (2009) 'Examining Emotion as Discourse: Emotion Codes and Presidential Speeches Justifying War', *Sociological Quarterly* 50(3): 497–524.

Loseke, D. R. and Kusenbach, M. (2008) 'The Social Construction of Emotion', in J. A. Holstein and J. F. Gubrium (eds) *Handbook of Constructionist Research*, pp. 511–30. New York: Guilford Press.

Lovelock, J. (2000) *Gaia: A New Look at Life on Earth*. Oxford: Oxford University Press.

(2009) *The Vanishing Face of Gaia: A Final Warning*. New York: Basic Books.

Lukacs, M. (2012) 'World's Biggest Geoengineering Experiment "Violates" UN Rules', *The Guardian*, 15 October, www.guardian.co.uk/environment/2012/oct/15/pacific-iron-fertilisation-geoengineering.

Lukes, S. (1991) *Moral Conflict and Politics*. Oxford: Clarendon Press.

(2005) 'Invasions of the Market', in M. Miller (ed) *Worlds of Capitalism: Institutions, Governance and Economic Change in the Era of Globalization*, pp. 289–311. London: Routledge.

Lupton, D. (1999) *Risk*. London: Routledge.

(2006) 'Sociology and Risk', in G. Mythen and S. Walklate (eds) *Beyond the Risk Society: Critical Reflections on Risk and Human Security*, pp. 11–24. Maidenhead: McGraw-Hill.

Lüthi, D., Le Floch, M., Bereiter, B., Blunier, T., Barnola, J.-M., Siegenthaler, U., Raynaud, D., Jouzel, J., Fischer, H., Kawamura, K., and Stocker, T. F. (2008) 'High-Resolution Carbon Dioxide Concentration Record 650,000–800,000 Years before Present', *Nature* 453(7193): 379–82.

Lynas, M. (2007) *Six Degrees: Our Future on a Hotter Planet*. London: HarperCollins.

Macalister, T. (2009) 'BP Shuts Alternative Energy HQ', *The Guardian*, 29 June, www.theguardian.com/business/2009/jun/28/bp-alternative-energy.

MacKenzie, D. (2006) *An Engine, Not a Camera: How Financial Models Shape Markets*. Cambridge, MA: MIT Press.

Makower, J. (2014) 'Exxon, Stranded Assets and the New Math', *GreenBiz.com*, 24 March, www.greenbiz.com/blog/2014/03/24/exxon-stranded-assets-and-new-math.

Mann, M. (2012) *The Hockey Stick and the Climate Wars: Dispatches from the Front Lines*. New York: Columbia University Press.

(2014) 'Earth Will Cross the Climate Danger Threshold by 2036', *Scientific American*, 18 March, www.scientificamerican.com/article/earth-will-cross-the-climate-danger-threshold-by-2036/.

Mann, M. E., Bradley, R. S., and Hughes, M. K. (1999) 'Northern Hemisphere Temperatures during the Past Millennium: Inferences, Uncertainties, and Limitations', *Geophysical Research Letters* 26(6): 759–62.

Manne, R. (2011) 'Bad News: Murdoch's *Australian* and the Shaping of the Nation', *Quarterly Essay* (43): 1–119.

Martin, B. and Wajcman, J. (2004) 'Markets, Contingency and Preferences: Contemporary Managers' Narrative Identities', *Sociological Review* 52(2): 240–64.

Marx, K. (1976) *Capital: A Critique of Political Economy*. Harmondsworth: Penguin.

Marx, K. and Engels, F. ([1848] 1998) *The Communist Manifesto*. London: Verso.

Masters, J. (2012) '2011's Billion-Dollar Disasters: Is Climate Change to Blame?', *Weatherwise* 65(2): 12–19.

Matten, D. and Crane, A. (2005) 'Corporate Citizenship: Toward an Extended Theoretical Conceptualization', *Academy of Management Review* 30(1): 166–79.

McAdams, D. P. (1996) 'Personality, Modernity, and the Storied Self: A Contemporary Framework for Studying Persons', *Psychological Inquiry* 7(4): 295.

(2006) *The Redemptive Self: Stories Americans Live By*. New York: Oxford University Press.

McCright, A. M. and Dunlap, R. E. (2003) 'Defeating Kyoto: The Conservative Movement's Impact on US Climate Change Policy', *Social Problems* 50(3): 348–73.

(2010) 'Anti-Reflexivity: The American Conservative Movement's Success in Undermining Climate Science and Policy', *Theory, Culture & Society* 27(2/3): 100–33.

(2011a) 'Cool Dudes: The Denial of Climate Change among Conservative White Males in the United States', *Global Environmental Change* 21(4): 1163–72.

(2011b) 'The Politicization of Climate Change and Polarization in the American Public's View of Global Warming, 2001–2010', *Sociological Quarterly* 52(2): 155–94.

McDonald's Australia. (2014) 'Meet Brad, 28, Sustainability Manager', 29 January, www.youtube.com/watch?v=_rBXdT2dWVw.

McKibben, B. (2010) *Eaarth: Making a Life on a Tough New Planet*. New York: Times Books.

McKibben, B.(2012) 'The Reckoning', *Rolling Stone* (1162): 52–58, 60.

McKibben, B. (2013a) 'Don't Imagine the Future – It's Already Here', *Organization* 20(5): 745–47.

(2013b) 'The Case for Fossil-Fuel Divestment', *Rolling Stone*, 22 February, www.rollingstone.com/politics/news/the-case-for-fossil-fuel-divestment-20130222.

(2013c) *Oil and Honey: The Education of an Unlikely Activist*. New York: Macmillan.

McNay, L. (1999) 'Gender and Narrative Identity', *Journal of Political Ideologies* 4(3): 315–36.

(2008) *Against Recognition*. Cambridge: Polity Press.

McPherson, G. R. (2013) *Going Dark*. Baltimore, MD: Publish America.

Meadows, D. H., Meadows, D. L., Randers, J., and Behrens, W. W. (1972) *The Limits to Growth*. New York: Potomac Associates.

Meinshausen, M., Meinshausen, N., Hare, W., Raper, S. C. B., Frieler, K., Knutti, R., Frame, D. J., and Allen, M. R. (2009) 'Greenhouse-Gas

Emission Targets for Limiting Global Warming to 2°C', *Nature* 458(7242): 1158–62.

Melillo, J. M., Richmond, T., and Yohe, G. W. (eds). (2014) *Climate Change Impacts in the United States: The Third National Climate Assessment.* Washington, DC: US Government Printing Office.

Meyerson, D. E. and Scully, M. A. (1995) 'Tempered Radicalism and the Politics of Ambivalence and Change', *Organization Science* 6(5): 585–600.

Miles, M. and Huberman, A. M. (1994) *Qualitative Data Analysis: An Expanded Sourcebook.* Thousand Oaks, CA: Sage.

Mills, E. (2009) 'A Global Review of Insurance Industry Responses to Climate Change', *Geneva Papers on Risk & Insurance – Issues & Practice* 34(3): 323–59.

Mitroff, I. I. and Pearson, C. M. (1993) *Crisis Management.* San Francisco: Jossey-Bass.

Mol, A. P. and Sonnenfeld, D. A. (2000) 'Ecological Modernisation around the World: An Introduction', in A. P. Mol and D. A. Sonnenfeld (eds) *Ecological Modernisation around the World: Perspectives and Critical Debates*, pp. 3–14. London: Frank Cass.

Mol, A. P. J. (2002) 'Ecological Modernization and the Global Economy', *Global Environmental Politics* 2(2): 92–115.

Mol, A. P. J. and Spaargaren, G. (2000) 'Ecological Modernisation Theory in Debate: A Review', *Environmental Politics* 9(1): 17–49.

Monbiot, G. (2011) 'Why Fukushima Made Me Stop Worrying and Love Nuclear Power', *The Guardian*, 22 March, www.theguardian.com/commentisfree/2011/mar/21/pro-nuclear-japan-fukushima.

(2013) 'This Transatlantic Trade Deal Is a Full-Frontal Assault on Democracy', *The Guardian*, 5 November, www.theguardian.com/commentisfree/2013/nov/04/us-trade-deal-full-frontal-assault-on-democracy.

Mooney, C. (2005a) *The Republican War on Science.* New York: Basic Books.

(2005b) 'Some Like It Hot', *Mother Jones*, May/June, www.motherjones.com/environment/2005/05/some-it-hot.

(2014) 'Why the Scientific Case against Fracking Keeps Getting Stronger', *Mother Jones*, 15 August, www.motherjones.com/environment/2014/08/inquiring-minds-anthony-ingraffea-science-fracking-methane.

Morgan, G. (1986) *Images of Organization.* Beverly Hills, CA: Sage.

Moser, S. C. (2007) 'More Bad News: The Risk of Neglecting Emotional Responses to Climate Change Information', in S. C. Moser and L. Dilling (eds) *Creating a Climate for Change: Communicating Climate Change and Facilitating Social Change*, pp. 64–80. New York: Cambridge University Press.

Naess, A. (1973) 'The Shallow and the Deep, Long-Range Ecology Movement. A Summary', *Inquiry* 16(1–4): 95–100.

Natural Capital Committee. (2014) *The State of Natural Capital: Restoring Our Natural Assets.* www.naturalcapitalcommittee.org/state-of-natural -capital-reports.html.

Nestlé. (2010) *Creating Shared Value and Rural Development Summary Report.* Vevey: Nestlé.

Neubacher, A. (2012) 'Interview with Richard Branson: "Climate Change Is a Huge Opportunity"', *Spiegel International,* 21 June, www .spiegel.de/international/business/richard-branson-discusses-climate -change-business-opportunities-a-839985.html.

Neuhoff, K. (2011) *Climate Policy after Copenhagen: The Role of Carbon Pricing.* Cambridge: Cambridge University Press.

New, M., Liverman, D., Schroder, H., and Anderson, K. (2011) 'Four Degrees and Beyond: The Potential for a Global Temperature Increase of Four Degrees and Its Implications', *Philosophical Transactions of the Royal Society A: Mathematical, Physical and Engineering Sciences* 369(1934): 6–19.

Newell, P. and Paterson, M. (2010) *Climate Capitalism: Global Warming and the Transformation of the Global Economy.* Cambridge: Cambridge University Press.

Nichols, W. (2014) 'Shell Rejects "Alarmist" Carbon Bubble Risks', BusinessGreen http://www.businessgreen.com/bg/analysis/2345604/ shell-rejects-alarmist-carbon-bubble-risks.

Nikiforuk, A. (2010) *Tar Sands: Dirty Oil and the Future of a Continent.* Vancouver: Greystone Books.

Nissan. (2010) 'Nissan Leaf Polar Bear', 10 September, www.youtube.com/ watch?v=VRZNA_3K2zA.

Nordhaus, T. and Shellenberger, M. (2007) *Break Through: From the Death of Environmentalism to the Politics of Possibility.* New York: Houghton Mifflin.

Nordhaus, W. D. and Kokkelenberg, E. C. (eds). (1999) *Nature's Numbers: Expanding the National Economic Accounts to Include the Environment.* Washington, DC: National Academy Press.

Norgaard, K. M. (2006) '"People Want to Protect Themselves a Little Bit": Emotions, Denial, and Social Movement Nonparticipation', *Sociological Inquiry* 76(3): 372–96.

Norman, W. and MacDonald, C. (2004) 'Getting to the Bottom of "Triple Bottom Line"', *Business Ethics Quarterly* 14(2): 243–62.

NSIDC. (2012) 'Arctic Sea Ice Extent Settles at Record Seasonal Minimum', *National Snow and Ice Data Center,* 19 September, http://nsidc.org/arcticseaicenews/2012/09/arctic-sea-ice -extent-settles-at-record-seasonal-minimum/.

Nyberg, D., Spicer, A., and Wright, C. (2013) 'Incorporating Citizens: Corporate Political Engagement with Climate Change in Australia', *Organization* 20(3): 433–53.

Nyberg, D. and Wright, C. (2012) 'Justifying Business Responses to Climate Change: Discursive Strategies of Similarity and Difference', *Environment and Planning A* 44(8): 1819–35.

(2013) 'Corporate Corruption of the Environment: Sustainability as a Process of Compromise', *The British Journal of Sociology* 64(3): 405–24.

O'Connor, J. (1988) 'Capitalism, Nature, Socialism a Theoretical Introduction', *Capitalism Nature Socialism* 1(1): 11–38.

O'Neill, S. and Nicholson-Cole, S. (2009) '"Fear Won't Do It": Promoting Positive Engagement with Climate Change through Visual and Iconic Representations', *Science Communication* 30(3): 355–79.

Oreskes, N. and Conway, E. M. (2010) *Merchants of Doubt: How a Handful of Scientists Obscured the Truth on Issues from Tobacco Smoke to Global Warming*. New York: Bloomsbury Press.

(2014) *The Collapse of Western Civilization: A View from the Future*. New York: Columbia University Press.

Orsato, R. J. (2009) *Sustainability Strategies: When Does It Pay to Be Green?* London: Palgrave Macmillan.

Ottman, J. A. (2011) *The New Rules of Green Marketing: Strategies, Tools, and Inspiration for Sustainable Branding*. San Francisco: Berrett-Koehler.

Owen, D. (2011) *The Conundrum: How Scientific Innovation, Increased Efficiency and Good Intentions Make Our Climate and Energy Problems Worse*. New York: Penguin.

PAGES 2k Consortium. (2013) 'Continental-Scale Temperature Variability during the Past Two Millennia', *Nature Geoscience* 6(5): 339–46.

Painter, J. (2011) *Poles Apart: The International Reporting of Climate Scepticism*. Oxford: Reuters Institute for the Study of Journalism.

Parkinson, G. (2014a) 'Greg Hunt: The "Extreme Left Is against Electricity"', *RenewEconomy*, 4 August, http://reneweconomy.com.au/2014/greg-hunt-the-extreme-left-is-against-electricity-44297.

(2014b) 'Solar's Dramatic Cost Fall May Herald Energy Price Deflation', *RenewEconomy*, 11 April, http://reneweconomy.com.au/2014/solars-dramatic-cost-fall-heralds-energy-price-deflation-76250.

Parsons, T. (1960) *Structure and Process in Modern Societies*. Glencoe: Free Press.

Patenaude, G. (2010) 'Climate Class for Business Schools', *Nature* 466(7302): 30.

Patrick, A. O. (2014) 'BHP's Andrew Mackenzie Brings Leftist Past to Bear in Defense of Global Coal Industry', *Washington Post*, 2 August, www.washingtonpost.com/world/asia_pacific/bhps-andrew-macken-zie-brings-leftist-past-to-bear-in-defense-of-global-coal-industry/2014/08/02/686a67a2-198d-11e4-9349-84d4a85be981_story.html.

Peabody Energy. (2013) *Advanced Energy for Life: Let's Brighten the Many Faces of Global Energy Poverty*. www.advancedenergyforlife.com/sites/default/files/Advanced%20Energy%20for%20Life%20Brochure_1.pdf.

Pearse, G. (2007) *High & Dry: John Howard, Climate Change and the Selling of Australia's Future*. Camberwell: Viking.

(2009) 'Quarry Vision: Coal, Climate Change and the End of the Resources Boom', *Quarterly Essay* 33: 1–122.

(2010) 'King Coal', *The Monthly* (May): 20–26.

(2012) *Greenwash: Big Brands and Carbon Scams*. Collingwood: Black Inc.

PERI. (2013) 'Toxic 100 Air Polluters', *Political Economy Research Institute, University of Massachusetts Amherst*, August, www.peri.umass.edu/toxicair_current/.

Peters, G. P., Marland, G., Le Quere, C., Boden, T., Canadell, J. G., and Raupach, M. R. (2012) 'Rapid Growth in CO_2 Emissions after the 2008–2009 Global Financial Crisis', *Nature Climate Change* 2(1): 2–4.

Peters, G. P., Minx, J. C., Weber, C. L., and Edenhofer, O. (2011) 'Growth in Emission Transfers Via International Trade from 1990 to 2008', *Proceedings of the National Academy of Sciences* 108(21): 8903–8.

Peters, T. and Waterman, R. (1982) *In Search of Excellence: Lessons from America's Best-Run Companies*. New York: Harper & Row.

Pew Research Center. (2013) *Climate Change and Financial Instability Seen as Top Global Threats*. Washington, DC: Pew Research Center, www.pewglobal.org/files/2013/06/Pew-Research-Center-Global-Attitudes-Project-Global-Threats-Report-FINAL-June-24-20131.pdf.

Phillips, M. (2013) 'On Being Green and Being Enterprising: Narrative and the Ecopreneurial Self', *Organization* 20(6): 794–817.

Pinkse, J. and Kolk, A. (2009) *International Business and Global Climate Change*. London: Routledge.

Plane Stupid. (2009) 'Polar Bear', 20 November, www.youtube.com/watch?v=fxis7Y1ikIQ.

Polanyi, K. (1957) *The Great Transformation*. Boston: Beacon Press.

Porter, M. E. and Kramer, M. R. (2006) 'Strategy & Society: The Link between Competitive Advantage and Corporate Social Responsibility', *Harvard Business Review* 84(12): 78–92.

(2011) 'Creating Shared Value', *Harvard Business Review* 89(1/2): 62–77.

Porter, M. E. and van der Linde, C. (1995) 'Green and Competitive: Ending the Stalemate', *Harvard Business Review* 73(5): 120–34.

Potter, W. (2011) *Green Is the New Red: The Journey from Activist to "Eco-Terrorist"*. San Francisco, CA: City Lights.

(2014) 'The Green Devil', *Foreign Policy*, 18 August, www.foreign policy.com/articles/2014/08/18/real_green_devil_australia_abbott_climate_disaster.

Power, M. (2004) *The Risk Management of Everything: Rethinking the Politics of Uncertainty*. London: Demos.

(2007) *Organized Uncertainty: Designing a World of Risk Management*. Oxford: Oxford University Press.

Prechel, H. (2000) *Big Business and the State: Historical Transitions and Corporate Transformation, 1880s–1990s*. Albany: SUNY Press.

PREP. (2012) *Value Chain Resilience: A Guide to Managing Climate Impacts in Companies and Communities*. Montreal: Partnership for Resilience and Environmental Preparedness, www.oxfamamerica.org/static/media/files/valuechainclimateresilience.pdf.

Preston, B. L. and Jones, R. N. (2006) *Climate Change Impacts on Australia and the Benefits of Early Action to Reduce Global Greenhouse Gas Emissions: A Consultancy Report for the Australian Business Roundtable on Climate Change*. Aspendale: CSIRO.

PricewaterhouseCoopers. (2014) *Two Degrees of Separation: Ambition and Reality – Low Carbon Economy Index 2014*. London: PricewaterhouseCoopers, www.pwc.co.uk/assets/pdf/low-carbon-economy-index-2014.pdf.

Prudham, S. (2009) 'Pimping Climate Change: Richard Branson, Global Warming, and the Performance of Green Capitalism', *Environment and Planning A* 41(7): 1594–613.

Pullman, E. (2012) 'Cozy Ties: Astroturf "Ethical Oil" and Conservative Alliance to Promote Tar Sands Expansion', *DeSmogCanada*, 13 January, http://desmog.ca/cozy-ties-astroturf-ethical-oil-and-conservative-alliance-promote-tar-sands-expansion.

Pulver, S. (2007) 'Making Sense of Corporate Environmentalism: An Environmental Contestation Approach to Analyzing the Causes and Consequences of the Climate Change Policy Split in the Oil Industry', *Organization & Environment* 20(1): 44–83.

Purser, R. E., Park, C., and Montuori, A. (1995) 'Limits to Anthropocentrism: Toward an Ecocentric Organization Paradigm?', *Academy of Management Review* 20(4): 1053–89.

Putnam, L. L. and Mumby, D. K. (1993) 'Organizations, Emotion and the Myth of Rationality', in S. Fineman (ed) *Emotion in Organizations*, pp. 36–57. London: Sage.

Rafaeli, A. and Sutton, R. I. (1987) 'Expression of Emotion as Part of the Work Role', *Academy of Management Review* 12(1): 23–37.

(1989) 'The Expression of Emotion in Organizational Life', in L. L. Cummings and B. Staw (eds) *Research in Organizational Behavior*, pp. 1–42. Greenwich, CT: JAI Press.

Randall, A. (2011) *Risk and Precaution*. Cambridge: Cambridge University Press.

Randall, R. (2009) 'Loss and Climate Change: The Cost of Parallel Narratives', *Ecopsychology* 1(3): 118–29.

Rasmussen, D. (1996) 'Rethinking Subjectivity: Narrative Identity and the Self', in R. Kearney (ed) *Paul Ricoeur: The Hermeneutics of Action*, pp. 159–72. London: Sage.

Readfearn, G. (2013) 'Australia's New Prime Minister Surrounded by Climate Science Denying Voices and Advisors', *DesmogBlog.com*, 9 October, www.desmogblog.com/2013/10/09/australia-s-new-prime-minister-surrounded-climate-science-denying-voices-and-advisors.

Renwick, D. W. S., Redman, T., and Maguire, S. (2013) 'Green Human Resource Management: A Review and Research Agenda', *International Journal of Management Reviews* 15(1): 1–14.

Ricœur, P. (1994) *Oneself as Another*. Chicago: University of Chicago Press.

Rignot, E. (2014) 'Global Warming: It's a Point of No Return in West Antarctica. What Happens Next?', *The Observer*, 18 May, www.theguardian.com/commentisfree/2014/may/17/climate-change-antarctica-glaciers-melting-global-warming-nasa.

Rignot, E., Mouginot, J., Morlighem, M., Seroussi, H., and Scheuchl, B. (2014) 'Widespread, Rapid Grounding Line Retreat of Pine Island, Thwaites, Smith, and Kohler Glaciers, West Antarctica, from 1992 to 2011', *Geophysical Research Letters* 41(10): 3502–9.

Rimmer, M. and Wood, C. (2014) 'The TPP Greenwashes Dirty Politics', *New Matilda*, 17 January, https://newmatilda.com/2014/01/17/tpp-greenwashes-dirty-politics.

Ritzer, G. (2004) *The McDonaldization of Society*. Thousand Oaks, CA: Pine Forge Press.

Rockström, J., Steffen, W., Noone, K., Persson, Å., Chapin, F. S., Lambin, E. F., Lenton, T. M., Scheffer, M., Folke, C., Schellnhuber, H. J., Nykvist, B., de Wit, C. A., Hughes, T., van der Leeuw, S., Rodhe, H., Sörlin, S., Snyder, P. K., Costanza, R., Svedin, U., Falkenmark, M., Karlberg, L., Corell, R. W., Fabry, V. J., Hansen, J., Walker, B., Liverman, D., Richardson, K., Crutzen, P., and Foley, J. A. (2009) 'A Safe Operating Space for Humanity', *Nature* 461(7263): 472–75.

Rogers, A. D., Sumaila, U. R., Hussain, S. S., and Baulcomb, C. (2014) *The High Seas and Us: Understanding the Value of High-Seas Ecosystems*. Oxford: Global Ocean Commission.

Ryan, C. (2012) 'Eye of the Storm', *Australian Financial Review (BOSS Magazine)*, 10 February: 14.

Saunders, A. (2014) 'Super Fund Aims to Send Fossil Fuels to Dustbin of History', *Sydney Morning Herald*, 4 September, www.smh.com .au/business/super-fund-aims-to-send-fossil-fuels-to-dustbin-of -history-20140904-10ckp6.html.

Sawyer, S. (2010) 'Human Energy', *Dialectical Anthropology* 34(1): 67–75.

Scherer, A. G. and Palazzo, G. (2011) 'The New Political Role of Business in a Globalized World: A Review of a New Perspective on CSR and Its Implications for the Firm, Governance, and Democracy', *Journal of Management Studies* 48(4): 899–931.

Schiermeier, Q. (2013) 'Did Climate Change Cause Typhoon Haiyan?', *Nature*, 11 November, www.nature.com/news/did-climate-change-cause-typhoon-haiyan-1.14139.

Schnaiberg, A. (1980) *The Environment: From Surplus to Scarcity.* New York: Oxford University.

Schnaiberg, A. and Gould, K. A. (1994) *Environment and Society: The Enduring Conflict.* New York: St. Martin's.

Schumpeter, J. A. (1942) *Capitalism, Socialism, and Democracy.* New York: Harper & Brothers.

Schwartz, J. (2014) 'Rockefellers, Heirs to an Oil Fortune, Will Divest Charity of Fossil Fuels', *New York Times*, 21 September, www.nytimes .com/2014/09/22/us/heirs-to-an-oil-fortune-join-the-divestment-drive .html.

Scott, W. R. (1991) 'Unpacking Institutional Arguments', in P. J. DiMaggio and W. W. Powell (eds) *The New Institutionalism in Organizational Analysis*, pp. 164–82. Chicago: University of Chicago Press.

Shamir, R. (2005) 'Corporate Social Responsibility: A Case of Hegemony and Counter-Hegemony', in B. de Sousa Santos and C. A. Rodríguez-Garavito (eds) pp. 91–117. Cambridge: Cambridge University Press.

(2008) 'The Age of Responsibilization: On Market-Embedded Morality', *Economy and Society* 37(1): 1–19.

Shapinker, M. (2014) 'Everything Is Not Awesome about Greenpeace's Assault on Lego', *Financial Times*, 15 October, www.ft.com/intl/cms/ s/0/7a8885fc-538c-11e4-8285-00144feab7de.html.

Shell. (2014) 'Shell Energy Scenarios to 2050', www.shell.com/global/ future-energy/scenarios/2050/acc-version-flash.html.

Shellenberger, M. and Nordhaus, T. (2004) *The Death of Environmentalism: Global Warming Politics in a Post-Environmental World.* Oakland, CA: Breakthrough Institute, www.thebreakthrough .org/images/Death_of_Environmentalism.pdf.

(eds). (2011) *Love Your Monsters: Postenvironmentalism and the Anthropocene*. Oakland, CA: Breakthrough Institute.

Shuttleworth, K. (2012) 'Agreement Entitles Whanganui River to Legal Identity', *New Zealand Herald*, 30 August, www.nzherald.co.nz/nz/news/article.cfm?c_id=1&objectid=10830586.

Skeggs, B. (2014) 'Values Beyond Value? Is Anything Beyond the Logic of Capital?', *The British Journal of Sociology* 65(1): 1–20.

Slawinski, N. and Bansal, P. (2012) 'A Matter of Time: The Temporal Perspectives of Organizational Responses to Climate Change', *Organization Studies* 33(11): 1537–63.

Slocum, R. (2004) 'Polar Bears and Energy-Efficient Lightbulbs: Strategies to Bring Climate Change Home', *Environment and Planning D* 22(3): 413–38.

Smit, B. and Skinner, M. W. (2002) 'Adaptation Options in Agriculture to Climate Change: A Typology', *Mitigation and Adaptation Strategies for Global Change* 7(1): 85–114.

Smith, G. (2014) 'U.S. Seen as Biggest Oil Producer after Overtaking Saudi Arabia', *Bloomberg Businessweek*, 5 July, www.bloomberg.com/news/2014-07-04/u-s-seen-as-biggest-oil-producer-after-overtaking-saudi.html.

Somers, M. R. (1994) 'The Narrative Constitution of Identity – A Relational and Network Approach', *Theory and Society* 23(5): 605–49.

Souder, W. (2012) *On a Farther Shore: The Life and Legacy of Rachel Carson*. New York: Crown.

Spaargaren, G. and Mol, A. P. J. (2013) 'Carbon Flows, Carbon Markets, and Low-Carbon Lifestyles: Reflecting on the Role of Markets in Climate Governance', *Environmental Politics* 22(1): 174–93.

St John, J. (2014) 'The Local and Global Impact of Tesla's Giga Factory', *Greentechgrid*, 4 September, www.greentechmedia.com/articles/read/The-Local-and-Global-Impact-of-Teslas-Giga-Factory.

Stark, D. (2009) *The Sense of Dissonance: Accounts of Economic Life*. Princeton: Princeton University Press.

Stearns, P. N. and Stearns, C. Z. (1985) 'Emotionology: Clarifying the History of Emotions and Emotional Standards', *The American Historical Review* 90(4): 813–36.

Steffen, W. (2013) *The Angry Summer*. Canberra: Climate Commission.

Steffen, W., Crutzen, P. J., and McNeill, J. R. (2007) 'The Anthropocene: Are Humans Now Overwhelming the Great Forces of Nature?', *AMBIO: A Journal of the Human Environment* 36(8): 614–21.

Stern, N. (2007) *The Economics of Climate Change: The Stern Review*. Cambridge: Cambridge University Press.

(2008) 'The Economics of Climate Change', *The American Economic Review* 98(2): 1–37.

Stern, N., Peters, S., Bakhshi, V., Bowen, A., Cameron, C., Catovsky, S., Crane, D., Cruickshank, S., Dietz, S., Edmonson, N., Garbett, S.-L., Hamid, L., Hoffman, G., Ingram, D., Jones, B., Patmore, N., Radcliffe, H., Sathiyarajah, R., Stock, M., Taylor, C., Vernon, T., Wanjie, H., and Zenghelis, D. (2006) *Stern Review: The Economics of Climate Change*. London: HM Treasury.

Stone, C. D. (1974) *Should Trees Have Standing? Toward Legal Rights for Natural Objects*. Los Altos, CA: W. Kaufmann.

Strauss, A. and Corbin, J. (1998) *Basics of Qualitative Research: Techniques and Procedures for Developing Grounded Theory*. Thousand Oaks, CA: Sage Publications.

Sturdy, A. (2003) 'Knowing the Unknowable? A Discussion of Methodological and Theoretical Issues in Emotion Research and Organizational Studies', *Organization* 10(1): 81–105.

Sturdy, A., Wright, C., and Wylie, N. (2015) *Management as Consultancy: Neo-Bureaucracy and the Consultant Manager*. Cambridge: Cambridge University Press.

Suchman, M. C. (1995) 'Managing Legitimacy: Strategic and Institutional Approaches', *Academy of Management Review* 20(3): 571–610.

Sumaila, U. R., Cheung, W. W., Lam, V. W., Pauly, D., and Herrick, S. (2011) 'Climate Change Impacts on the Biophysics and Economics of World Fisheries', *Nature Climate Change* 1(9): 449–56.

Sunstein, C. R. (2007) 'Of Montreal and Kyoto: A Tale of Two Protocols', *Harvard Environmental Law Review* 31(1): 1–65.

Swyngedouw, E. (2010) 'Apocalypse Forever?: Post-Political Populism and the Spectre of Climate Change', *Theory, Culture & Society* 27(2/3): 213–32.

(2011) 'Depoliticized Environments: The End of Nature, Climate Change and the Post-Political Condition', *Royal Institute of Philosophy Supplements* 69: 253–74.

Szerszynski, B. (2010) 'Reading and Writing the Weather: Climate Technics and the Moment of Responsibility', *Theory, Culture & Society* 27(2/3): 9–30.

Tams, S. and Marshall, J. (2011) 'Responsible Careers: Systemic Reflexivity in Shifting Landscapes', *Human Relations* 64(1): 109–31.

Taylor, L. (2011) 'No Holds Barred as Industry "Lobby" Fights Tax', *Sydney Morning Herald*, 11 October, www.smh.com.au/federal-politics/ political-opinion/no-holds-barred-as-industry-lobby-fights-tax-2011 1010-1lhmc.html.

(2014) 'Renewable Energy Target Review Backs Closure of Scheme to New Entrants', *The Guardian*, 28 August, www.theguardian. com/environment/2014/aug/28/renewable-energy-target-review -calls-scheme-closed-new-entrants.

TED. (2007) 'John Doerr Sees Salvation and Profit in Greentech', *TED Ideas Worth Spreading*, www.ted.com/talks/john_doerr_sees_salvation_and_profit_in_greentech.html.

The Nature Conservancy. (2014) *Working with Companies*, www.nature.org/about-us/working-with-companies/companies-we-work-with/index.htm.

The World Bank. (2012) *Turn Down the Heat: Why a 4°C Warmer World Must Be Avoided*. Washington, DC: World Bank, http://documents.worldbank.org/curated/en/2012/11/17097815/turn-down-heat-4%C2%B0c-warmer-world-must-be-avoided.

The World Bank. (2014) *Turn Down the Heat: Confronting the New Climate Normal*. Washington, DC: World Bank Group, http://documents.worldbank.org/curated/en/2014/11/20404287/turn-down-heat-confronting-new-climate-normal-vol-2-2-main-report.

Thévenot, L. (2001) 'Organized Complexity: Conventions of Coordination and the Composition of Economic Arrangements', *European Journal of Social Theory* 4(4): 405–25.

(2007) 'The Plurality of Cognitive Formats and Engagements', *European Journal of Social Theory* 10(3): 409–23.

Thévenot, L., Moody, M., and Lafaye, C. (2000) 'Forms of Valuing Nature: Arguments and Modes of Justification in French and American Environmental Disputes', in M. Lamont and L. Thévenot (eds) *Rethinking Comparative Cultural Sociology: Repertoires of Evaluation in France and the United States*, pp. 229–72. Cambridge: Cambridge University Press.

Thornborrow, T. and Brown, A. D. (2009) '"Being Regimented": Aspiration, Discipline and Identity Work in the British Parachute Regiment', *Organization Studies* 30(4): 355–76.

Torfing, J. (2009) 'Power and Discourse: Towards an Anti-Foundationalist Concept of Power', in S. R. Clegg and M. Haugaard (eds) *The Sage Handbook on Power*, pp. 108–24. London: Sage.

Trenberth, K. E. (2012) 'Framing the Way to Relate Climate Extremes to Climate Change', *Climatic Change* 115(2): 283–90.

Unilever. (2013) 'Unilever Launches Project Sunlight – a New Initiative to Motivate People to Live More Sustainably', 20 November, http://www.unilever.co.uk/media-centre/pressreleases/2013pressreleases/Project-Sunlight.aspx.

United States Government. (1973) *Energy Reorganization Act of 1973. Hearings, Ninety-Third Congress, First Session, on H.R. 11510*. Washington, DC: US Government Printing Office.

Useem, M. (1982) 'Classwide Rationality in the Politics of Managers and Directors of Large Corporations in the United States and Great Britain', *Administrative Science Quarterly* 27(2): 199–226.

Valente, M. and Crane, A. (2010) 'Public Responsibility and Private Enterprise in Developing Countries', *California Management Review* 52(3): 52–78.

Van Aalst, M. K. (2006) 'The Impacts of Climate Change on the Risk of Natural Disasters', *Disasters* 30(1): 5–18.

van Huijstee, M., Pollock, L., Glasbergen, P., and Leroy, P. (2011) 'Challenges for NGOs Partnering with Corporations: WWF Netherlands and the Environmental Defense Fund', *Environmental Values* 20(1): 43–74.

Van Maanen, J. and Kunda, G. (1989) '"Real Feelings:" Emotional Expression and Organizational Culture', in L. L. Cummings and B. M. Staw (eds) *Research in Organizational Behavior*, 11, pp. 43–104. Greenwich, CT: JAI Press.

Van Maanen, J., Sørensen, J. B., and Mitchell, T. R. (2007) 'The Interplay between Theory and Method', *Academy of Management Review* 32(4): 1145–54.

Van Noorden, R. (2011) 'How the Financial Crisis Barely Dented Carbon Emissions', *Nature.com*, 4 December, http://blogs.nature.com/news/2011/12/how_the_financial_crisis_barel.html.

Vaughan, A. (2010) 'No Pressure: The Fall-Out from Richard Curtis's Explosive Climate Film', *The Guardian*, 5 October, www.theguardian.com/environment/green-living-blog/2010/oct/04/10-10-activism.

Vidal, J. (2005) 'Revealed: How Oil Giant Influenced Bush', *The Guardian*, 8 June, www.theguardian.com/news/2005/jun/08/usnews.climatechange.

  (2012) 'Will Philippines Negotiator's Tears Change Our Course on Climate Change?', *The Guardian*, 6 December, www.theguardian.com/global-development/poverty-matters/2012/dec/06/philippines-delegator-tears-climate-change.

Vos, J. (2009) 'Actions Speak Louder Than Words: Greenwashing in Corporate America', *Notre Dame Journal of Law Ethics & Public Policy* 23: 673–97.

Wagner, G. and Weitzman, M. L. (2012) 'Playing God', *Foreign Policy*, 24 October, www.foreignpolicy.com/articles/2012/10/22/playing_god.

Walzer, M. (1973) 'Political Action: The Problem of Dirty Hands', *Philosophy and Public Affairs* 2(2): 160–80.

  (1983) *Spheres of Justice: A Defense of Pluralism and Equality*. New York: Basic Books.

Warden, G. (2009) 'Why I'm Concerned about Climate Change', *Ward Off Climate Change*, www.garywarden.com.au/page/Why-Im-Concerned-about-Climate-Change.aspx.

Watson, T. (1994) *In Search of Management: Culture, Chaos and Control in Managerial Work*. London: Thompson Business Press.

(2008) 'Managing Identity: Identity Work, Personal Predicaments and Structural Circumstances', *Organization* 15(1): 121–43.

Watson, T. J. (2009) 'Narrative, Life Story and Manager Identity: A Case Study in Autobiographical Identity Work', *Human Relations* 62(3): 425–52.

Weart, S. (2011) 'The Development of the Concept of Dangerous Anthropogenic Climate Change', in J. S. Dryzek, R. B. Norgaard, and D. Schlosberg (eds) *Oxford Handbook of Climate Change and Society*, pp. 67–81. Oxford: Oxford University Press.

Weart, S. R. (2003) *The Discovery of Global Warming*. Cambridge, MA: Harvard University Press.

Weigel, D. (2014) 'Rolling Coal', *Slate*, 3 July, www.slate.com/articles/news_and_politics/politics/2014/07/rolling_coal_conservatives_who_show_their_annoyance_with_liberals_obama.html.

Welch, I. (2014) 'Why Divestment Fails', *New York Times*, 9 May, www.nytimes.com/2014/05/10/opinion/why-divestment-fails.html.

West, M. (2014) 'Schoolchildren Embroiled in Coal-Seam Gas Dispute', *Sydney Morning Herald*, 7 June, www.smh.com.au/business/school children-embroiled-in-coalseam-gas-dispute-20140606-39ogq.html.

Wetherell, M. and Potter, J. (1989) 'Narrative Characters and Accounting for Violence', in J. Shotter and K. J. Gergen (eds) *Texts of Identity. Inquiries in Social Construction*, pp. 206–19. Thousand Oaks, CA: Sage.

Willmott, H. (1993) 'Strength Is Ignorance; Slavery Is Freedom: Managing Culture in Modern Organizations', *Journal of Management Studies* 30(4): 515–52.

Willow, A. and Wylie, S. (2014) 'Politics, Ecology, and the New Anthropology of Energy: Exploring the Emerging Frontiers of Hydraulic Fracking', *Journal of Political Ecology* 21: 222–36.

Winston, A. S. (2014) 'GE Is Avoiding Hard Choices about Ecomagination', *HBR Blog Network*, 1 August, http://blogs.hbr.org/2014/08/ges-failure-of-ecomagination/.

Wolf, J. and Moser, S. C. (2011) 'Individual Understandings, Perceptions, and Engagement with Climate Change: Insights from in-Depth Studies across the World', *Wiley Interdisciplinary Reviews: Climate Change* 2(4): 547–69.

Woody, T. (2013) 'Why You Might Buy Electricity from Elon Musk Some Day', *The Atlantic*, 25 November, www.theatlantic.com/technology/archive/2013/11/why-you-might-buy-electricity-from-elon-musk-some-day/281824/.

World Bank Group/Ecofys. (2014) *State and Trends of Carbon Pricing 2014*. Washington, DC: World Bank Group.

Wright, C. and Nyberg, D. (2012) 'Working with Passion: Emotionology, Corporate Environmentalism and Climate Change', *Human Relations* 65(12): 1561–87.

(2014) 'Creative Self-Destruction: Corporate Responses to Climate Change as Political Myths', *Environmental Politics* 23(2): 205–23.

Wright, C., Nyberg, D., De Cock, C., and Whiteman, G. (2013) 'Future Imaginings: Organizing in Response to Climate Change', *Organization* 20(5): 647–58.

Wright, C., Nyberg, D., and Grant, D. (2012) '"Hippies on the Third Floor": Climate Change, Narrative Identity and the Micro-Politics of Corporate Environmentalism', *Organization Studies* 33(11): 1451–75.

Yaziji, M. and Doh, J. (2009) *NGOs and Corporations: Conflict and Collaboration*. Cambridge: Cambridge University Press.

York, R. (2004) 'The Treadmill of (Diversifying) Production', *Organization & Environment* 17(3): 355–62.

Yusoff, K. (2010) 'Biopolitical Economies and the Political Aesthetics of Climate Change', *Theory, Culture & Society* 27(2/3): 73–99.

(2013) 'The Geoengine: Geoengineering and the Geopolitics of Planetary Modification', *Environment and Planning A* 45(12): 2799–808.

Yusoff, K. and Gabrys, J. (2011) 'Climate Change and the Imagination', *Wiley Interdisciplinary Reviews: Climate Change* 2(4): 516–34.

Zinn, H. (2003) *A People's History of the United States: 1492–Present*. New York: HarperCollins.

Žižek, S. (1989) *The Sublime Object of Ideology*. London: Verso.

Index

Made in the USA
Monee, IL
06 June 2021

70102888R00148